I0893142

Duerksen's book is well-researched, timely and cre
those wondering what direction the Spirit is leadin
changing times. In *Christ-Follower's in Other Religions* you will come to see how God is at work in the world; not limited to what has traditionally been called by the West, 'the Church'. Whether you understand what is happening as fact or imaginary, the book shows this movement is not something new, but continues to resurface throughout the ages, forcing us to ask the deepest questions about who God is and what is God up to? And, equally important, what must we do to follow?

Randy S. Woodley, PhD, author of
Becoming Rooted: One Hundred Days of Reconnecting with Sacred Earth

This timely corrective work is long overdue. Building on a heritage of earlier efforts, the last two centuries of Protestant Christian mission has been one of the most well-funded, privatized, individualistic international industries on the planet. The concepts of 'Christianizing' conquest and comity contracts continue to prioritize human effort over spirit-led obedience and partnership. This western missionary pandemic has infected the world and continues to infect the world through the efforts of equally well intentioned and un-informed non-western global workers today. Duerksen brings us back to 'imaginaries' that allow us to recover the original invitation to participate with a Spirit-led global initiative in and (shockingly!) through other religious traditions. This re-discovery of another dimension of the work of the *missio dei* stands in judgment on all locally inspired attempts to 'bring' God to *panta ta ethne*. Just as mission changed the church in Acts 15, may we as the church be humble enough to be converted by this insight into God's insider work in the world yet again.

Paul De Neui, Professor of Missiology, North Park Seminary, and editor of
Emerging Faith: Lessons from Mission History in Asia
and *Gift and Duty: Where Grace and Merit Meet*

Establishing a position of openness to the possibility that the Holy Spirit may be present and active in places not labelled 'Christian' or 'church', Darren Duerksen aims to understand selected 'insider movements' in their own terms, rather than in relation to the global mission strategies of others. Closely argued from the growing literature in the field – from insiders themselves and from those who accompany and study the movements, this volume will challenge, and may provoke, but it offers new imaginaries for reading the scriptures and understanding salvation, conversion and family to other 'Christ-followers' in the West who are willing to receive it.

Kirsteen Kim, Paul E. Pierson Professor of World Christianity and Associate Dean for the Center for Missiological Research, Fuller Theological Seminary

As someone who has worked for two decades to find ways beyond the impasses regarding the so-called exclusivism and inclusivism in historic debates in theology of religions, I welcome how Darren Duerken's book shows so clearly not only how the former isms are misleading rather than illuminating, and also why: because we have dated understandings of the so-called religions that do not match up to the hybridity, historicity, and dynamic movements of people on faith journeys that intersect with, combine, and mutually inform across religious lines. Yet, and herein the other genius of this volume: many of these multiple-religious practitioners are also Jesus-followers, thus challenging Christian self-understandings of faithful discipleship in an era of globalization. *Christ-Followers in Other Religions* will challenge preconceived notions about Christian commitment in a world of many faiths.

Amos Yong, Dean of the School of Mission and Theology and Professor of Theology and Mission, Fuller Theological Seminary, and author of *Mission after Pentecost: The Witness of the Spirit from Genesis to Revelation* and *The Hermeneutical Spirit: Theological Interpretation and the Scriptural Imagination for the 21st Century*

In this important work, Darren Duerksen tackles multiple complex, and mystery filled issues in mission: religion, hybridity in identity, the work of the Spirit outside of our typically expected manifestations, and more. That in and of itself would be ambitious, but in his concluding chapter he also reveals one of his aims: mending missiology. Thus, while Darren has a pastoral and practical and ultimately field-rooted grasp of the issues he invites us to explore, he also encourages us to imagine an encompassing vision for a future, a future in which we don't just imagine something happening 'out there' but also something different among 'us', we who do and think about missiology. I will be relying on this book in some of my own writing projects, and highly comment it to you.

Kevin Higgins, General Director Frontier Ventures

There are many reasons to commend this book, including introductions to some wonderful lovers of Christ outside of Christianity. Nothing is more commendable than the restraint of the book, the respect for people working out discipleship to Jesus in contexts foreign to Western Christian life. Duerksen not only models this respectful restraint, he provides a satisfying paradigm that accounts for and supports these differences within the body of Christ. Many helpful examples of specific areas of tension and rethinking are outlined, often noting that there is not one simple solution that all insider followers of Jesus agree on. This book deserves a wide readership among all who are interested in new movements toward Christ across the globe.

H. L. Richard, author of *Following Jesus in the Hindu Context* and editor of *Cultural Gaps: Benjamin Robinson's Experience with Hindu Traditions*

Darren Duerksen has provided a much-needed compass on the seemingly threatening terrain of insider movements within other religious worlds. His personal blend of grassroots research and comprehensive missiological perspective carries a credibility and a savvy as we look to respond to this emergent interreligious phenomenon. He does not skirt the difficult issues of syncretism, inter-textuality, and conversion, and he exudes that wonderful manner of walking expectantly and patiently alongside those who follow Jesus from these other religious worlds. This is an easily consumable manual for all who seek to discern the Spirit's creative handiwork on the religious borderlands of the 21st century.

Brad Gill, Editor, International Journal for Frontier Missiology

In this thought-provoking text, Duerksen explores the alternative missiological imaginaries that are emerging from insider movements, which both challenge and have the potential to enrich Western understandings of Christianity and mission practice. Centered around two key questions, "How is God working among and through insider Christ-followers?" and "What might we learn from this work of the Spirit?", the author provides a new framework through which to recognize the mission of God in multi-religious contexts. Well-researched and compelling, this book is an essential read for mission practitioners, scholars, and students engaged in, or preparing to enter, cross-cultural ministry.

Sarita Gallagher Edwards, author of *Breaking through the Boundaries: Biblical Perspectives on Mission from the Outside In*

In this book, Duerksen considers from the perspective of the Spirit followers of Christ in other religions. In the process, he opens exciting, informative, and humbling vistas. *Christ-Followers in Other Religions* will challenge (and perhaps change!) your paradigm of Christian mission.

Robert K. Johnston, Senior Professor of Theology and Culture, Fuller Theological Seminary and author of *God's Wider Presence*

Darren Duerksen has spent much of his career as a missionary and researcher listening to Christ followers in other religious traditions, and this book shares the deep respect he has for their witness. In fact he thinks learning from them suggests a new missiological imagination that sees the triune God working within and across religious traditions. The results are impressive, offering fresh insights into the role of Scripture, conversion, even the meaning of salvation that will nourish new ways of thinking about witness to people of other faiths.

William Dyrness, Senior Professor of Theology and Culture, Fuller Theological Seminary, Pasadena, California. Author most recently of *The Facts on the Ground: A Wisdom Theology of Culture*

Christ-Followers in Other Religions

The Global Witness of Insider Movements

Series Preface

Regnum Studies in Mission are born from the lived experience of Christians and Christian communities in mission, especially but not solely in the fast growing churches among the poor of the world. These churches have more to tell than stories of growth. They are making significant impacts on their cultures in the cause of Christ. They are producing 'cultural products' which express the reality of Christian faith, hope and love in their societies.

Regnum Studies in Mission are the fruit often of rigorous research to the highest international standards and always of authentic Christian engagement in the transformation of people and societies. And these are for the world. The formation of Christian theology, missiology and practice in the twenty-first century will depend to a great extent on the active participation of growing churches contributing biblical and culturally appropriate expressions of Christian practice to inform World Christianity.

Series Editors

REGNUM STUDIES IN MISSION

Christ-Followers in Other Religions

The Global Witness of Insider Movements

Darren Todd Duerksen

First edition published 2022 by Regnum Books International

Regnum is an imprint of the Oxford Centre for Mission Studies
St. Philip and St. James Church, Woodstock Road
Oxford, OX2 6HR, UK
www.regnumbooks.net

09 08 07 06 05 04 03 8 7 6 5 4 3 2 1

British Library Cataloguing in Publication Data
A catalogue record for this book is available from the British Library

ISBN: 978-1-5064-9748-8
eBook ISBN: 978-1-5064-9749-5

Typeset by Words by Design

Cover images © Jyoti Sahi, used with permission
The Urdu text at the bottom translates John 13:8 literally,
"If I do not wash you, you are not partner (sharīk) with me."

Distributed by Fortress Press in the US, Canada, India, and Brazil

Contents

Preface

One day early in the writing of this book I was compelled to take off my shoes. It was a reminder that the places where I moved – the lives of followers of Christ in other religions – were sacred spaces. None of these communities are perfect; none our religious communities are perfect either. But they bear an image and make confessions that prompt respect, and reverence. As an outsider venturing into a landscape of God's profound design I thought of God's instruction as Moses gazed on the burning bush. I also thought about the practice of many religionists, including Christians, when entering a church, temple, gurdwara, or mosque. Remove your shoes, honor God, and show respect to the people and spaces God has said are holy. It was a practice I often observed throughout the research and writing of this book.

The intended audiences for this book are academic scholars of mission as well as interested and informed mission students and practitioners. For the sake of the former I utilize footnotes to refer to various technical and more detailed discussions of some of the topics referenced in the main text, which non-scholars can skip over should they choose. I apologize to scholars who may wish that I integrate the more technical and detailed arguments into the main text of the book and deal with them more directly, but I trust that this format will help non-scholars engage with the main issues presented, as well as offer a doorway to those interested in exploring certain topics in greater detail.

You may not feel compelled to physically remove your shoes as you read this book – which would be understandable. Part of what you are doing is evaluating the degree to which what I present in these pages is indeed holy, bearing God's mark, whether you agree with my assessments, and what you think our response should be. That is the is the role and beauty of books. They are a conversation of sorts, and you will exit the conversation with your own ideas and conclusions. I can only tell you that, for me, as a White North American Protestant/Evangelical/Mennonite who has been a missionary and thus has had personal connections to the legacy of colonial mission practice, I have learned to take off my shoes. There is often much more holiness in some places than I initially attributed to them. You can, and will, do as you please.

Native American activist Vine Deloria Jr has remarked that "Native people do not need white people to understand them."[1] His comment reminds me of the skepticism I encountered among Hindu Christ-followers in India when I initially asked to conduct research among some of their groups. It was not uncommon for foreigners, usually White men, to come to them with such requests, they told me. The resulting books and articles were often inaccurate, written entirely for the benefit of a foreign audience, and potentially exposed the Christ-followers to scrutiny and criticism from Christian and Hindu groups. They would agree with Deloria's assessment – why do they need to explain themselves to us?

I sympathize with Deloria's sentiment and the colonial power struggles that inform it. Too often Western Christians have placed the burden of proof on non-Western Christians to explain themselves, their theologies, practices, and other choices, to us. In so doing, Christians betray our assumption that these people and groups are somehow less-than and need to prove to us otherwise. The same is certainly the case, even more so, with Christ-followers among non-Christian communities.

But I also in part disagree with Deloria. White people do need to understand Native people. North American Presbyterians, or any other denomination, do need to understand African Pentecostals and the many other expressions of global Christianity. Christians do need to understand Hindu, Muslim, Buddhist, or Native Christ-followers. Not to prove their worth or legitimacy or theological orthodoxy. But rather to help Western Christians see new things about their shared faith and humanity. White people need to understand Native people if for no other reason than to help White people see that, while their vision of life has strengths, it also has profound limitations. The same holds true for the Christian faith. People from various denominations can glean important truths of their shared faith from each other. And, in a like manner, might Christians have something to learn – indeed something they *need* to learn – from non-Christian Christ-followers?

It is true that the very questions I pose and the frameworks I use to analyze these topics are often not the questions and frameworks of the Christ-followers I discuss themselves. They are rather *etic* ones I bring to the discussion, from outside their context. Meta-analyses such as this study often require this, and I am aware that such approaches run the risk of colonizing the theology and experiences of those we analyze. I hope my mindfulness of this to a certain degree overcomes, or at least minimizes, some of this by giving priority to insiders' stories and frameworks and receiving their feedback on the ideas and draft. But, as always, the thoughts and analysis I provide are my own, with all the limitations that brings.

---

[1] As paraphrased by Cheryl Bear-Barnetson, *Introduction to First Nations Ministry* (Cleveland, TN: Cherohala Press, 2013), 30.

I am very grateful for the help and feedback I received from many Christ-followers I have interacted with over the years, and particularly in the work on this book. These include Sarah Ardu, Marie Bauer, Cheryl Bear, Dayanand Bharati, Casey Church, Frank Decker, Paul De Neui, Gavriel Geffen, Brad Gill, Kevin Higgins, Robert Johnston, Beat Jost, Joshua Kalapati and the staff at the Madras Christian College Archives, Paul Pennington, Jan Hendrik Prenger, John Ridgway, Brother "Somsak", Michael Steltenkamp, John Stephenson, Harley Talman, Jonathan Tan, John Travis, Brother "Vijay", Banpote Wetchgama, Randy Woodley, Emelito Acoba Yango, Amos Yong, and Brother "Yussef".

Thanks also to numerous friends and colleagues who provided feedback and encouragement along the way, including Mark Baker, Bill Dyrness, Ron Herms, Quentin Kinnison, and H.L. Richard. Also, I'm grateful to my students at Fresno Pacific University and Seminary who read drafts of the book and, though required reading, engaged thoughtfully and critically with its content, and helped sharpen my own thinking.

I also want to thank my program assistant Karl Gurney who conducted research on various topics, and Launa Grunau who helped with editing.

Thanks to Fresno Pacific University for the sabbatical during which I was able to conduct a large part of the research for the book. Also, to First Mennonite Church, Reedley, who kindly gave me use of their library as a place to do my work.

As many authors know, a project like this requires not only their own sacrifices, but those of their family as well. I'm grateful to my children and particularly to my wife, Shahna. Thank you so much for your encouragement and for giving me ample time and space to do this work.

Lastly, I am extremely grateful for all the insider Christ-followers who shared their stories with me; some listed above, some not listed because of security, and some who shared their stories through a trusted friend. You gifted me with your wisdom and stories, often being very vulnerable in the process. I hope in at least some small way this book honors you and the work God is doing in and through you.

Fresno, California
Pentecost, June 5, 2022

Section One

Insiders and Missiological Imaginaries

1: Introduction: New Missiological Imaginaries

"Sometimes I DO wonder, am I a Sikh follower of Jesus or am I Christian? What will my kids be? These are some big issues." As my friend Jaspreet and I talked one evening at his house in rural northwest India, it was getting dark and the countryside was settling into its evening rhythms. Jaspreet was in a reflective mood. "This culture thing is a big thing. It's an identity crisis among the nomads like me," he said.

Ten years earlier Jaspreet was forced to leave his family and community when his father found out Jaspreet had become a Christian. Jaspreet was then mentored and trained by various pastors and became a pastor and church-planter for a local Christian denomination. But though he had been rejected by his Sikh community and had a growing and fulfilling ministry in the Christian community, he felt like a religious "nomad": someone wandering from place to place without a clear sense of a permanent home. Normally he projected the persona of a very confident Christian pastor. But in this vulnerable moment he revealed the quandary of not being a part of the Sikh community via his family any longer while not fully feeling a part of the Christian community.

Jaspreet is not alone in his questions and discomfort. Every year thousands of people from non-Christian religious communities begin following Christ.[1] The guidance they receive as they do so is often remarkably similar – they are told they need to leave their old "religion" in favor of following Christ. Inevitably this creates tension, which they are taught is a conflict of loyalty. The answer to this conflict, of course, is that they should be ready to leave anything, even "father and mother" (Matt. 10:37), for the sake of being faithful to Jesus. But for many this dichotomous choice brings not only relational pain, social displacement, and even the threat of death, but also questions. Is this really the only option available to them? Or might it be possible to follow Christ as revealed in the Bible while also remaining a part of their own social and religious communities?

---

[1] Center for the Study of Global Christianity, *Christianity in its Global Context, 1970–2020* (South Hamilton, MA: Gordon-Conwell Theological Seminary, 2013), 13. www.globalchristianity.org/globalcontext, Accessed March 1, 2019.

This book is about individual Christ-followers, and the groups some of them lead or are a part of, who in recent years have begun to grow and develop a different pathway for following Christ. Often referred to (by Western Christians) as "insider Christ-followers," these believers seek to follow Christ while remaining a part of their religious communities. But they do so not by "converting" religions or leaving their communities to join a Christian church. In fact, though they follow Christ and prioritize biblical Scripture, they do not consider themselves "Christian."

The existence of insider Christ-followers and groups has raised many questions regarding if and how such Christ-followers can remain a part of their non-Christian religious traditions while maintaining a faith that is biblically orthodox.[2] But perhaps more importantly, and the focus of this book, is the question of what these Christ-followers in other religious traditions might teach Christ-followers from "Christian" communities and traditions about the mission of God. Insiders themselves are not, of course, normally concerned with academic debates on theologies of mission and religion. Rather, theirs are theologies of practicality and necessity or, as Samuel Escobar and other Latin American theologians notably called them, "theologies of the road."[3] These are worked out as they daily seek to faithfully follow Jesus while honoring their families and various commitments. But their experiences and insights form nascent theologies of mission that can teach non-insider Christ-followers (Christians) alternative ways to understand God's mission in and through religious communities.[4]

---

[2] For a collection of articles that provides an overview of some history, examples, case studies, and theological and missiological discussions of insider movements see Harley Talman and John Jay Travis (eds), *Understanding Insider Movements: Disciples of Jesus Within Diverse Religious Communities* (Pasadena, CA: William Carey Library, 2015). For some critiques of insider movements see Gary Corwin, "A Humble Appeal to C5/Insider Movement Mulsim Ministry Advocates to Consider Ten Questions," *International Journal for Frontier Missiology* 24:1 (2007), 5-20; Timothy Tennent, "The Challenge of Churchless Christianity: An Evangelical Assessment," *International Bulletin of Missionary Research* 29:4 (2005), 171-177; Ayman S. Ibrahim and Ant Greenham (eds), *Muslim Conversions to Christ: A Critique of Insider Movements in Islamic Contexts* (New York: Peter Lang, 2018).

[3] Escobar and his colleagues drew this imagery from the work of John Mackay. See Samuel Escobar, "Doing Theology on Christ's Road," in Jeffrey P. Greenman and Gene L. Green (eds), *Global Theology in Evangelical Perspective: Exploring the Contextual Nature of Theology and Mission* (Downers Grove, IL: IVP Academic, 2012), 69-71; John Alexander Mackay, *A Preface to Christian Theology* (The James Sprunt Lectures, 1940: New York: Macmillan, 1941).

[4] Though in this book I am using the term "insider" in a very narrow sense to refer to those who follow Christ in non-Christian traditions, in reality *all* Christ-followers are "insiders" to their own religious and cultural traditions. In addition, it is a truism that all Christ-followers are also "outsiders." As Amos Yong has noted, "While it is obvious how we are 'insiders' to our own tradition, it is also important to note that

Insider groups and those walking alongside them believe that there can and should be new paths of Christ-centered discipleship that challenge many of the common Christian assumptions and approaches towards religious traditions. They do this by addressing one of Jaspreet's core concerns – the question of identity. This, many insiders would say, is where they differ from the many "contextualization" approaches to evangelism and church.[5] Though many Christ-following Christians may contextualize and adapt various forms of their faith and worship, such as music styles, sermon styles, clothes, architecture, and various other practices, they still identify themselves as "Christian." For example, in India some Christian leaders have begun calling their meetings and church gatherings "*satsangs*," a term traditionally used by Hindus to refer to worship gatherings. But, though these Christian groups are adapting a term that originates in Hindu traditions, they continue to maintain a separate Christian religious identity.[6] Insider Hindu followers of Jesus, on the other hand, might not only call their worship gatherings "*satsangs*," but continue to identify themselves as Hindu. For them contextualizing the name of a worship gathering does not fully capture the core issue; they do not desire to be Christians who look or sound a little more Hindu, but to be Hindus who are truly following Christ.[7]

As one could imagine, the ways in which insiders integrate their faith in Christ with their religious identity vary widely depending on their religious, cultural, and political context. For example, because most Muslims believe

---

we are theological 'outsiders' even to the Christian tradition insofar as we are still not yet fully converted to the image of Christ (on this side of the eschaton)." Amos Yong, *The Cosmic Breath: Spirit and Nature in the Christianity-Buddhism-Science Trialogue* (Boston: Brill, 2012), 28.

[5] John Travis' well-known "C-scale," which charts the socio-religious forms and identities of Christ-followers in the Muslim world, makes what many see as a crucial distinction between C3/4 and C5. Christ-followers in the C3 and C4 categories use Muslim forms of worship and give them "new biblical meaning." Those in the C5 category do this as well, but do not leave their Muslim community and thus see themselves still as Muslims. John Travis, "The C1 to C6 Spectrum: A Practical Tool for Defining Six Types of 'Christ-Centered Communities' ('C') Found in the Muslim Context," *Evangelical Missions Quarterly* 34:4 (1998), 407-408.

[6] See also Phil Parshall's case study of contextualized churches of Muslim Background Believers in "Lombaro" who similarly embrace a non-Muslim identity while maintaining some Muslim practices (like sitting on the floor, praying with hands lifted up Muslim-style, etc.). Phil Parshall, *Muslim Evangelism: Contemporary Approaches to Contextualization* (Downers Grove, IL: InterVarsity Press, 2003), 25-30.

[7] See Darren Duerksen, *Ecclesial Identities in a Multi-Faith Context: Jesus Truth-Gatherings (Yeshu Satsangs) Among Hindus and Sikhs in Northwest India* (American Society of Missiology Monograph Series: Eugene, OR: Pickwick Publications, 2015).

declaring the *shahada*[8] is a core practice for their religious identity, some Muslim followers of Christ are comfortable declaring it in their prayers (usually also modifying its words or meaning). Other insiders, however, do not agree with saying the *shahada* in prayer, even though they still claim a Muslim identity. In addition, insiders and insider groups change over time; they may affirm a particular practice or teaching at one point and then modify or change their approach in response to further study or interaction with others. Religious and theological categories are rarely neat or fixed in the lived realities of everyday life, including those of insiders.

Imaging God's Mission Anew

Despite much diversity, insider Christ-followers' overall approach to religious identity presents us with a unique opportunity to reconsider the relationship between God and his mission among religious traditions through what I will call *alternative missiological imaginaries*. Drawing from Charles Taylor's "social imaginary,"[9] an imaginary in this sense is not a "fantasy" as understood in the popular sense, nor disembodied and disengaged ideas and thoughts – "insubstantial dreams" – conjured up in the individual's mind with little or no basis in reality.[10] Rather, for Taylor, a social imaginary is a type of knowledge about the world that runs "much broader and deeper than the intellectual schemes people may entertain when they think about social reality in a disengaged mode."[11] Such imaginaries are not normally expressed through theoretical ideas and arguments, but instead through "images, stories, and legends."[12] Not only this, but these images and stories often have a dynamic relationship with shared social practices. As James K.A. Smith summarizes, an imaginary signals that "our most basic way of intending and constituting the world is visceral and tactile – it runs off the fuel of 'images' provided by the senses."[13] We have, as it were, shared images that reflect the way we think our social worlds operate, or should operate, and we express these not so much through intellectual theories about those worlds but rather

---

[8] A declaration that says, "there is no deity but Allah and Muhammad is his prophet."

[9] This also reflects phraseology from Latin American missiologist Samuel Cueva ("prophetic missiological imagination") in Samuel Cueva, *Mission Partnership in Creative Tension: An Analysis of Relationships Within the Evangelical Missions Movement with Special Reference to Peru and Britain from 1987–2006* (Carlisle, UK: Langham Monographs, 2015), 378.

[10] Charles Taylor, *Modern Social Imaginaries* (Durham: Duke University Press, 2004), 183.

[11] Taylor, *Modern Social Imaginaries*, 23.

[12] Taylor, *Modern Social Imaginaries*, 23.

[13] James K.A. Smith, *Desiring the Kingdom: Worship, Worldview, and Cultural Formation* (Grand Rapids, MI: Baker Academic, 2009), 66.

through our practices. These practices not only help us navigate our social worlds successfully, or at least with some approximate success, but also express and enact a deep, unarticulated knowledge about the way we think the world does and should work.[14]

Our *missiological* imaginaries operate in a very similar way. Few Christ-followers have clearly formulated their own theories or theologies of mission in relation to their faith in Christ. But this does not mean they are mission-less, devoid of any sense of how their faith in Christ shapes and navigates their moral and social lives and relationships. As they integrate their faith in Christ in their lives, they, like all Christ-followers, develop an imaginary of what their faith in Christ calls them to do and be in their world, including their religious world. They imagine the ways in which their faith calls them to relate to others, how to respond to and transform expectations, and how their faith impacts what Taylor calls "the deeper normative notions and images which underlie these expectations."[15]

For some the term "imaginary" may seem new, or even unnecessary. However, it is helpful to talk about an imaginary rather than just a *theory* of mission or missiology. This is because, first, our focus here is on the way the faith of ordinary people orients their identity, relationships, and practices as expressed not so much in theoretical terms as in images, stories, experiences, and practices. Second, theory is often developed by an elite group using elite categories and concerns, whereas an imaginary is shaped and shared by a wider group of people. Third, an imaginary is or flows out of "a common understanding which makes possible common practices, and a widely shared sense of legitimacy."[16]

In light of this, I suggest that insider Christ-followers are working out missiological imaginaries regarding God's mission in and through religious communities that are alternatives to the dominant missiologies of Christians, and particularly Western Christians. The specifics of these alternative imaginaries, and what they seek to counter, vary depending on the context. Often, as we will see, insiders are countering aspects of the colonial heritage of Christian mission in their region, including the sense that to follow Christ is to join a Western religion that competes with and threatens local religious and cultural communities. Along with this, many insiders are countering some of the more competitive and combative Christian missiologies and

---

[14] See Hans Alma and Guido Vanheeswijck, "Introduction," in Hans Alma and Guido Vanheeswijck (eds) *Social Imaginaries in a Globalizing World* (Boston: De Gruyter, 2018), 21-46.
[15] Charles Taylor, *A Secular Age* (Cambridge, MA: Harvard University Press, 2007), 171.
[16] Taylor, *A Secular Age*, 171-172.

approaches to other religious communities, many of whose origins and/or energy seem to emanate from Western churches, scholars, and institutions.[17]

This is not to discount the experience of countless people who have converted out of other religious traditions to Christianity. Their testimonies and their encounters with and salvation by God's grace are rightly to be celebrated. The imaginaries that insiders seek to present do not, in my mind, negate those who have experienced and promote Christian conversion. However, it is common for imaginaries to become so ingrained, so taken for granted, so dominant, that it becomes hard to conceive, let alone accept, alternative possibilities. As Taylor says about the "modern" social imaginary on which he focuses, "(it) has now become so self-evident to us that we have trouble seeing it as one possible conception among others."[18] When a particular way of conceiving the world becomes so dominant we have a hard time realizing how contingent our imaginaries are.[19] The argument here is not that insiders' alternative missiological imaginaries are the "correct" or even necessarily always the best way of orienting a Christ-following faith in relation to other religious traditions. But the questions they raise could, and perhaps should, help us realize that existing conversionist imaginaries too may not be the only, or always the best, ones and that Christian Christ-followers may have much to learn from insiders and the perspectives that they would share with us.

Preparing for New Imaginaries

The project of this book is to observe and reflect on the imaginaries, or theologies of the road, of various insider Christ-followers. To do this, in subsequent chapters I will examine various examples of insider groups and the factors that have helped shape their missiological imaginaries. But since much of the debate regarding insider groups has occurred within Western Christian mission circles it will be helpful to briefly consider some of developments in Western mission thinking that has led to this discussion. Thus, for the remainder of this chapter I will trace the influence of two particular developments – the concept of "people movements" and recent theories regarding "indigenization" or "contextualization." I will then describe the overall argument and outline of the coming chapters and how

---

[17] "Western" is in many ways an outdated and very inexact term, but alternatives such as "Global North" (as opposed to Global South) are equally inexact. I thus use "Western" as shorthand for ideas, theologies, and practices whose locus of origin and development has been Europe and North America. This is not to ignore the fact that scholars and leaders from other regions, including those of the "Global South," have contributed to and promoted these ideas as well.

[18] Taylor, *Modern Social Imaginaries*, 2.

[19] Smith, *Desiring the Kingdom*, 28 n12.

they will help us understand aspects of insiders' alternative missiological imaginary.

Beyond People Groups

As is well known among mission workers and scholars, when Donald McGavran developed his concept of "People Movements" starting in the 1950s he had grown critical of evangelistic strategies that led to the extraction of Christian converts from their communities. Such evangelism, he observed, often resulted in small, stunted churches that were disconnected from the wider communities. The solution, McGavran envisioned, was "Christward movements of peoples"[20] who considered and made decisions to follow Christ as a group. If and where this could happen, new Christ-followers would not need to leave their social group but would instead remain within it and develop styles of teaching, worship, evangelism and gathering appropriate to their contexts. This formed the backdrop for what McGavran later called the Homogenous Unit Principle (HUP), in which "people like to become Christians without crossing racial, linguistic, or class barriers."[21]

One of McGavran's important contributions through the HUP was to recognize and challenge the impact of Western individualism on modern mission approaches. Missionaries had long pondered the strongly communal nature of many societies, how this often kept individuals from converting to Christianity, and how it often marginalized those who did. Because of this they concluded that social structures and communities were a significant barrier to the spread of the gospel, hindering the autonomy of individuals to determine their own choices. But McGavran challenged this view and, by extension, the Western value on personal autonomy that it reflected. Instead, he suggested that social structures, though broken and sinful, did not have to be seen as barriers; they could also be the means through which the gospel could spread. Even more, his reinterpretation of the concept of *ethne* (peoples) in passages such as Matthew 28:19 as cultural groups that included "tongues, tribes, castes, and lineages"[22] hinted at the possibility that social groupings were not only a sociological tool or means for evangelism, but that they were somehow theologically integral to the present and future contour and nature of God's people (Rev. 5:9, 7:9).[23]

But, despite its innovation and influence, from an insider perspective McGavran's people group theory had two significant weaknesses. First, for all his focus on *social* and *ethnic* groups, McGavran never specifically

---

[20] Donald Anderson McGavran, *The Bridges of God: A Study in the Strategy of Missions* (New York: World Dominion Press, 1955), 81.
[21] Donald Anderson McGavran, *Understanding Church Growth*, 3rd ed. (Grand Rapids, MI: Eerdmans, 1990), 163.
[22] McGavran, *Understanding Church Growth*, 40.
[23] McGavran, *Understanding Church Growth*, 293.

discussed if or how his theory applied to *religious* communities and identities.[24] It did not take long, however, for mission workers to see the implications of people group theory for religious communities. For example, in 1977 Presbyterian missionary John Wilder analyzed the ways in which early Hebrew Christianity and the contemporary Messianic Judaism movement could be seen as analogues for a possible "people movement to Christ which remains within Islam."[25] Starting in the 1970s many missiologists and mission workers developed McGavran's insights still further, arguing for an openness to and pursuit of people movements that remain within *religious* communities.[26]

Another potential weakness of McGavran's work, at least as it impacted religious communities, was his strong focus on creating a new and more effective mission "strategy."[27] Because of its pragmatic focus and application to church-planting methods, mission workers have often used the HUP to evaluate and analyze social identities in terms of their utilitarian means for evangelistic ends. And though, as we saw above, McGavran hinted at a deeper theological meaning and purpose for social identities, missionaries have sometimes been prone to analyze a social identity simply as a "device for niche marketing."[28] In doing so some have sometimes run the risk of trivializing the importance of these identities for persons of that community and minimizing the possibility that such identities reflected something more theologically profound about God's creation and purposes. In contrast, and as we will see in subsequent chapters, many insider groups implicitly and explicitly critique reducing their identity and their relationships to a strategic tool.

Despite these weaknesses, there can be little doubt that McGavran's emphasis on people groups formed an important basis for Western Christians

---

[24] McGavran in fact seemed curiously unaware of the implications that his thinking could have for these. For example, when assessing a movement of Hindu Christ-followers in South India led by Subba Rao he feared that the movement would be "more likely to develop into a form of Hinduism than into a form of Christianity." Donald Anderson McGavran, *Ethnic Realities and the Church: Lessons from India* (Pasadena, CA: William Carey Library, 1979), 219. My thanks to H.L. Richard for this insight into McGavran's thinking.

[25] John Wilder, "Some Reflections on Possibilities for People Movements among Muslims," *Missiology* 5:3 (1977), 310.

[26] Much of this initially developed in relation to Muslim communities. For a helpful overview of this early literature see Christian J. Anderson, "Islam as Gospel Receptacle: US Evangelical Missionaries and the Reimagining of Christianity's Relationship with Islam During the 1970s and 1980s," publication forthcoming.

[27] As seen even in the subtitle of his book *The Bridges of God: A Study in the Strategy of Missions.*

[28] Eddie Gibbs, "How Appropriate is the Church Growth Paradigm?" in C.H. Kraft (ed.) *Appropriate Christianity* (Pasadena, CA: William Carey Library, 2005), 301.

to consider the ways in which the gospel could develop "within," and not just call individuals to leave, religious communities.

Beyond Contextualization

A second and closely related development in recent decades, which has helped to create within Western mission workers and scholars an openness to the alternative missiological imaginaries of insider groups, has been the discussion of and work in indigenization or contextualization. Though these concepts are relevant to insider groups in several ways, I will briefly describe two ways in which contextualization has opened up the possibilities of new missiological imaginaries.

One regards the ways in which the category of "religion" was gradually understood. An initial impulse of contextualization was the positive evaluation of cultures. That is, every culture has the potential to translate and express faith in Christ. But what about the particularly *religious* traditions and practices of a cultural community? Interestingly, though perhaps not surprisingly, many early discussions on contextualization often ignored or conveniently bracketed considerations of religious traditions or subsumed these under the wider category of "culture" and other aspects of society. For example, in his address to the American Society of Missiology in 1976, Louis J. Luzbetak argued that new churches should be allowed to "express Gospel values in their own local cultural patterns, values, philosophy, traditions and structures."[29] But where does "religion" fit into this description? It is hard to know. Was Luzbetak implicitly viewing things "religious" as aspects of "values, philosophy, traditions," etc.? Or was he avoiding what some Christians may have regarded as a more controversial application of contextualization?

In contrast to Luzbetak there were other mission workers and scholars before and during this time who more directly addressed how the gospel might be contextualized within a community's religious rituals and practices. Some even began to ask an additional question: might the gospel be contextualized within a religious community's *identity*? Interestingly, questions along these lines had already been raised periodically throughout the late 19th and 20th centuries in India by Christians who had long interacted with other religious communities.[30] In 1966 the debate was renewed via an article by Kaj Baago, a Danish missionary and professor teaching in India. Critiquing the colonial mission heritage and its closedness to other religions, he asks,

---

[29] Louis J. Luzbetak, "Two Centuries of Cultural Adaptation in American Church Action: Censure or Challenge?" *Missiology* 5:1 (1977), 66.

[30] Several prominent Indian leaders in this regard were Brahmabandhab Upadhyaya, Sadhu Sundar Singh, Pandipeddi Chenchiah, and Vengal Chakkariah.

> Must Buddhists, Hindus and Muslims become Christians in order to belong to Christ? Do they have to be incorporated into church organizations which are utterly alien to their religious traditions? Do they have to call themselves Christians – a word which to them signifies a follower of the Western religion? Should they necessarily adopt the Christian traditions, customs and rites which often have their root in Western culture more than in the Gospel? Are all these things conditions for belonging to Christ?[31]

The answer, he asserts, is "no." It is Christ, not a religion or its institutions, that has supreme importance. Provocatively, he suggests that, if Christians did not monopolize Christ and were instead open to Christ being incarnated in all religions, it would lead not to people leaving their religions but to "the creation of Hindu Christianity or Buddhist Christianity."[32] Baago's article prompted further research and debate,[33] including a study by scholars at Gurukul Theological Seminary on persons they had identified and called "Unbaptized Believers in Christ" – people who followed Christ but did not take baptism and membership in a church.[34] One of these scholars, Herbert Hoefer, was surprised to find in his subsequent research that there were perhaps several thousand such persons in the city and vicinity of Madras (Chennai) who, though often having simple beliefs, demonstrated practices and understandings of Christ that, Hoefer felt, made them a part of "Jesus' flock" though "not in our (Christian) fold."[35]

Discussions regarding the ways in which the gospel could be contextualized to other religious traditions continued in various Catholic, Ecumenical, and Evangelical circles throughout the 1980s and 90s. Some of these reflected positive, or at least sympathetic, evaluations of religious traditions as part of the process of contextualizing the gospel for those communities.[36] However, and as mentioned above, many have preferred to

---

[31] Kaj Baago, "The Post-Colonial Crisis of Missions," *International Review of Missions* 55 (1966), 331.

[32] Baago, "The Post-Colonial Crisis of Missions," 332.

[33] One of these was the well-known correspondence and debate between Indian scholar M.M. Thomas and British missionary Lesslie Newbigin. For an overview, see Hunsberger's and Richard's review of these debates. George Hunsberger, "Conversion and Community: Revisiting the Lesslie Newbigin–M.M. Thomas Debate," *The International Bulletin of Missionary Research* 22:3 (1998) 112-117; H.L. Richard, "Community Dynamics in India and the Praxis of "Church," *International Journal of Frontier Missiology* 24:4 (2007), 185-194.

[34] J. Paul Rajashekar, "The Question of Unbaptized Believers in the History of Mission in India," in Herbert Hoefer (ed.), *Debate on Mission* (Chennai, India: Gurukul Lutheran Theological College and Research Institute, 1979), 323-341.

[35] Herbert Hoefer, *Churchless Christianity* (Pasadena, CA: William Carey Library, 2001), 164.

[36] Scott Moreau, "Contextualization that is Comprehensive," *Missiology* 34:3 (2006), 325-335; A. Scott Moreau, *Contextualizing the Faith: A Holistic Approach* (Grand Rapids, MI: Baker Academic, 2018).

focus on non-religious cultural practices or, at the very most, specific religious rituals or practices, rather than religious identity per se. This perhaps more limited view of contextualization is something that the alternative imaginary provided by insiders challenges and seeks to further develop.

If contextualization initiated a more positive view of culture in general, and a potentially positive view of religious traditions, a second way contextualization has opened up pathways for new missiological imaginaries is in the area of what is often called "discernment." *How* might a person or group decide what beliefs and practices were appropriate for a context and for expressing faith in Christ? One of the more influential frameworks for discernment has been Paul Hiebert's "critical contextualization."[37] In this Hiebert proposes a four-step process designed to help groups of Christ-followers avoid the pitfalls of "noncontextualization" and syncretism, or what he calls "uncritical contextualization."[38] The steps – exegesis of culture, exegesis of the Scripture, critical response, and new contextualized practices – together with Hiebert's analysis of cultural theory and his embrace of critical realism, have provided a framework that has informed conversation on the topic since the 1980s and continues to prompt further elaborations.[39]

Hiebert's emphasis on exegeting culture and Scripture and thoughtfully analyzing these together has certainly been and continues to be the basis of helpful frameworks for discernment. But notice the strong reliance, and perhaps even over-reliance, on the rational analysis of beliefs. Hiebert, and many mission workers of recent decades, were and have been strongly influenced by the symbolic anthropology of Clifford Geertz, who argued that components of culture and religions, like symbols and rituals, were external markers of internal beliefs and worldviews.[40] Hiebert, for example, says that symbols "link physical things with mental concepts, and these concepts can

---

[37] Paul G. Hiebert, "Critical Contextualization," *Missiology* 12 (1984), 287-296; Paul G. Hiebert, "Critical Contextualization," *International Bulletin of Missionary Research* 11:3 (1987), 104-112.

[38] Hiebert, "Critical Contextualization," (1987), 106-108.

[39] R. Daniel Shaw, for example, has recently sought to supplement Hiebert's framework with a better understanding of the complex processes involved when people are faced with making changes in their beliefs and practices. As such he combines critical contextualization with a model of the "cognitive adjustments" people may need to make in order to move their understanding and rituals towards "God's truth" and intention. R. Daniel Shaw, "The Dynamics of Ritual and Ceremony: Transforming Traditional Rites to Their Intended Purpose," in R. Daniel Shaw and William R. Burrows (eds), *Traditional Ritual as Christian Worship: Dangerous Syncretism or Necessary Hybridity?* (Maryknoll: Orbis Books, 2018), 15-16.

[40] Geertz, Hiebert, and other anthropologists based this on the semiotic theory of Charles Peirce, where the symbol received meaning both from the person(s) perceiving/using it and from the object which it signified.

be distinguished from the form and immediate context of the symbols… symbols thus become labels for abstract concepts."[41] In a similar way, rituals "give visible expression to the deep cultural norms that order the way people think, feel, and evaluate their worlds."[42]

The insistence that the "outward" forms of a culture or religion receive meaning from the beliefs of its people, while not necessarily wrong, nonetheless overlooks other reasons why these could be important for people and communities. We can mention two. First, as Talal Asad pointed out in his classic *Genealogies of Religion*, this way of understanding symbols and rituals "insists on the primacy of meaning without regard to the processes by which meanings are constructed."[43] In other words, while symbols/rituals do have meanings or "beliefs" that they reflect and realities they point to, for many or most communities this is not their primary significance. Symbols/rituals do not call persons to "decode" the meaning behind them, but rather to engage through them in proper activity or "performance."[44] It is only in relation to their "articulations in and of social life," through what they call people to do and be, that we can understand symbols/rituals.[45]

What is the point or goal of the activity or performance of symbols/rituals? These can be numerous but, for many communities, including religious communities, symbols/rituals teach people how to live and be in the world, how to relate to each other and the divine. Thus, symbols/rituals have often been the material means for developing in and through the body important virtues and moral dispositions.[46] As such, for many religious traditions (including early/medieval Christianity) relationship with God, or the divine, was not achieved by mastering the right beliefs (expressed outwardly through symbols/rituals), but rather through using symbols/rituals to teach the body

---

[41] Paul G. Hiebert, *Cultural Anthropology*, 2nd ed. (Grand Rapids, MI: Baker, 1983), 115.

[42] Paul G. Hiebert, *The Gospel in Human Contexts: Anthropological Explorations for Contemporary Missions* (Grand Rapids, MI: Baker Academic, 2009), 156.

[43] Talal Asad, *Genealogies of Religion: Discipline and Reasons of Power in Christianity and Islam* (Baltimore: Johns Hopkins University Press, 1993), 43. Asad argues that the emphasis on meaning is uniquely a "modern, privatized Christian one because and to the extent that it emphasizes the priority of belief as a state of mind rather than as constituting activity in the world." Asad, *Genealogies of Religion*, 47.

[44] As Asad says, "Apt performance involves not symbols to be interpreted but activities to be acquired… it presupposes no obscure meanings, but rather the formation of physical and linguistic skills." Asad, *Genealogies of Religion*, 62.

[45] Asad, *Genealogies of Religion*, 53. Interestingly, in his later work Hiebert seems to acknowledge the activity/performance of symbols/rituals, though he does not develop it and still leaves it subservient to the cognitive. See Hiebert, *The Gospel in Human Contexts*, 155.

[46] Asad develops this further through Mauss' use of *habitus*.

how to live as God would desire.[47] In the early and medieval church, for example, rituals and sacraments were "not the representation of cultural metaphors; they (were) parts of a Christian program for creating in its performers, by means of regulated practice, the 'mental and moral dispositions appropriate to Christians.'"[48]

A second and related oversight that comes from an overemphasis on beliefs is an underdeveloped account of the role played by intuition or *emotions* in religious practices, contextualizing, and decision making.[49] This is perhaps understandable, since the enlightenment emphasis on the scientific method and rationality has led many to view emotions as epistemically unreliable means for gaining knowledge. Modern Christian leaders and scholars often reflect this same assessment; Dallas Willard summarizes this view well when he says, "Feelings are, with a few exceptions, good servants. But they are disastrous masters."[50]

Certainly, as Willard further argues, feelings can be both good and destructive, and the latter particularly often need to be transformed by processes of spiritual formation. However, such sidelining of emotions also reinforces an overall Western bias, privileging the role of rationality in epistemology, and perhaps does not give a full enough account of the full measure by which we make decisions, including the role of emotions and intuition. In contrast, recent scholarship, particularly in neuroscience, reveals that our intuition, or the "influence of nonconscious emotional information on an otherwise unrelated decision or judgement,"[51] processes information before conscious cognition does. Intuition works quickly and effortlessly, and helps our cognition frame the choices available to it. As Catherine Elgin shows, emotions provide important "epistemic access" to situations, ideas, or properties that we combine with beliefs to help build our understanding. It is true, she agrees, that emotions can be variable, fallible, and sensitive to circumstances, but this does not disqualify them as a means for *some* level of

---

[47] "The inability to enter into communion with God becomes a function of untaught bodies." Asad, *Genealogies of Religion*, 77.

[48] Asad, *Genealogies of Religion*, 78, quoting Hugh of St. Victor.

[49] By this I am not referring to the cultivation of emotions such as joy in the context of missional witness as discussed in Evelyne A. Reisacher, *Joyful Witness in the Muslim World: Sharing the Gospel in Everyday Encounters* (Grand Rapids, MI: Baker Academic, 2016).

[50] Dallas Willard, *Renovation of the Heart: Putting on the Character of Christ* (Colorado Springs: NavPress, 2002), 122.

[51] Chris Donkin Galang Lufityanto and Joel Pearson, "Measuring Intuition: Nonconscious Emotional Information Boosts Decision Accuracy and Confidence," *Psychological Science* 27:5 (2016), 623.

insight.[52] Rather, emotions can often help us access important information. For example, emotions can direct our focus and help us to notice things we might otherwise miss and suggest to us certain things that are worth noticing.[53] A person's fear of big dogs may make her particularly attuned not only to the presence of dogs in a park, but also cause her to note the various sizes and shapes of dogs in a way that someone who is indifferent to dogs may not notice.

The point here is that intuition with its nonconscious emotional information provides important guidance and information in the decision-making process, information that cognitive methods for discerning cultural and religious meaning may miss or discount. How, for instance, might the emotional well-being that a person experiences through a ritual be a helpful commentary on what that person and his community deem to be a good, flourishing community? If a particular religious ritual is rejected as inappropriate for a Christ-follower, what emotional commentary might be lost, along with its insight into important cultural values? Or, in discussing a topic such as conversion, how might people's feelings on the topic, even if variable and fallible, nonetheless provide information and commentary regarding its impact? Recall from above Jaspreet's pain-filled pondering over his rejection and displacement from his Sikh family, and his worry about his children's relationship to them. Jaspreet's emotions highlighted and made salient certain realities, and raised corresponding missiological questions, that rational discussions regarding contextualization might simply miss.

The Purpose of This Book

People group and contextualization theories are just two of the various developments in recent Western missiology and practice that has created an openness to the alternative missiological imaginaries of insider groups. These two, however, have been particularly important in helping to dislodge dominant imaginaries among Western mission workers and scholars regarding the relationship of Christ-followers to their own non-Christian religious traditions and communities. This does not mean that they were completely adequate; as suggested above each theory has limitations that subsequent scholarship, and insider imaginaries themselves, would highlight and challenge. Such critique is similar to what we will see throughout this book, where the practices and impulses of insider Christ-followers affirm but also challenge numerous aspects of Western notions of mission.

---

[52] Catherine Z. Elgin, "Emotion and Understanding," in Georg Brun, Ulvi Doguoglu, and Dominique Kuenzle (eds) *Epistemology and Emotions* (New York: Routledge, 2016), 37.

[53] Elgin, "Emotion and Understanding," 44.

The argument of this book is that insider movements are shaping alternative missiological imaginaries from which other Christ-followers can learn, or re-learn, insights about God and his mission. How might God be at work in various ways in the midst of these movements despite imperfections, whatever these might be? And how might our own understanding of the gospel, the nature of revelation, and the practice of Christian mission, be enhanced and enriched?

I begin the next chapter by defining and discussing the key concepts of "religion," "religious traditions," and, more importantly in my estimation, people's *religiosity*. These, I will argue, always reflect a mixture, or hybrid, of influence. I suggest that the faith of *all* followers of Christ, past and present, has been and is characterized by a contextual, hybrid religiosity. This helps us understand that the process creating missiological imaginaries, including those of insiders, has always existed.

In chapter 3 I build on this observation by suggesting that such hybrid religiosity is not something to fear, but rather a reality in which God is often at work. As we learn from insiders, as well as missiologists who study the biblical role of the Holy Spirit in creation and in the midst of religious traditions, we find that the Spirit may sometimes speak through religious traditions in ways that enrich biblical, Christ-following faith.

In chapters 4–5 I seek to share the voices of various insiders themselves in history (chapter 4) and in our present time (chapter 5). These examples and case studies provide a grounding for our continued discussion of the alternative imaginaries that these groups provide in the areas of revelation and religious scripture (chapters 6 and 7), salvation (chapter 8), religious conversion (chapter 9), and community and relationships (chapter 10). I will then conclude by suggesting some of larger missiological themes that these insights may challenge Western Christians to adopt as we continue in our witness in the 21st century.

Some Christians have been concerned about, and even highly critical of, insider groups. This book, as you have now seen, is not seeking to answer questions about the biblical legitimacy of insiders or to defend them. As mentioned above, most of these groups are indifferent to Western missiological debates. Rather, my interest is to consider what the alternative missiological imaginaries of insiders may teach Christ-followers in various contexts, including the West, about new responses and postures towards religious communities as we continue into the 21st century. Such imaginaries may dislodge the dominance of received approaches, and may even challenge Western and other dominant Christians' assumed role as caretakers of mission.

2: Religion and Hybrid Religiosity

In 625 CE the Nestorian Christian missionary Alopen arrived in China and introduced teaching on Christianity, or what became known as the *Jingjiao* (Brilliant Teaching). While we lack many details as to Alopen's missionary approach and theology, it is apparent that he and the Persian-Nestorian missionaries with him interacted closely with Buddhist monks and were comfortable adopting Buddhist and Dao concepts and terminology through which to talk about God, creation, Christ, and other Christian topics.[1]

But evidently not everyone, including some Buddhist leaders, were entirely comfortable with this approach. One text from the time by what seems to have been a Buddhist writer recounts how two monks, one a Nestorian Christian and the other an Indian Buddhist, collaborated to translate a Buddhist text and present it to the Imperial Majesty. However, when they presented their translation to the Imperial Majesty he was critical of it, feeling that the "principles (of the dharma) had been obscured and that (their) rendering was without context."[2] This affirmed, at least for his Majesty, that it was best if the Christian monk stuck to propagating the teaching of the *mishihe-jiao* (Messiah) and the Buddhist monk the Buddhist sutras. In this way, says the writer, "(His Majesty) wished that the ways of teaching should be clearly discerned from each other so that the people would not be confused. True and false teaching (should) remain different like the Jing- and the Wei-river flow separately."[3] Interestingly, the writer and his audience would know that the Wei River was quite muddy, while the Jing was relatively clean. In other words, he implies that the false, muddy (Christian) Wei River should not be allowed to contaminate or pollute the true, pure waters of the (Buddhist) Jing.[4]

---

[1] Ralph Covell, *Confucius, the Buddha, and Christ: A History of the Gospel in Chinese* (Eugene, OR: Wipf and Stock, 2004), 25-26.

[2] As translated by Max Deeg, "The 'Brilliant Teaching': The Rise and Fall of 'Nestorianism' (Jingjiao) in Tang China," *Japanese Religions* 31:2 (2006), 98.

[3] As translated by Deeg, "The 'Brilliant Teaching', 98.

[4] Charles M. Stang, "The 'Nestorian' (jingjiao) Monument and its Theology of the Cross," in E. Keser-Kayaalp H. Teule, K. Akalın, N. Doru, M.S. Toprak (eds), *Syriac in its Multi-cultural Context* (Louvain: Peeters, 2017), 110.

The writer of this text shares an anxiety common among many religionists, or persons engaged in religious traditions (including Christ-followers): when interacting with other religions might the "purity" of our own religious identity and beliefs become "polluted"? If so, how do we ensure that our own tradition's integrity is protected? Such questions are often a chief concern of critics of insider Christ-followers. If such Christ-followers remain a part of and even positively evaluate and re-evaluate aspects of their religious tradition, are they not in danger of syncretizing and "muddying" the river of Christianity with the waters of a different tradition?

These are important concerns which any discussion of mission among non-Christian religions, including insider groups, need to take into account. In this and the next chapter, I will address them from two perspectives. First, we need to consider the nature of religious traditions and religiosity, and how mixture or hybridity is a constant reality of these, whether intended or accepted or not. Of course, such mixture often occurs slowly, over time, and almost imperceptibly. Thus, the Buddhist chronicler, like many religionists, perhaps downplayed the hybrid history of his own tradition and obscured the ways in which it itself reflected a unique interaction between Indian Buddhism, Chinese Daoism, and Confucianism.[5] His own Chinese-Buddhist "river" was itself the amalgamation of numerous previous streams and rivers. Such is the case in various ways with all religious traditions.

But a further perspective and argument of this book, addressed in the next chapter, is that, while the process of hybridization in religious traditions and religiosity is in some ways unavoidable, it is not something that Christ-followers necessarily need to fear. Rather, God is often involved in such processes, revealing himself, providing new witness, and inspiring new expressions of worship within and through various religious traditions. And while Christ-followers are certainly called to discern if/how God is at work in the midst of these religious traditions, we do well to first approach such traditions with what Robert Johnston calls a "hermeneutic of open generosity and possibility" in order to better see if and how God's Spirit may be at work.[6] This is something with which insider groups can help us, since they are regularly discerning if and how God is at work in the midst of their respective religious communities and traditions, and how to live in that community as Christ-followers.

[5] Peter N. Gregory, *Tsung-Mi and the Sinification of Buddhism* (Honolulu: University of Hawaii Press, 2002), 3-14.
[6] Robert K. Johnston, *God's Wider Presence: Reconsidering General Revelation* (Grand Rapids, MI: Baker Academic, 2014), 214.

The Worlds of "Religion"

When we talk about the possibility of God working in the midst of a "religion," a "religious tradition," or people's "religiosity," what do we mean? Paul Tillich famously described religion as "the state of being grasped by an ultimate concern... which itself contains the answers to the question of the meaning of our life."[7] We could add to this the contribution of some religious studies scholars, such as Christian Smith, who define religion in terms of practices (and corresponding beliefs) that seek various protections and blessings from divine powers.[8] These and other scholars would thus broadly describe "religion" as that part of personhood and society that senses and pursues the transcendent and expresses this pursuit in culturally specific ways.

Such definitions are not without contention, as students and scholars of religious studies know all too well; a survey of the variety of definitions can lead one to sense how difficult it becomes to use *religion* to consistently refer to anything beyond the most general and vague reference and characteristics.[9] Recognizing this over 60 years ago, Wilfred Cantwell Smith leveled his well-known criticism against the concept of *religion* contending that, while people have probably been *religious* for time immemorial, the systematization of this into what we call *religion* is a very modern invention.[10] In addition, no less modern is the organization of systems of belief into so-called "world religions." Because of this many agree with proposals such as that of H.L. Richard that, at the very least, we should talk not about *religions* but instead religious *traditions* – Hinduisms, Islams, and Christianities – to indicate the plural and contextually specific ways these are expressed.[11]

---

[7] Paul Tillich, *The Future of Religions* (New York: Harper & Row, 1966), 3. In a similar way William Dyrness calls religion an "inbuilt longing for God – the spaces humans construct to look for and even find God." William A. Dyrness, *Insider Jesus: Theological Reflections on New Christian Movements* (Downers Grove, IL: IVP Academic, 2016), 101.

[8] Religion, says Smith, is "a complex of culturally prescribed practices, based on premises about the existence and nature of superhuman powers, whether personal or impersonal, which seek to help practitioners gain access to and communicate or align themselves with these powers, in hopes of realizing human goods and avoiding things bad." Christian Smith, *Religion: What it is, How it Works, and Why it Matters* (Princeton, NJ: Princeton University Press, 2017), 22.

[9] For one overview of this debate see Brent Nongbri, *Before Religion: A History of a Modern Concept* (New Haven: Yale University Press, 2013), chapter 2.

[10] Wilfred Cantwell Smith, *The Meaning and End of Religion: A New Approach to the Religious Traditions of Mankind* (New York: Macmillan, 1963).

[11] H.L. Richard, "Religious Syncretism as a Syncretistic Concept: The Inadequacy of the 'World Religions' Paradigm in Cross-Cultural Encounter," *International Journal for Frontier Missiology* 31:4 Winter (2014): 211. For this reason I will most often reference *religious traditions* rather than *religions* per se.

But though it is helpful to consider *what* a religion or religious tradition is, perhaps even more important is the question of what religious traditions *do* for people. On a very basic level, as Christian Smith indicates, people engage in religious traditions because they believe these will help them to realize particular human goods, address particular concerns, and avoid certain evils.[12] Some of these goods will be explicitly religious insofar as they can only be obtained by seeking to access God, a deity, or some other power and gaining some blessing or protection from harm. However, people may value aspects of a religious tradition or community that are not unique to a religious setting or group. These could include social identity, community, moral order and meaning, social order, and artistic creativity. But though these are not unique to religious traditions per se, they are often experienced and perhaps accentuated in unique ways through the religious setting. For instance, the social support that a person may feel at church may not be unique to the Christian religious setting, since the person could in theory have a similar experience in a context that made no reference to God or any other divine power. But the fellowship is experienced as uniquely *religious* insofar as it is derived, at some point and in some way, from core religious concerns.

Some of the "goods" of religious traditions like those listed above can be readily observed and discussed by religionists themselves. Other goods or benefits, however, are perhaps less clear or explicit. In fact, an important but often overlooked benefit of religious traditions is the sense of emotional well-being that they provide people. In the previous chapter I noted recent scholarship highlighting the ways in which emotions are an important part of our deliberation process. Relatedly, it is becoming increasingly apparent that religious traditions, practices, and communities provide profound emotional benefits and help people navigate and interpret emotion-filled experiences. Stephen Asma, for example, draws on affective neuroscience to argue that religions are important to people because of the often unconscious emotional benefits they provide. Whatever the specific metaphysical claims of a given religious tradition, he says, people turn to religious practices and "use" them to constructively channel emotions such as grief and sorrow, and to cultivate emotions such as joy and empathy.[13] People are, as sociologist Randall Collins says, "emotional energy seekers," evaluating things like religious

---

[12] Smith, *Religion: What it is, How it Works, and Why it Matters*, 191.

[13] For example, he says that religions often do not repress or repudiate sorrow but rather help people process it "in a manner that leaves the grieving person relatively vital, functioning, and even potentially happy, albeit transformed by the nontrivial loss of the loved one." Stephen T. Asma, *Why We Need Religion* (New York, NY: Oxford University Press, 2018), 42.

practices and experiences in terms of the positive emotions these generate for them.[14]

Though such analysis runs the risk, like any functional theory, of reducing religious traditions and assessing them in terms of their unconscious purposes, Asma and Collins raise an issue that is often missed in analyses of religious traditions. That is, people's rational deliberations about their religious beliefs and practices are often second order, coming after and being shaped by deep, emotion-laden commitments. We direct these "affective commitments," as Asma calls them, towards people and things that we deeply care about, whether it is the beauty and character of a spouse or the existence of our God.[15] As evangelists often recognize, people rarely become Christian because of the evangelist's box-tight rational arguments about the existence of the Christian God or the historical evidence of Jesus' death and resurrection. Rather, more often than not, people turn to Christ because, at that moment in their lives, Christ meets a deeply felt need or concern. This does not discount rational belief per se. Rather it highlights the truism that religious traditions not only provide important and helpful beliefs, but also address and affirm perceptions of well-being that persons experience in and through the religious practices and context in which they are involved.

"Socio-Religious" Identities

Religious traditions, I am noting, matter to people for a wide variety of reasons. And while some of these reasons are ideological, religious traditions often matter most because of the various ways they shape and affirm things important to us, including identities, social relationships, and sense of emotional well-being. It is thus impossible for religionists to truly silo their tradition and practices into "religious" boxes of life which they unpack during a "religious" event or worship service and pack away again at its conclusion. Religious traditions just do not work that way, in any context. This is particularly the case in non-Western contexts where enlightenment separations of "religion" from other spheres of life have traditionally made little sense.

Because religious traditions provide, shape, and affirm various "goods" that are important to people, it makes sense that such traditions often closely interact with other aspects of a context that we value, such as politics, ethnicity, etc.[16] It is because of this that religious traditions can become

---

[14] Randall Collins, *Interaction Ritual Chains* (Princeton, NJ: Princeton University Press, 2004), 373. See also Smith, *Religion: What it is, How it Works, and Why it Matters*, 222-225.

[15] Asma, *Why We Need Religion*, 119.

[16] Martin Riesebrodt, *The Promise of Salvation: A Theory of Religions*, trans. Steven Rendall (Chicago: University of Chicago Press, 2010), 14. See also Genevieve Zubrzycki, "Religion, Religious Tradition, and Nationalism: Jewish Revival in

deeply tied to ethnic, national, and/or linguistic identities, even becoming for many people more important than their religion's access to divine power. More orthodox religionists may disparage such people as "nominal" and their cultural-religious world and identity as somehow less than authentic. But from the experience of the religionists themselves this interaction between religious tradition and ethnicity, nationality, etc. can create a powerful social identity. Thus, someone from Ireland may identify as "Catholic" or someone from Jordan as a "Muslim," even if they rarely participate in practices that avail themselves of God's power. Such people identify themselves to be part of a religious tradition that has interacted with ethnic, national, and political interests and identities, creating a new, composite identity to which they ascribe.

Recognizing the way in which religious traditions may interact with other social factors helps us understand just how complex religious identities can be. When a person claims to be "Muslim," what is she saying? At the outset it is difficult to know. At the very least it is probable that she is claiming a particular religious tradition that has emerged out of practices directed towards Allah that seek various goods and avoid evils. But this tradition has other features, including a sense of obligation towards a community and certain moral expectations that have in turn interacted with other social features such as ethnic identity. For a woman to be Muslim may mean to not only practice Muslim prayer, but to also honor her family and its heritage and values, which may in turn be closely tied to an ethnic or national culture.

The interaction between a religious tradition and the "worlds" – personal, historical, social, ethnic, etc. – with which it may interact helps us understand why some persons and scholars are drawn to hyphenate categories related to religious identity, such as "socio-religious," "politico-religious," etc. Because a religious tradition and identity emerges out of numerous interactions, these terms seek to qualify and highlight a particular aspect of their identity. For example, as I have pointed out above, over time the religious practices of a particular context may have interacted with wider social practices and interests, giving rise to a composite identity that includes religious, ethnic, class, or other social identities. In such a context a Muslim follower of Jesus may claim that, for her, "Muslim" is a socio-religious identity, indicating that her religious tradition and identity has interacted and continues to interact with social (family, community, ethnic, national) identities. This tells us something of what she wants to emphasize, though little else about her evaluation of other aspects of her tradition, such as practices directed towards Allah.[17]

Poland and 'Religious Heritage' in Quebec," *Journal for the Scientific Study of Religion* 51:3 (2012), 442-455.

[17] In fact, because religious traditions are often quite extensive and include many different components, it would be impossible for a person or group to value each

But though hyphenated identities and terms such as *socio-religious* open up a rich discussion about the intricacies of identity, they leave aside a crucial question for our discussion: in what ways are insider Christ-followers *outside*, or distinct and different, from their religious communities? Is there an alternative term that helps to capture the ways in which a person is both inside *and* outside their religious tradition? Abu Jaz, a Muslim-background believer in Christ, prefers to describe himself and the groups he leads as *Cultural Insiders, Theological Outsiders* (CITO).[18] On the one hand he disagrees with the common mission approach that teaches Muslims to follow Christ by disconnecting from their communities and families socially, culturally, and religiously. But he is also nervous of insider approaches that, in his estimation, adopt practices like reciting the Muslim *shahada* and potentially blur important theological distinctives. He is, he claims, remaining culturally inside his community by contextualizing various practices and terms, but staying theologically outside using biblical revelation as the sole source of teaching. As Gene Daniels adds, if followers of Christ keep themselves "outside" of generally accepted Islamic theology, including Islamic understandings of God, salvation, and Jesus, they can better avoid syncretism.[19]

Missiologist Fred Farrokh similarly wants terminology that clarifies the ways in which Christ-followers are "inside" and "outside" their community and tradition, but suggests that it is unhelpful to talk about *cultural* insiderness. This is because culture, for Farrokh, is primarily about being able "to communicate effectively in a given context, understanding at a deep level what is going on around him or her, and responding accordingly."[20] No one ever truly loses this ability to culturally understand and communicate with

---

component equally. Rather it is most common for people and groups to prioritize different aspects of a tradition, and to do so as part of their identity formation. Thus, a person may prioritize aspects of a religious tradition and de-emphasize others, depending on how those aspects contribute to their sets of concerns. For example, within the Christian tradition various denominations prioritize and engage certain aspects of the tradition over others, thereby creating a particular identity or sub-tradition.

[18] Abu Jaz, "The Cultural Insider, Theological Outsider (CITO): A Conversation with Abu Jaz," *International Journal for Frontier Missiology* 32:2 (Summer 2015); see also Abu Jaz, "Our Believing Community is a Cultural Insider but Theological Outsider (CITO)," in Ayman S. Ibrahim and Ant Greenham (eds), *Muslim Conversions to Christ: A Critique of Insider Movements in Islamic Contexts* (New York: Peter Lang, 2018).

[19] Gene Daniels and L.D. Waterman, "Bridging the 'Socio-Religious' Divide: A Conversation Between Two Missiologists," *International Journal for Frontier Missiology* 30:2 (Summer 2013), 63, 66.

[20] Fred Farrokh, "Will the Umma Veto SITO? Assessing the Impact of Theological Deviation on Social Acceptability in Muslim Communities," *International Journal for Frontier Missiology* 32:2 (Summer 2015), 70.

their community, unless they make very strong efforts to do so. What is more pertinent for Farrokh is the question of what he calls the *social* insiderness, or "how a person is accepted by and in good standing within the mainstream of (his or her) society."[21] It is very possible for persons to be a cultural insider in terms of their cultural knowledge and communication "but still be socially ostracized and no longer accepted as members in good standing."[22]

In light of this distinction Farrokh prefers to talk about *Social Insiders, Theological Outsiders* (SITO). Similar to Abu Jaz and others he maintains that Christ-followers have an obligation to remain theologically separate from their religious community and tradition. However, if they do so, will their community continue to embrace them socially? From the responses of interviews that he conducts with numerous Muslims and Muslim-background believers, Farrokh is skeptical. Though some Muslims will allow for theological diversity in their community, others will regard a theological outsider as misguided and in need of correction, or an apostate. In either case the community may shame the person and not give them the same social status as before, making them social outsiders. Farrokh concludes that, "while attaining SITO status is a commendable missiological goal… it appears unlikely that the *umma* (Muslim community) at large will tolerate, let alone embrace, believers in Christ as social insiders."[23]

In part Abu Jaz, Farrokh, and others are identifying the reality I have described above – religious identities are impacted and shaped by a variety of concerns and commitments, including doctrinal/theological, cultural, social, and political, amongst others. Given this, they ask, which aspects of these commitments are appropriate for a follower of Christ to retain and remain "inside," and which ones should be rejected? And, does it not make sense that the doctrinal/theological claims of a religious tradition would be most contentious, the one from which Christ-followers should most clearly stand apart?

But notice that it is here where, in an effort to preserve Christian distinctiveness, many are apt to draw solid boundary lines where dotted lines may be more appropriate. In the case of theologies, what theology ever truly stands "outside" its context? It is true that the gospel derives from outside all contexts. It is, however, always and in every case revealed *within* a context. It is also true that biblical revelation should and always will challenge certain claims. Here Abu Jaz is right to raise the question about certain Muslim claims and the way in which biblical revelation may well challenge them. In this case, and in all cases, the authority for the gospel's challenge comes from "outside" a context.

---

[21] Farrokh, "Will the Umma Veto SITO?" 71.
[22] Farrokh, "Will the Umma Veto SITO?" 71.
[23] Farrokh, "Will the Umma Veto SITO?" 78-79.

However, is rejection and theological outsiderness the only option? It is here that the imaginary of insider Christ-followers would seek to bring additional possibilities. For one, the gospel does not only replace, but can also transform. This is something I will explore in more depth in the coming chapters, but I here suggest that religious communities and traditions may in some cases be open to change and transformation in various ways. In addition, as often happens, a Christ-follower's own understanding of the gospel can be deepened and even, at points, transformed. That is, even while the gospel transforms people and their context and traditions, those same traditions help them in turn see aspects of God and his purposes that were perhaps latent in other contexts. A Muslim Christ-follower may have gained an appreciation for the power and holiness of God – in part through the influence of their Muslim tradition – that many Western Evangelical Christians, with their focus on God's relatability and immanence, sometimes minimize.[24] I will return to the question of if and how God reveals himself through other religious traditions. But here I want to suggest that, while claiming the status of a "theological outsider" may provide comfort to some Christians worried about syncretism, the reality is that theology always interacts with and is shaped by and inside its context.

Religiosity

I have thus far argued that religions are multi-faceted, that religionists may value a religious identity for a wide variety of reasons, and that a Christ-follower can seek to transform and be "inside" that community and tradition in a variety of ways. However, what I have begun to hint at, and what we need to explore more fully, are the ways in which people *do things* with religious traditions. That is, religious traditions and their contexts not only act on people, but people draw on them to address their concerns, realize certain goods, and avoid certain evils. This highlights what I call people's *religiosity*. Though on a popular level this term can imply someone who is excessive or slavish in his devotion to a religion, I use it here simply to refer to what religious studies scholar Martin Riesebrodt has described as a person's or group's "subjective appropriation and interpretation" of a religious tradition at any given time.[25] How often or the ways in which a person, family, or smaller group venerates a deity, offers *salah* (Muslim

---

[24] This is the argument of Evangelical theologians such as Gerald McDermott and Harold Netland. See chapter 3 of Gerald R. McDermott and Harold A. Netland, *A Trinitarian Theology of Religions: An Evangelical Proposal* (Oxford: Oxford University Press, 2014).

[25] Riesebrodt, *The Promise of Salvation*, 76. Riesebrodt and Smith prefer the term *religiousness*.

prayer), venerates spirits, or meditates are matters of their religiosity.[26] A person's or group's religiosity, we could say, is the mix of beliefs, practices, symbols, etc. that they subjectively select and activate, often to pursue certain goods, gain protections, or avoid bad things, for immediate and/or longer term well-being.

The subjectivity afforded by the concept of religiosity is important because not every member of a religious community and tradition has an equal level of religiosity; nor do they express it in the same way. Among insider Christ-followers, for example, some have practiced a high amount of religiosity in their religious community and continue this level of religiosity (though in modified ways) as they follow Jesus. Others, though a part of a religious tradition, identified more strongly with their tradition's social identity and were less concerned about and observant in their religiosity. For them being a Hindu, Muslim, Buddhist, etc. was not expressed primarily through their religiosity, but rather through identification with other aspects of the religious tradition, such as its connection to a family or ethnic identity. However, after placing their faith in Christ, these persons embraced religious practices, often by modifying ones from their religious tradition to express and pursue their faith in Christ.

Hybrid Religiosity

A person's or group's religiosity is, then, the point where a person or group interacts with and interprets a wider religious tradition for their own context, reflective of their own interests and concerns. Religiosity thus grows out of and reflects religious traditions while also re-imagining and reshaping them for present contexts. But, and as our example from the beginning of the chapter shows, people's religiosities, and the traditions they reflect, are often not the theologically "pure" rivers that they imagine them to be. Rather, these have normally interacted with and been influenced by various contextual factors, including other religious traditions. As regards Christianity, for example, scholars have long noted the fact that, from a social science perspective, the Christian faith has always syncretized, absorbed, transformed, and been transformed by various contextual factors. As Gerald Arbuckle summarizes in his lengthy study on the matter, "At no point in time is there ever a pure Christianity. It has never existed and never will. The fact is that both the faith of Israel and the faith of the first Christian generations developed processes of inculturation involving syncretism in assimilating influences of other cultures."[27]

---

[26] See also Smith, *Religion: What it is, How it Works, and Why it Matters*, 47.

[27] Gerald A. Arbuckle, *Culture, Inculturation, and Theologians: A Post-Modern Critique* (Collegeville, MN: Liturgical Press, 2010), 183-184.

That Christianity adapts and modifies aspects of the culture in which it resides is often acknowledged and accepted. However, the prospect that Christian beliefs and practices could be subject to "syncretism" has been of great concern to Christian leaders and missionaries for some time, as we saw above. Though syncretism, from a social science standpoint, can refer to a neutral and inevitable type of mixing, for Christian mission workers and scholars it often has more negative connotations. Gailyn Van Rheenen, for example, articulates the common Evangelical perspective that syncretism blends Christian and non-Christian beliefs and practices such that "Christianity loses its distinctiveness and speaks with a voice reflective of its culture."[28]

Sometimes terms acquire so much baggage – so many varied and imprecise meanings – that it becomes more worthwhile to search for a different term entirely. In this case is there a concept that does not instantly prejudice the mixing process, as "syncretism" does for many, nor is restricted to the important but limited methods of "contextualization" or "inculturation," as I discussed in chapter 1?[29] One possibility, as suggested in a recent study by William Burrows and Daniel Shaw, is "hybridity." In horticulture this term refers to the process of crossing genetically diverse plants in order to create a new plant, or a "hybrid."[30] For scholars in social sciences, as well as Missiologists like Burrows and Shaw, it can be used to refer to the dialectic nature of culture and cultural norms and to challenge the tendency, particular on a popular level, to essentialize cultural and religious traditions. It focuses on, as Joel Kuortti and Jopi Nyman describe, "the emergent cultural phenomena stemming from cultural contact and mixing." As well, hybridity points to a "site of transformation and change where fixed identities based on essentialisms are called into question."[31]

Of course, like any concept and analogy, hybridity is not a perfect match to describe all that inevitably occurs in the interaction between God's

---

[28] Gailyn Van Rheenen, "Syncretism and Contextualization: The Church on a Journey Defining Itself," in *Contextualization and Syncretism: Navigating Cultural Currents*, ed. Gailyn Van Rheenen (Pasadena, CA: William Carey Library, 2006), 8. Van Rheenen quotes John Orme to say that "Syncretism is like 'an odorless, tasteless gas, likened to carbon monoxide which is seeping into our atmosphere.'" John Orme, *IFMA News* 55:2 (Summer 2004), as quoted in Van Rheenen, "Syncretism and Contextualization," 3.

[29] See also William Dyrness' discussion of the limitations of contextualization in Dyrness, *Insider Jesus*, 1-27.

[30] William R. Burrows, "Theological Ideals, Cross-Cultural Realities: Syncretism and Hybridity in Christian Culture Crossing," in R. Daniel Shaw and William R. Burrows (eds), *Traditional Ritual as Christian Worship: Dangerous Syncretism or Necessary Hybridity?* (Maryknoll: Orbis Books, 2018), 27.

[31] Joel Kuortti and Jopi Nyman, "Introduction: Hybridity Today," in Joel Kuortti and Jopi Nyman (eds), *Reconstructing Hybridity: Post-Colonial Studies in Transition* (New York: Rodopi, 2007), 3.

revelation and human culture. For example, Swami Dayanand Bharati, a Hindu follower of Christ, objects to the implied idea that his faith is a "hybrid" of Christianity (as expressed in Western and Indian churches) and Hinduism.[32] Rather, he seeks to interpret biblical scripture and to make sense of what it means to follow Jesus in light of his family's Hindu traditions. This is an important point; for many insiders at least, hybrid religiosity is *not* the mixing of two religious traditions. Though it could, and probably does, often include aspects of this; for insiders it involves the interaction and crossing of God's revelation with a particular religious tradition. In this sense hybridity points to the natural and normal processes whereby people make sense of the gospel through their own practices and symbols. It is, as William Dyrness and I have described, a result of a "reverse hermeneutic," where the gospel is interpreted always and everywhere through the lenses of the cultural context.[33]

As mentioned above, this hybridity happens through people's particular expressions of religiosity; their "subjective appropriation and interpretation" of a religious tradition.[34] Religiosity is itself a hybrid in two senses. First, a given expression is the result of past cultural interactions, however recent and/or long ago they occurred. These past interactions are often opaque to the religionist, shrouded in history. But second, a person's or group's religiosity reflects the current interactions between their cultural/religious context and their understanding of the gospel. Religiosity is thus always dynamic, reflecting the interactions of people past and present and their ongoing assessments of what in their religious practices and beliefs to prioritize, highlight, affirm, or modify. Thus, the hybrid religiosity of insiders, on which we focus, is not as a process unique to them, but something they shape and express in unique ways.

Conclusion

In one sense it is understandable that the Chinese Imperial Majesty was concerned to keep the Christian "river" from mixing with and contaminating the Buddhist "river." As has happened in history, and as Christian missionaries have been highly aware, such hybrid processes sometimes can indeed dilute what is distinctively central to a religious tradition. Because of this many missionaries have sought out language and guidelines to guard against syncretism and to help the Christian faith in various contexts remain

---

[32] My thanks to Swami Dayanand Bharati for his insights during personal discussion on this topic.

[33] See Darren T. Duerksen and William A. Dyrness, *Seeking Church: Emerging Witnesses to the Kingdom* (Downers Grove, IL: IVP Academic, 2019), 28-29, 71-73.

[34] Riesebrodt, The Promise of Salvation, 76.

distinct and theologically "outside" other religious traditions. But the Imperial Majesty was perhaps mistaken in the assumption that he could completely prevent hybridity, including theological, from occurring. Rather, people's lived religion is always expressed through the hybrid religiosities they have learned and, in many cases, further hybridized and made to work for themselves and their particular concerns. For our purposes, and as we know from Church history, it is certainly possible that such hybrid religiosity could dilute biblical revelation beyond recognition. But here we can also raise a sign of hope, for in our concerns over religious hybridity we often miss or forget the ways in which God himself can, and often is, seen in and through other "rivers." It is to this that we next turn.

3: God's Activity in Hybrid Religiosity

In the previous chapter I argued that the theologies of Christ-followers – including Christian Christ-followers – are never completely shaped "outside" of a context; they are always informed and shaped by the cultural and religious traditions and practices of a people. Hybrid religiosity is, in short, an unavoidable, emergent process.[1] But how do we evaluate it missiologically? Is it an aspect of a broken creation that needs to be guarded against? We certainly have evidence of instances when the Christian gospel was hybridized with political and even military aspirations and led to disastrous consequences. Witness the medieval crusades. We could add the examples of various religious movements that had initial Christian influence but hybridized with other philosophies and revelations in ways that obscured biblical understandings of Christ. But though such examples exist, might there also be instances in which hybrid religiosity actually reflects the work and purposes of God? If so, what new missiological imaginaries emerge from this work? In the following chapters we will meet various insider Christ-followers and hear their accounts of how God has led and worked in their lives and religious traditions. But before considering some of their stories we need to explore a fundamental question: while religious traditions themselves, like any aspect of creation, are certainly broken and sinful, in what way might God be evident in and reveal himself in the midst of these, and for what purpose?

The Spirit's Role in the *Missio Trinitas*

We can begin with a fundamental query: how does God relate to other religious traditions? There are different ways by which we could categorize the answers of Christian scholars to this question. One way is to consider which person of the trinity is thought to, in a sense, take the lead in the interaction with the tradition. Perhaps the most common has been to take a

[1] Though I do not describe it in depth my perspective is influenced by critical realism and emergence theory. For a discussion on emergence as a theological process, particularly in relation to ecclesiology, see chapter 3 of Duerksen and Dyrness, *Seeking Church*.

Christocentric approach.[2] And because the person and work of Christ are connected to questions of salvation, this approach has also often forefronted questions of if/how a tradition provides salvation through Christ. Christocentric approaches thus often begin with and highlight salvific distinctives of the Christian tradition based on Christ and then explore ways in which Christianity may agree or disagree with other religious traditions.

Countering this have been theocentric approaches, such as that of John Hick. Often such approaches have sought more general and pluralistic understandings of God or a higher power in an effort to emphasize commonality versus difference. Why is commonality important for such scholars? The answers vary, but as Veli-Matti Kärkkäinen has discussed, these are often motivated by a desire to establish between religious communities equality, justice, and tolerance.[3]

In response to both of these have been scholars, including those from Pentecostal traditions, that have proposed an approach that begins with the Spirit. Here the enquiry begins not with questions of Christ's distinctiveness, or with common understandings of God or a higher power, but with enquiries into how the Spirit might already be at work in and through religious traditions. These would ask, how might our understanding of God's mission and work among other religious traditions shift or change if we make the Spirit, rather than Christ or the Father, our starting point?

This is an important question. Most Christian traditions have understood the Spirit primarily to be that aspect of God that sanctifies, perfects, and empowers individual Christ-followers. If and when the Spirit was seen to have any relationship to other religious traditions it was to provide boldness to Christ-followers for evangelism and, particularly among Pentecostals, to empower them to perform miracles that would help bring people to faith in Christ.[4]

Recapturing the Spirit's Wider Role

Beginning in the 1970s, however, some questioned whether traditional understandings of the Spirit were too restrictive and if the Holy Spirit might instead have a wider role in God's mission, particularly among other religious traditions. Work in this area was initiated by Orthodox, Roman Catholic, and ecumenical Protestant scholars[5] and, by the 1990s, joined by

---

[2] For a helpful overview of these approaches see chapter 14 of Veli-Matti Kärkkäinen, *Trinity and Revelation: A Constructive Christian Theology for the Pluralistic World Vol 2* (Grand Rapids, MI: Eerdmans, 2014).

[3] Kärkkäinen, *Trinity and Revelation*, 357.

[4] For example, see John Wimber and Kevin Springer, *Power Evangelism* (San Francisco: Harper & Row, 1986).

[5] Some key voices initiating this conversation: from an Eastern Orthodox perspective, George Khodr, "Christianity in a Pluralist World: The Economy of the

Evangelical/Pentecostal theologians such as Clark Pinnock, Amos Yong and Kirsteen Kim.[6] And though the discussions have been diverse, one of the motivations has been to help theologies of religion move beyond the "impasse,"[7] as Yong has called it, that has developed around questions of Christ, salvation, and other religious traditions.[8]

Holy Spirit," in Stanley J. Samartha (ed.), *Living Faiths and the Ecumenical Movement* (Geneva: World Council of Churches, 1971), 131-142. From a Roman Catholic perspective, Jacques Dupuis, "The Cosmic Influence of the Holy Spirit and the Gospel Message," in Jacques Dupuis (ed.), *Jesus Christ and His Spirit: Theological Approaches* (Bangalore: Theological Publications in India, 1977), 181-210; Dupuis, "The Cosmic Economy of the Spirit and the Sacred Scriptures of Religious Traditions," in Jacques Dupuis (ed.), *Jesus Christ and His Spirit: Theological Approaches* (Bangalore: Theological Publications in India, 1977), 211-228. From an ecumenical Protestant perspective, S.J. Samartha, "The Holy Spirit and People of Various Faiths, Cultures, and Ideologies," in S. J. Samartha (ed.), *Holy Spirit* (Nashville: Tidings, 1974), 20-39.

[6] Clark H. Pinnock, *Flame of Love: A Theology of the Holy Spirit* (Downers Grove: InterVarsity Press, 1996); Amos Yong, "'Not Knowing Where the Spirit Blows…' On Envisioning a Pentecostal-Charismatic Theology of Religions," *Journal of Pentecostal Theology* 14 (April 1999), 81-112; Amos Yong, *Discerning the Spirit(s): A Pentecostal-Charismatic Contribution to Christian Theology of Religions* (Sheffield: Sheffield Academic Press, 2000); Amos Yong, *Beyond the Impasse: Toward a Pneumatological Theology of Religions* (Grand Rapids, MI: Baker Academic, 2003); Amos Yong, "The Holy Spirit and the World Religions: On the Christian Discernment of Spirit(s) 'after' Buddhism," *Buddhist-Christian Studies* 24:1 (2004), 191-207; Kirsteen Kim, *Mission in the Spirit: The Holy Spirit in Indian Christian Theologies* (Delhi: ISPCK, 2003); Kirsteen Kim, *The Holy Spirit in the World: A Global Conversation* (Maryknoll, NY: Orbis, 2007).

[7] Yong, *Discerning the Spirit(s)*, 33.

[8] Yong's pneumatology of religions has received various critiques, often questioning whether he makes too substantial a distinction between the work of the Spirit and that of Christ. See Keith E. Johnson, "Does the Doctrine of the Trinity Hold the Key to a Christian Theology of Religions? An Evaluation of Three Recent Proposals," *Southern Baptist Journal of Theology* 10:1 (2006), 24-47; Chapter 4, "Divine Relations in the Theology of Religions," in Keith E. Johnson, *Rethinking the Trinity and Religious Pluralism: An Augustinian Assessment* (Downers Grove, IL: IVP Academic, 2011); James R.A. Merrick, "The Spirit of Truth as Agent in False Religions? A Critique of Amos Yong's Pneumatological Theology of Religions with Reference to Current Trends," *Trinity Journal* 29:1 (2008), 107-125; Chapter 6, "Inclusivism II: Evangelical Expressions," in Todd Miles, *A God of Many Understandings? The Gospel and Theology of Religions* (Nashville: B&H Academic, 2010). See also his and Tony Richie's response to these in Amos Yong, *Pneumatology and the Christian-Buddhist Dialogue: Does the Spirit Blow through the Middle Way?* (Boston: Brill, 2012), 243-249; Tony Richie, "The Spirit of Truth as Guide into All Truth: A Response to R.A. James Merrick, "The Spirit of Truth as Agent in False Religions? A Critique of Amos Yong's Pneumatological Theology of Religions with Reference to Current Trends," *Cyberjournal for Pentecostal-Charismatic Research* 19 (January 2010).

According to this approach, how does biblical scripture help us understand the wider work of God's Spirit? On the one hand it is certainly the case that one of the purposes of the Spirit is to give gifts to Christ-followers (1 Cor. 12), help produce "fruit" within them (Gal. 5:22-23), and testify to Christ and his work (John 15:26). But how, and through whom, does the Spirit extend these gifts? As Paul indicates in the above passages the Spirit gives gifts to individual believers, and often does this directly or through the church community. But might the Spirit also gift people who are not Christ-followers? Or, from a different angle, might the Spirit provide gifts to Christ-followers, but do so through people or traditions that are not specifically identified with Christ? This of course opens up the question of if and how the Spirit offers good things, gifts, outside of the Christian community, including through other religious traditions. We will return to this question later in the chapter.

But though the Spirit is that aspect of God that gives gifts to people, theologians examining the role of the Spirit would caution us from reducing and minimizing the work of the Spirit to only this. In Genesis 1, for example, the Spirit-breath (*ruach*) of God is present and sweeps across the face of the waters. This, together with images evoked by the psalmist, presents God's Spirit as universally present across creation. As Psalm 33:6 says, "By the word of the Lord the heavens were made; their starry host by the breath [*ruach*] of his mouth."

God's Spirit-breath is not only instrumental in creating the wider natural order, but also in creating humanity. When God puts Spirit-breath into people in Genesis 2, the text indicates that God's Spirit brings continued animation and life – that God's Spirit not only *begins* life, but also in some ways *sustains* it. Psalm 104:29-30 poetically expresses this when it says,

> When you hide your face,
> they are terrified;
> when you take away their breath,
> they die and return to the dust.
> When you send your Spirit,
> they are created,
> and you renew the face of the ground.

As Walter Brueggemann says, this text asserts that "the world has no capacity for generativity on its own. Its life depends on closeness to and reliance on the God who breathes."[9] And even though in Genesis 3 God's image in persons becomes marred through sin, there is no indication that the Spirit-breath of God leaves creation or created beings. Rather, God's Spirit

---

[9] Walter Brueggemann, *Theology of the Old Testament: Testimony, Dispute, Advocacy* (Minneapolis: Augsburg Fortress, 1997), 156.

is portrayed as what Steven M. Studebaker calls "a liminal agent who operates at the threshold between death and life and chaos and order."[10] Despite the brokenness and distortions in the created order caused by sin there remains a pneumatological dimension in which the Spirit seeks to sustain life in creation and with every individual.

This suggests that God's Spirit is not only involved in the work of creation, but also instrumental in the ongoing work of re-creation. In the First Testament this is implied in the poetic language of Psalms such as discussed above, as well as instances when God's Spirit comes upon leaders and individuals in order to make his will and wisdom known to his people. In the New Testament the Spirit's re-creating work is instrumental in the incarnation of Jesus, where the Spirit overshadows Mary (Luke 1:35) and continues to be present and active in Jesus' life, death, and resurrection.[11] The work of re-creation continues in Acts, starting with the catalyzing events on the Day of Pentecost. Here God's Spirit is not only "poured out" on Christ's immediate disciples, but his presence is seen by Peter as a fulfillment of his universal movement among "all flesh" (Acts 2:17). The Spirit is, as John V. Taylor says, the "go-between God,"[12] bridging the Trinity with creation for the purpose of re-creation. In addition, Peter's reference to the prophecy by Joel indicates that the Spirit's work of re-creation is part of God's overall eschatological plan. As Paul would later say to the church in Rome, the Spirit "groans" in and through us, moving us and creation towards liberation from our "bondage to decay" (8:21-27). The Holy Spirit is, as Amos Yong says, "the universal presence and activity of God… that spans the entirety of God's work from original creation, to re-creation, to final creation."[13]

The Spirit and the Son

The Spirit, I am emphasizing, is the liminal "go-between" God and the "principal actor" in God's re-creative activities,[14] both within and for the people of God as well as with and for God's wider creation. But how does the Spirit then connect with Christ and his salvific work? To answer this some recall Irenaeus' famous analogy of the Trinity – the Father with two hands, one the Son and the other the Spirit – extended out to others but connected to

[10] Steven M. Studebaker, *From Pentecost to the Triune God: A Pentecostal Trinitarian Theology* (Grand Rapids, MI: Eerdmans, 2012), 68.
[11] Yong, *Beyond the Impasse*, 38.
[12] John V. Taylor, *The Go-Between God: The Holy Spirit and the Christian Mission* (Philadelphia: Fortress Press, 1972), 19-22.
[13] Yong, *Beyond the Impasse*, 42; See also Amos Yong, *The Missiological Spirit: Christian Mission Theology in the Third Millennium Global Context* (Eugene, OR: Cascade, 2014), 192.
[14] Studebaker, *From Pentecost to the Triune God*, 68.

each other through the Father.[15] This, however, can evoke a misleading picture of two separate beings with a disconnected relationship to each other. Rather, as Veli-Matti Kärkkäinen has shown, a pneumatological approach is not adequate unless understood within the framework of the mission of the Trinity – the *missio trinitas* – particularly as it includes the close interrelationship of the Spirit and the Son. For, regardless of the stance Christians take on the ancient debate of whether the Spirit came from the Father or from the Son, Scripture is clear that the Spirit leads people towards the teachings, actions, and person of Jesus (John 14:26, John 16:13-15). As Jacques Dupuis summarizes, "The Spirit is the 'point of entry' of God's self-communication to human beings; but the Spirit of God is, at one and the same time, the Spirit of Christ, communicated by him in virtue of his resurrection from the dead."[16] I will return to this point momentarily.

The Spirit and Other Religious Traditions

But the inquisitive reader will wonder, "In what ways might God's Spirit be at work in other religious traditions? Surely this is the crux of the matter." Indeed. And to pursue this let's return to the point made above, that the Spirit may provide "gifts" to and through people other than Christ-followers.

Certainly one of the gifts that the Spirit provides is revelation. As Jesus said, the Spirit would guide people into "all the truth" (John 16:13). In what ways does the Spirit provide gifts of revelation to people? Robert Johnston, in his book *God's Wider Presence*, describes what Christian tradition has often thought to be three primary sources of general revelation – or general knowledge – about God.[17] First, *creation*, such as mountains, oceans, the skies, etc., provide people with a variety of impressions, including a sense of awe or transcendent experience connected to God. Second, a generally shared sense of *conscience*, stemming perhaps from people's creation in God's image, provides people with values that reflect God's moral order.[18] Third, *culture*, and particularly the ability to create and celebrate truth and goodness,

---

[15] A. Cleveland Coxe, *Ante-Nicene Fathers: The Writings of the Fathers down to A.D. 325. Volume 1: The Apostolic Fathers, Justin Martyr, Irenaeus*, ed. Alexander Roberts and James Donaldson. (New York: Christian Literature Publishing, 1885), 463.

[16] Jacques Dupuis, *Toward a Christian Theology of Religious Pluralism* (Maryknoll, NY: Orbis Books, 1997), 197.

[17] Johnston, *God's Wider Presence*, 190-199.

[18] In his classic text *Mere Christianity* C.S. Lewis appeals to conscience as a source of general revelation when he claims that, across cultures and religious traditions, human beings "have this curious idea that they ought to behave in a certain way, and cannot really get rid of it… They know the Law of Nature." C.S. Lewis, *Mere Christianity* (New York: HarperOne, 2001), 8.

can in a similar way reflect an innate capacity given by and reflecting something of God's design.

But though truths about God can indeed be known through creation, conscience, and culture, Johnston raises an important point. Too often Christ-followers have interpreted the medium itself as that which does the revealing. This, however, would be a serious misunderstanding of the way God reveals himself. It is *not*, as Johnston shows, the mountains, or sense of morality, or a profound musical piece that is doing the revealing. Rather, when revelation occurs it is because God's Spirit is there, at that moment, in that experience. Revelation is always an event, one brought by the Spirit. Creation, conscience, and culture may indeed be recordings or evidence of God's past activity and have value insofar as they bear witness to that activity. However, when they serve as sources of present revelation to people it is not because people are logically deducing God's past activity. Rather, revelation occurs if and when God reveals himself through his Spirit.[19]

The Spirit Reveals (Not the Religious Tradition)

But if this is the case, what does this mean for the Spirit's work in religious traditions? Johnston highlights three implications important for our discussion. First, religious traditions, like any other part of culture, can be a medium through which God reveals himself. As Johnston shows, in addition to the natural works of creation, God also reveals himself through the cultural and religious reflections of non-covenant people. Biblical writers/compilers themselves recognized this and included such insights into the biblical scripture, including sections of Proverbs (30:1-14; 31:1-9; 22:17–24:22), narratives regarding non-Israelite leaders (2 Chron. 2:3-16, 25:20-27, 26:22-23, and Gen. 14:17-20), and Psalms such as 19 and 29.[20] Israel's context, including its surrounding neighbors as well as the peoples that inhabited its own land, provided many traditions of wisdom that in turn had a profound influence on its own scriptures.[21] In addition to the wisdom literature and sayings that Israel incorporated and adapted from other cultures we could add the stories about the non-covenant people that received dreams from God, many of which did not need interpretation by others, such as those like Abimelech, Laban, and Balaam.[22] Such inclusion of the work and revelation of God through non-covenant persons extends into the New Testament, such as the philosophy and poetry included in Acts 14 and 17.

---

[19] Johnston, *God's Wider Presence*, 120-121.

[20] Johnston, *God's Wider Presence*, 67-94. See also chapter 4 of William A. Dyrness, *The Facts on the Ground: A Wisdom Theology of Culture* (Eugene, OR: Cascade, 2022).

[21] Dyrness, *The Facts on the Ground*, 84.

[22] Johnston, *God's Wider Presence*, 94-104.

In other words, many biblical writers/compilers did not seem to have a problem with the idea that other cultural and religious traditions could be mediums of God's revelation. Of course, some readers may respond by asserting that the above passages are "special" or one-offs. But, as Johnston shows, the biblical narratives do not really agree with such an assessment. God reveals himself as he chooses, and sometimes does so via other religious traditions. Of course, and again, it is not cultures or religious traditions themselves that reveal God; it is only God who reveals God, and he chooses to do so through his (and people's) created order in various ways.

But what about the recordings of God's past work and revelation? Here, just as creation, conscience, and culture can display God's past handiwork or show his "footprints," might also religious traditions display these? As we saw in chapter 2, religious traditions are a human response to a desire to access transcendent powers for various reasons. They are, as William Dyrness says, "the practices associated with the human search for God… the spaces humans construct to look for and even find God."[23] As people search after transcendent powers, they create written, practical, ritual, and material responses that serve as records to their pursuit. These responses are often very incomplete, or even misguided.[24] But Johnston would alert us to the possibility that people may have, by God's Spirit, glimpsed some of God's gifts in themselves and creation, prompting them to reflect on and record these in various ways. There is, as this would suggest, a close relationship between people's own perceptiveness and the work of God's Spirit. As Avery Dulles says, "Revelation should not be understood as an insertion of fully formulated divine truths into the continuum of human knowledge, but rather as the process by which God, working within human history and human tradition, enables his spiritual creatures to discern more profoundly the true meaning of their existence."[25]

Perhaps then, for this reason, when a Muslim expresses compassion for the poor by offering to someone *zakat* (Muslim offering), or a Hindu performs a dance that celebrates a harvest, it is possible that these may be records of his Spirit's past revelation to people. Such would not be unlike First Testament authors who sensed that a prayer, song, or proverb from another religious tradition reflected truth about God and included it in their own record of wisdom or worship (as Proverbs 30:1-4 or Psalm 29 seem to have been). In this sense some religious traditions, scriptures, rituals, etc. may contain *some* records of people's encounters with God's Spirit. These,

---

[23] Dyrness, *Insider Jesus*, 101.

[24] Dyrness, *Insider Jesus*, 39.

[25] Avery Dulles, "Revelation and Discovery," in William Kelly (ed.), *Theology and Discovery: Essays in Honor of Karl Rahner, S.J.* (Wilwaukee, WI: Marquette University Press, 1980), 21.

we could say, are evidence of God's footprints – testimony to his past presence and activity – in and through those traditions.

But, to reiterate, though a religious tradition may have traces of God's past work and revelation, discerning whether or not an action, song, prayer, etc. might reflect God's past activity is something that occurs in the present and is again led by God's Spirit. The creation of cultural wisdom and religious tradition is the work of persons; revelation is the work of God. However, as Dyrness points out, "If we listen closely to the former, we sometimes end up hearing the latter."[26] In other words, and as we'll explore more in a moment, hearing God in and through a culture's religious tradition, or discerning the past and present footprints of God, can never be done apart from God's Spirit.

Before proceeding, it is important to stress that, just because persons may receive glimpses and revelations of God through religious traditions, this does not mean that such traditions are salvific. They are not. Religious traditions, including Christianity, do not bring salvation to people – only God through Christ can save persons. Rather, and again, theologically speaking, religious traditions are created by persons as part of their search for and response to God (Acts 17). Through their religious practices and traditions people seek to make sense of the divine and/or the created order. Religious traditions are, as we have said and William Dyrness argues, the accumulation of wisdom – the "ongoing and dramatic response to God's presence and activity in (created) order, as this points toward (or away from) the final (eschatological) purposes God has for that creation."[27]

But though they do not bring salvation, religious traditions can and often do reflect people's encounter with God's Spirit. Because of this we can now better understand the ways in which hybrid religiosity may, at times, reflect God's work. Religiosity is always hybrid – an interaction and engagement in a particular time and space.[28] As Willie Jennings has expressed it, moral sensibilities are "space textured."[29] As we discussed in the last chapter, from a phenomenological perspective the religiosity of people – their interpretation and expression of a religious tradition at any given time – are always "textured" by the space in which they occur. This is particularly the case in the midst of migration and other processes of movement and interaction. And though, as mentioned at the beginning of the chapter, hybrid religiosity has at times distorted the message of scripture and witness of Christ, it is possible that some are also records of an experience of the Spirit's revelation and work in a person and community. Perhaps a person reads a passage of biblical scripture and, by the power of the Spirit, gains new

---

[26] Dyrness, *The Facts on the Ground*, 190.
[27] Dyrness, *The Facts on the Ground*, 31.
[28] Dyrness, *The Facts on the Ground*, 82.
[29] Willie James Jennings, *The Christian Imagination: Theology and the Origins of Race* (New Haven, Conn: Yale University Press, 2010), 54.

understanding about God's love which she then captures in a song that uses local styles and terminology for God's love and power. The result, we could say, is a hybrid expression of her religiosity – her interpretation of a Spirit-given insight through a religious tradition and practice.

As we will see in the next chapter, insider Christ-followers see their religious tradition and identity as a rich seedbed of past, present, and future encounters with the Spirit of Christ, but do not claim that *all* expressions of religiosity reflect the work of the Spirit. Insiders would agree that there is much in their traditions that needs to be discerned and countered. But there is also much that is good, which leads to Johnston's next point.

The Spirit's Purposes

A second implication that Johnston suggests regarding the Spirit's work in religious traditions can be introduced with a question: *why* does God choose to reveal himself outside of his covenant people, including among various religious traditions? One purpose, and the one most theologians have assumed, is that such revelation is part of God's effort to make himself known throughout the earth, and to ultimately convict people of their sin. The classic text for this view is Romans 1, where God makes known his "invisible attributes, his eternal power and divine nature" to humanity such that they are without excuse for their sin.[30] But while this may be one of the Spirit's purposes, the eschatological work of the Spirit – moving creation towards its re-creation in Christ – suggests something more. As suggested above, God's Spirit also desires to provide gifts that bring his goodness. As Johnston says, "It is not enough to say that general revelation helps preserve the world from destruction; the Spirit's revelatory presence must also be seen as providing humankind, including adherents of other faiths, all that is good."[31] That is, just as God's Spirit is presently transforming creation, conscience, and culture in anticipation of the ultimate re-creation and establishment of God's kingdom, the Spirit may indeed desire to include religious traditions as part of this project.

To biblically understand just how this might be we can turn to God's work at Pentecost in Acts 1 and 2. Here God both reaffirms his historical work through Israel while also giving a glimpse of the universal scope and mission of his Spirit. One of the central foci of this passage is the communication of the gospel to "all peoples" via their various languages; as the Spirit came

---

[30] Johnston convincingly argues that Paul, in Romans 1 and 2, is not primarily trying to describe the nature of God's general revelation. He explains, "Paul's focus in his opening argument in Romans is elsewhere. He is focused not on those occasions when God's revelatory Presence breaks through and we respond in awe and obedience, but rather on humankind's selfishness in regularly closing off such awareness of God's Presence." Johnston, *God's Wider Presence*, 126.

[31] Johnston, *God's Wider Presence*, 211.

upon the Christ-followers they began to speak in other tongues about the wonders of God (2:11). This was primarily for the benefit of people staying in Jerusalem who came from other regions and whose first language was presumably not the Aramaic that the disciples would have normally and naturally been speaking.

But, as Amos Yong contends, Acts 2 suggests that the Pentecost miracle is not only a linguistic event but also a picture of the ways in which God intended to pour out his Spirit on "all people." As the text suggests, and as we ourselves know, language is intricately connected to cultural identity. As such, the tongues of Pentecost signified the many cultures of the ancient Mediterranean world (2:9-11). Moreover, as Yong points out, language and culture "are related to religious traditions, even if each is a distinguishable aspect of human life."[32] The narrative suggests that God desires to renew, and even speak through, all aspects of culture. What it does not say explicitly, but certainly leaves open, is the possibility that this could also include religious traditions.

And why wouldn't it? As Yong again points out, "Why would this reconciling work of the Spirit (and of Christ) not include the redemption of the religious sphere of human life? This reconciliatory work is especially important since religions, no less than other dimensions of human experience, are fallen and in need of redemption."[33] The key point here again is not only to emphasize the presence of God's Spirit with his creation and their activities, including their religious activities, but also *why* God's Spirit would remain with, and even "sustain," other religious traditions. As Peter's speech makes clear, the presence of God's Spirit and his work in "all flesh" is part of his eschatological redemption and reconciliation of all things in Christ. In other words, God wants to bring all things, including religious traditions, towards completion in Christ. Yong summarizes this point saying, "the religions are neither accidents of history nor encroachments on divine providence but are, in various ways, instruments of the Holy Spirit working out the divine purposes in the world…"[34]

Discerning the Spirit

Johnston highlights a third and final implication for our understanding of the Spirit's work among religious traditions, including those of insider Christ-followers. As suggested above, though religious traditions often contain records of the Spirit's gifts and revelation, they are also imperfect searches

---

[32] Yong, *The Missiological Spirit*, 113.

[33] Yong, *The Missiological Spirit*, 48. Or, as Clark Pinnock has said, "it would be strange if the Spirit excused himself from the very arena of culture where people search for meaning." Pinnock, *Flame of Love*, 203.

[34] Amos Yong, *The Spirit Poured Out on All Flesh: Pentecostalism and the Possibility of Global Theology* (Grand Rapids, MI: Baker Academic, 2005), 236.

for God or transcendent powers at best, and misguided, destructive, or even demonic responses to those at worst. Because of this, the process of discernment is crucial. How should Christ-followers discern the Spirit's presence, and what should they look for? Christian theologians and mission scholars suggest a number of possibilities. For Jürgen Moltmann the work of the Spirit is that which affirms life. This is because the Spirit is the "divine wellspring of life – the source of life created, life preserved and life daily renewed, and finally the source of the eternal life of all created being."[35] Clark Pinnock similarly sees the work of the Spirit as that which affirms life, particularly as revealed by Christ. Reminding us that the ultimate test of the spirits, and the Spirit, is Christological (1 John 4:2-3) he suggests that the presence of the Spirit will be found "wherever we see traces of Jesus in the world and people opening up to his ideals."[36] What particular ideals? "Wherever, for example, we find self-sacrificing love, care about community, longings for justice, wherever people love one another, care for the sick, make peace not war, wherever there is beauty and concord, generosity and forgiveness, the cup of cold water, we know the Spirit of Jesus is present. Other Spirits do not promote broken and contrite hearts."[37]

Amos Yong has pursued the question of discernment at length in various places, including his exploration of the Spirit in Buddhism. In *Pneumatology and the Christian-Buddhist Dialogue: Does the Spirit Blow Through the Middle Way?* Yong seeks to bring the biblical texts and norm of Jesus Christ into dialogue with a true openness to the categories of Buddhism. It is important, Yong asserts, that Christ-followers do not import a rigidly formed picture of what the Spirit's activity may look like – what is "good" in one context may look slightly different in another. Overall, however, Yong finds that criteria such as the fruit of the Spirit are applicable and evident in traditions such as Theravada Buddhism.[38] The Spirit is certainly present in these ways. And yet, because many Buddhists understand the telos of their journey to be annihilation through *nirvana*, the Spirit's presence is provisional. Some Buddhist teaching does not evidence the ultimate, eschatological criterion of "conformation to the image of the Son culminating in glorification (Rom. 6– 8, esp. 8:29-30)."[39] Thus, for Moltmann, Pinnock, Yong, and others, a Muslim's generosity, a Buddhist proverb, or a Native American's concern for the land could well reflect the Spirit's presence insofar as these are "traces of Jesus in the world." But these traces ultimately

[35] Jürgen Moltmann, *The Spirit of Life: A Universal Affirmation* (Philadelphia: Fortress Press, 1992), 42. See Johnston's discussion of Moltmann's theology of the Holy Spirit: Johnston, *God's Wider Presence*, 178-187.
[36] Pinnock, *Flame of Love*, 209.
[37] Pinnock, *Flame of Love*, 209-210.
[38] Yong, *Pneumatology and the Christian-Buddhist Dialogue*, 175.
[39] Yong, *Pneumatology and the Christian-Buddhist Dialogue*, 176.

serve as signposts that direct persons towards Christ and becoming more like Christ.

As we start to conclude our discussion of the work of God's Spirit in other religious traditions we need to address one additional question: since we are proposing a trinitarian framework, how does Christ, along with questions regarding salvation, relate to the Spirit's work of revelation and re-creation among religious traditions?

The Christ/Spirit "Hermeneutical Spiral"

As mentioned above, the analogy of the Spirit and the Son forming the two hands of the Father could lead some to minimize the interrelationship of the Spirit and Son. After all, a right hand can act completely independent of and without any reference to the left hand.

But such is not the case with the Trinity, and particularly with the way the Spirit relates to the Son. The Spirit, as we have said, is the Spirit of Christ. I am thus not indicating that the Spirit's desire to be present and work within religious traditions means that every religionist does or will experience God's salvation regardless of their knowledge of or response to Jesus. Nor am I saying that all people, by simply following their religious traditions, will ultimately be saved. I do not believe that to be consistent with Scripture, nor do many Christ-following insiders seem to believe this.

Rather, even if we begin with and give much attention to the work of the Spirit, eventually every religionist can and should be challenged by what Yong calls "the Christological scandal of particularity."[40] Salvation occurs only through Christ (however we may understand the details of this), and the Spirit's work of re-creation finds its ultimate fulfillment through Christ. Insiders discussed in the following chapters, in their testimonies and lives, agree with this. However, their testimonies also show that, in their estimation, it is not just the Christian's presentation of Christ that has caused scandal and offense in their religious communities. Rather, the scandal often comes from a Christian's identity and unrelatable religiosity that can sever Christians from their religious community and tradition. It is this offense, as we will see, that many insider Christ-followers seek to counter. They are not shy of the Christological claims of Jesus and his Lordship but believe that these can be embraced within their traditions. They sense that, in some way, the Spirit has been present with them and their community and is leading them and their community to Christ from *within* their religious traditions.

Thus, giving initial attention to the work of the Spirit does not diminish Christ. On the contrary, the work of the Spirit in and through other religious traditions reveals a continually expanding vision of Jesus as the Christ. And,

---

[40] Yong, *The Missiological Spirit*, 6.

while doing this, the Spirit also continually shapes and reshapes religious traditions while moving them towards an eschatological convergence with the glory of Christ, even if we can only dimly perceive the nature of that convergence at present.[41]

Conclusion: The Mission of the Trinity and Hybrid Religiosity

Why is this foray into the Trinity's work among religious traditions, and hybrid religiosity, important for our discussion of insider Christ-followers? It is certainly *not* because insiders themselves are reading and taking note of these discussions and interpreting their faith in these categories. Instead, such approaches – and usually those that begin with and only consider Christocentric/soteriological concerns – underlie Western Christians' debates about religious traditions and insiders. And whereas questions regarding Christ and salvation are crucial concerns, our discussion suggests that a trinitarian understanding of God's work may help us to better understand the alternative missiological imaginaries of insiders. In particular, we should not prematurely dismiss the ways in which God's Spirit may be revealing and doing a re-creative work in the midst of other religious traditions, with the ultimate goal of reconciling all things to God in Christ (Col. 1:19-20).

Might this thus mean that the alternative missiological imaginaries of insiders are part of the larger project of revitalizing, renewing, and reshaping their religious tradition towards the eschatological purposes of God? If this is a possibility it opens up missiological space to understand insiders and their hybrid religiosity not so much as evangelistic strategy or contextualization, but more as a genuine desire on their behalf to follow Christ and his teachings while not rejecting, and perhaps instead moving with, the Spirit deeper into their own religious traditions. What does this look like? We turn in the next section to historical and contemporary case studies of various insider people and groups to consider how this might be the case.

[41] Yong, *Pneumatology and the Christian-Buddhist Dialogue*, 245.

Section Two

Case Studies of Insider Christ-Followers

4: Insider Christ-Follower Imaginaries in History

The argument I have been making thus far is that, first, *all* Christ-oriented groups, and all religious groups in general, hybridize their religiosity in various ways. We need to disabuse ourselves of the notion that a "pure" expression of the Christian faith is possible. It simply is not, at least on this side of the eschaton. But this does not mean that we should not make efforts to discern God's revelation, nor that those efforts are pointless. Rather, God's Spirit is at work in the hybridizing process, continually guiding all people towards the completion of all things in Christ. Second, insider groups provide for us a unique example of this; through them and their hybrid religiosities the Spirit is creating new missiological imaginaries – new ways of missional being in the religious world.

This creates an openness, at least theoretically and theologically, to the things that insiders may say to us. With this as our framework, it is now the right stage in our discussion to introduce the stories of various insiders, past and present. In this chapter I discuss the stories of two Christ-followers in other religious traditions from the early 20th century. Our look at past examples illustrates the fact that Christ-followers in various contexts (and the missionaries who were with them) have long wrestled with issues related to hybrid religiosities, and hybrid Christianities in particular. They framed these discussions in terms of the analytical tools, Western and non-Western, that were available to them, just as we in more recent years have utilized the methods of social sciences and related postcolonial frameworks.

For our present discussion I have intentionally chosen people who were not theologians in any trained sense. These are people who, during their lifetimes, embraced Christ and sought to faithfully live out their faith in the context of their religious communities. In addition, though they did not start groups or movements, or at least groups that sustained the imaginaries they held, they share concerns and impulses from which we can learn, and that are emulated by other insider Christ-followers to the present day.

Black Elk: A Lakota Native-American Christ-Follower

When a Lakota *wicasa wakan*, or medicine man, living in South Dakota accepted Catholic baptism in 1904 few people suspected the innovations and controversy his faith journey would create. Black Elk (1863–1950) was one of many Lakota who embraced the teaching of Christian missionaries, including Catholic Jesuits, who had begun work in their area. But though Black Elk became Catholic he also, in his own way, hybridized and re-imagined his new faith in light of his Lakota traditions and the trauma his people experienced in the late 19th and early 20th centuries.

Black Elk was born on the Great Plains at a time when the US government was quickly taking away territory from the Lakota and other tribes through a series of military actions. Eventually he and his tribe were forced to settle onto the Pine Ridge reservation in 1880. He was deeply impacted by the violence and injustice that he and his people experienced, and his people's need for hope and renewal would be a theme that he would carry throughout his life.

Another theme important to Black Elk was the desire to be a source of healing for his people. At the age of nine he had a vision in which he went into the clouds to meet with six grandfathers. In the vision they gave instructions and showed Black Elk numerous sights, including a red road down which he would lead his people for healing and prosperity.[1] The grandfathers also gave him gifts: a bow and arrow with which to destroy his people's enemies, and a wooden cup of water with which he was to save humanity.[2] This vision foreshadowed his later eventual calling and role as a *wicasa wakan*, through which he developed his own *yuwipi* (healing) ceremony to heal people of various ailments.[3]

Perhaps a third theme important for Black Elk was an interest in other traditions, including – ironically enough – the White culture responsible for his people's oppression. In 1886 Black Elk left Pine Ridge and spent over two years performing in New York and throughout Europe with Buffalo Bill's Wild West Show and the "Mexican Joe" Shelley Show, motivated in part to learn more about the White culture and their religious beliefs.[4] While on that trip he learned about Christianity from an Episcopal teacher/chaplain

---

[1] Raymond J. DeMallie (ed.), *The Sixth Grandfather: Black Elk's Teachings Given to John G. Neihardt* (Lincoln: University of Nebraska Press, 1984), 122.

[2] DeMallie, *The Sixth Grandfather*, 119.

[3] In a *yuwipi* ceremony the *wicasa wakan* would often wrap himself in a special blanket and call on various spirits who might respond with sounds or voices and foretell certain events, diagnose and cure an illness, or bring other insights. Michael F. Steltenkamp, *Nicholas Black Elk: Medicine Man, Missionary, Mystic* (Norman: University of Oklahoma Press, 2009), 25.

[4] Clyde Holler, *Black Elk's Religion: The Sun Dance and Lakota Catholicism* (Syracuse, NY: Syracuse University Press, 1995), 8; DeMallie, *The Sixth Grandfather*, 7.

traveling with the show and was intrigued by the European church services and rituals that he observed.[5]

When Black Elk returned from his travels to Pine Ridge in 1889 he found his tribal community grappling with drought, crop failures, disease, death, and increasing disillusionment over the US government's failure to uphold treaty agreements.[6] Through his role as a *wicasa wakan* he again sought to help his people, but soon experienced his own personal hardships, including the death of his first wife in 1901 and ongoing physical ailments. In 1904, when he was 41 years old, Black Elk was invited by a Jesuit to receive medical help and teaching at a local Catholic mission.[7] Black Elk accepted the invitation, listened to the priest's teaching, and after a two-week stay accepted baptism and the Christian name Nicholas.[8]

Black Elk quickly excelled in memorizing and explaining bblical scripture and teachings.[9] Because of this he was soon appointed as a missionary and tasked with traveling to other reservations to evangelize and establish new Catholic groups; a role he had till 1916. When funding for this role was stopped Black Elk continued to serve as a catechist, teaching, preaching, and praying for his Lakota community in Pine Ridge.[10]

In 1932, however, the image of Black Elk as the faithful Catholic convert and catechist was challenged. It was in that year that poet/writer John Neihardt published his now-famous *Black Elk Speaks*, based on interviews he conducted with Black Elk in 1930.[11] In it, Black Elk recollects his early

---

[5] He says in one report to his tribe, "So my relatives, the Lakota people, now I know the white men's customs well. One custom is very good. Whoever believes in God will find good ways – that is what I mean." Printed in the *Iapi Oaye,* a Dakota-language missionary newspaper. DeMallie, *The Sixth Grandfather*, 8.

[6] Steltenkamp, *Nicholas Black Elk*, 59. Not coincidentally, that year Black Elk and many from his tribe participated in the ghost dance – a growing messianic religious movement that was banned by the US government because of its vision of the imminent overthrow of White colonial rule. Despite the ban many Lakota, including Black Elk, continued to participate in the ghost dance, leading to the violent suppression and massacre at Wounded Knee in 1890.

[7] The Jesuits had been conducting mission work among the Lakota since the 1850s and at Pine Ridge reservation since 1887. Damien Costello, *Black Elk: Colonialism and Lakota Catholicism* (Maryknoll, NY: Orbis, 2005), 27-28.

[8] DeMallie, *The Sixth Grandfather*, 14.

[9] DeMallie, *The Sixth Grandfather*, 16.

[10] Black Elk's commitment to the church, particularly in his early years, seems to have been very sincere, though some scholars dispute this. For a sampling of those skeptical of the authenticity of Black Elk's conversion see Julian Rice, *Black Elk's Story: Distinguishing Its Lakota Purpose* (Albuquerque: University of New Mexico Press, 1991); Holler, *Black Elk's Religion.* Those who argue for his sincerity include Michael F. Steltenkamp, *Black Elk: Holy Man of the Oglala* (Norman: University of Oklahoma Press, 1993); Costello, *Black Elk.*

[11] John G. Neihardt, *Black Elk Speaks: Being the Life Story of a Holy Man of the Oglala Sioux* (Lincoln, NE: University of Nebraska Press, 1988 [1932]).

life and his tribe's experiences, including the Wounded Knee massacre in 1890. He also recounts the "great vision" he had when he was nine years old that foretold how he would lead his people into a new and good way. But much to the consternation of Catholic leaders, Neihardt's narrative did not address Black Elk's life after 1890, including his turn to the Catholic faith. And of perhaps even greater concern, Black Elk gave no indication that his early life, rituals, and visions, deeply entrenched in Lakota traditions and devoid of any overt Christian references, were in any way invalid or questionable.

Scholars, Native American traditionalists, and Catholics have long debated Black Elk's positive recollection of his indigenous traditions and spirituality. Did Black Elk at that point in his life experience a renewal of his indigenous religious tradition, and a corresponding doubt about his Catholic faith?[12] Had he been sincere in his Catholic faith to begin with? On the one hand he did stop his work as a catechist around this time,[13] continued to tell White scholars about his traditions,[14] and even began to regularly perform in a summer tourist show in the role of a *wicasa wakan*.[15] On the other hand, Black Elk took steps to reassure his Catholic leaders that he was still a devoted Catholic, and continued to observe Mass and Catholic rituals as he was able up till his death in 1950 at the age of 87.[16]

Though some in both camps – Native American traditionalists and Roman Catholics – have contended for a Black Elk that exclusively represents their respective traditions, others have sensed a fundamental flaw in these readings. That is, these rely on a dichotomous interpretive framework that would have struck Black Elk as utterly foreign.[17] Contrary to the method used

---

[12] DeMallie expresses this opinion, saying "It was as if something long bound up inside the old man had broken free at last, an impulse to save that entire system of knowledge that his vision represented and that for more than twenty-five years he had denied." DeMallie, *The Sixth Grandfather*, 28.

[13] Though, as Costello points out, Black Elk was 67 old and his health was weakening at this point. Costello, *Black Elk*, 160 n6.

[14] Black Elk gave interviews to Joseph Epes Brown for what became the book *The Sacred Pipe: Black Elk's Account of the Seven Rites of the Oglala Sioux* (Norman, OK: University of Oklahoma Press, 1953). He also gave another set of interviews to John Neihardt which informed his book *When the Tree Flowered: An Authentic Tale of the Sioux Indians* (New York: Macmillan, 1951).

[15] DeMallie, *The Sixth Grandfather*, 63-66.

[16] After the publication of *Black Elk Speaks* Black Elk wrote a letter to his Catholic community and leaders reassuring them that "I know that the Catholic religion is good, better than the Sun dance or the Ghost dance." DeMallie, *The Sixth Grandfather*, 60.

[17] Representing this more nuanced view, though not agreeing with each other in many areas, would be Holler, *Black Elk's Religion*; Steltenkamp, *Nicholas Black Elk*; Joshua Thomas, "Native Hermeneutics: Reverse Typology and Remythologization, or: The Theological Genius of Black Elk's Dual Participation,"

by some Christians, Black Elk did not simply interpret Lakota traditions through a Christian lens, where Christianity would remain untouched and either fulfill Lakota traditions or replace those that contradicted the gospel. Neither, as some scholars have suggested, does it seem that Black Elk kept each tradition separate and adeptly shifted from one to the other as the social situation necessitated.[18] Relatedly, and to use similar insights from Sergei Kan's study of Native Tlingit Christians, neither does it seem that Black Elk treated Christianity "simply as a protective veneer underneath which timeless precolonial beliefs and values survive(d) intact."[19]

It seems more likely that, and as Joshua Thomas has shown, for Black Elk each tradition interpreted the other in a cyclical fashion.[20] Each tradition spoke to the other, not in a linear fashion, but in a dialogue. For Black Elk, Christ and his salvific, good way became central and reshaped the Lakota traditions and trajectory, but the latter also reshaped the work and significance of Christ. This cyclical interpretation formed the basis of Black Elk's hybrid religiosity and people's misunderstanding of him, particularly in his later years. To illustrate this we can see how two examples of this hybridity – the imagery in his early vision and his description of the Lakota Sun Dance –shaped for Black Elk a particular missiological imaginary.

Black Elk's Vision of the Red Road and Flowering Stick

The "great vision" that Black Elk had at nine years of age was, for him, a pivotal event that he sought to understand and fulfill throughout his life. The initial vision is lengthy[21] and filled with imagery that was not always easy for others to interpret, particularly since Black Elk himself did not always provide commentary on them.[22] One aspect of the vision that has received considerable attention, however, is the black and red roads shown to him by the grandfathers. According to the grandfathers the black road is "a fearful

---

Transactions of the Charles S. Peirce Society 53:3 (2017), 447-465; Hans Stefan Gustafson, "Descandalizing Multiple Religious Identity with Help from Nicholas Black Elk and His Spirituality: An Exercise in Interreligious Learning," *Journal of Ecumenical Studies* 51:1 (2016), 80-113.

[18] This is Clive Holler's overall thesis. Holler, *Black Elk's Religion.*

[19] Sergei Kan, *Memory Eternal: Tlingit Culture and Russian Orthodox Christianity Through Two Centuries* (Seattle: University of Washington Press, 1999), xx.

[20] Thomas contrasts this with the linear typologies of various Christian traditions, such as the Puritans, where an older type (often in the Old Testament) is a foreshadow of its antitype fulfillment (usually in the New Testament). Thomas, "Native Hermeneutics" 457.

[21] The text of the great vision is nearly 30 pages long in DeMallie's transcription of Neihardt's interview notes.

[22] DeMallie remarks that Neihardt most likely did not comprehend the meaning of the vision, but understood the importance of trying to communicate it to others. DeMallie, *The Sixth Grandfather*, 37.

road, a road of troubles and of war," and one which Black Elk would walk on and through to defeat his enemies.[23] However, the grandfathers also show him a red road, the good way, on which he would lead his nation. This road leads away from pain and violence and towards a sacred circle or hoop which represented life, peace, and good relationships with each other. In reflecting on these Black Elk at one point has both sadness and hope for his people, saying, "I thought of my vision, and how it was promised me that my people should have a place in this earth where they could be happy every day. I thought of them on the wrong road now, but maybe they could be brought back into the hoop again and to the good road."[24]

Similarly, in a subsequent vision he sees an eschatological scene that includes

> a beautiful land where many, many people were camping in a great circle. I could see that they were happy and had plenty. Everywhere there were drying racks full of meat. The air was clear and beautiful with a living light that was everywhere. All around the circle, feeding on the green, green grass, were fat and happy horses; and animals of all kinds were scattered all over the green hills, and singing hunters were returning with their meat.[25]

Taken on its own, the road imagery seems to indicate that Black Elk is being called to help restore the Lakota people by leading them back to their rich traditions. And it is certainly this interpretation that Neihardt sought to communicate.[26] But, as Catholic Black Elk scholar Michael Steltenkamp has shown, we cannot fully understand Black Elk's description of the red road, as well as other images in his vision, apart from his faith in Christ and a particular Christian teaching tool that Black Elk was fond of: the Two Roads Map.[27]

In the late 19th and early 20th centuries many Christian denominations published and used a pictorial depiction of salvation history, often called "ladders of salvation."[28] These provided teachers a concise, colorful, and creative way to summarize the biblical story starting with creation, moving through the history of Israel, and culminating with the life of Christ, the church, and the eventual return and triumph of Christ. The Jesuits provided for their catechists a version of such a map which, similar to others, featured

---

23 Neihardt, *Black Elk Speaks*, 29.
24 Neihardt, *Black Elk Speaks*, 239.
25 Neihardt, *Black Elk Speaks*, 242.
26 This interpretation has been widely embraced by Native American communities more broadly, such that the "red road" has become synonymous with Native American traditions generally.
27 In fact, it is likely that Black Elk's recollection and interpretation of his vision evolved over time.
28 Steltenkamp, *Nicholas Black Elk*, 115.

a road going up the middle. The road was black as it tracked history through the Old Testament stories and then, from the birth of Christ to the end of history, it became red. In addition, on both sides of the map were two roads leading in opposite directions – one towards heaven and the other towards hell. Black Elk was given his own copy which, as an illiterate catechist, he valued and used as one of his primary teaching tools.[29]

By the time Black Elk recounted his vision to Neihardt he had been using the Two Roads Map for nearly three decades. Its images had begun to be a part of his imaginary and were infused with the vision and hopes he carried for his people. Thus, when he tells Neihardt, "I had been appointed by my vision to be an intercessor of my people with the spirit powers and... sometime in the future I'd bring my people out of the black road into the red road,"[30] it is apparent that the way of abundance was integrally connected to Christ.[31]

That the red road was closely connected to the way of Christ in the Two Roads Map is further supported by another image important for Black Elk – a flowering, sacred stick or tree. In his vision this tree stood in the center of a hoop and was a source of hope. In its presence the birds sing and people and animals all rejoice. Black Elk says of it,

> Behold it, from there we shall multiply; for it is the greatest of the greatest sticks. This stick will take care of the people... We live under it like chickens under the wing. We live under the flowering stick like under the wing of a hen. Depending on the sacred stick we shall walk and it will be with us always.[32]

The imagery of the stick certainly lends itself to many Lakota images, including a cherry branch stick used in religious ceremonies, the order of God or the Great Spirit (*Wankan Tanka*), and the flourishing of the Lakota nation.[33] But the stick also seems to indicate the presence, and perhaps the cross, of Christ. In this, notice how Black Elk seems to describe it using imagery from Matthew 23:37 and Luke 13:34, where Jesus expresses his longing to gather his children "as a hen gathers her young under her wings," and Jesus' promise in Matthew 28:20 that "I am with you always."

---

[29] Black Elk's daughter and others told Steltenkamp how Black Elk would often use his map in teaching children and adults, and taught them to use it as well. Steltenkamp, *Black Elk*, 99-102.

[30] DeMallie, *The Sixth Grandfather*, 293.

[31] As Steltenkamp summarizes, "Instead of solely recounting an unaltered vision from a boyhood experience, the holy-man might have provided [Neihardt] with a synthesis of religious images that engaged him from boyhood through adulthood – that is, vision images fused with images from the Two Roads Map." Steltenkamp, *Nicholas Black Elk*, 117.

[32] DeMallie, *The Sixth Grandfather*, 129.

[33] Steltenkamp, *Nicholas Black Elk*, 121.

So were the images of the vision Christian, or Native American? Here again, rather than force a choice on Black Elk, it would seem that each tradition interprets the other in a cyclical way. Christ's road and presence becomes a pathway and source of hope for the Lakota people, and the flourishing and good news that Christ offers is integrally tied up with the hopes and longings of the Lakota people.

Black Elk's Interpretation of the Sun Dance

As another example of Black Elk's hybrid religiosity, every year the Lakota would anticipate the annual return and hunt of the buffalo with the Sun Dance. This ritual lasted for several days and could include anyone from the village who wished to join. On the last day, however, the dance itself was reserved for a select group of young men who would go through a purification ceremony, go to the dance space, and then pierce themselves with skewers that were tied to a central pole. As they danced, they pulled against the pole with the goal of ripping the skewers out of their skin, an action that empowered them and signaled their pledge for the upcoming hunt.[34]

Starting in 1947, when he was 81 years old, Black Elk gave a series of interviews to Joseph Epes Brown, a scholar of Native American culture and history. In it, Black Elk describes at length aspects of the Sun Dance as he taught it to be practiced. And here, as in the case of the vision he described to Neihardt, the tradition is best understood as a process of hybrid religiosity, a cyclical interpretation between Lakota tradition and his Christian faith.[35]

One way this can be seen is the way in which Black Elk's instructions for the Sun Dance seem to interact with Christ's passion.[36] For example, as the young men prepare themselves to be pierced they should say, "All this may be difficult to do, yet for the good of the people it must be done. Help me, O Grandfather, and give to me the courage and strength to stand the sufferings which I am about to undergo."[37] Notice how Black Elk's version of these words sound reminiscent of Jesus' prayer in the Garden of Gethsemane. As such, Black Elk's version of this prayer shifts the emphasis away from empowerment and pledge for the hunt, and instead has the dancers identify with Christ's suffering.[38] As Black Elk says, "In this great rite you are to offer your body as a sacrifice in behalf of all the people, and through you the people

---

[34] The Sun Dance was made illegal in 1883 and reinstated in the late 1920s.

[35] The hybridity of Black Elk's Sun Dance is more obvious than that of his vision, such that numerous scholars have commented on it. DeMallie, *The Sixth Grandfather*, 71; Holler, *Black Elk's Religion*, 139-178.

[36] The following draws from Costello's analysis of Black Elk's Sun Dance. Costello, *Black Elk*, 120-122.

[37] Brown, *The Sacred Pipe*, 79.

[38] Thomas, "Native Hermeneutics," 456.

will gain understanding and strength."[39] As another example, at the end of the ceremony the pronouncement is made, "O *Wakan Tanka* (God, Great Spirit), this sacred place is Yours. Upon it all has been finished. We rejoice!"[40] Notice again how this echoes Jesus' final words on the cross in John 19:30, and again indicates that the dancers are identifying with Jesus' actions on the cross.

In addition to interpreting the Sun Dance in a way that seeks to identify with Christ's suffering, Black Elk also sought to connect it to the real suffering that the Lakota have experienced. Along these lines another of Black Elk's pronouncements says, "By your actions today you have strengthened the sacred hoop of our nation. You have made a sacred center which will always be with you, and you have created a closer relationship with all things of the universe."[41] Thus, whereas the Sun Dance was originally a purification and renewal rite in preparation for a successful hunt, it now serves to renew the identity of the people, but does so around Christ.

Conclusion: A Distinct Imaginary

Black Elk's hybrid religiosity sought a mutual renewal of both his people's traditions as well as the significance of Christ. But, one may wonder, what does our discussion of Black Elk have to do with insider Christ-followers and alternative missiological imaginaries? It is true that, unlike the insider Christ-followers we are discussing, Black Elk never distanced himself from a Christian, and in this case a Catholic Christian, identity. But notice that for Black Elk, as for other Native American Christ-followers that we will meet, to be Lakota was a singular identity. It was only with the coming of missionaries and a modern conception of a thing called "religion" that some sought to separate those things religious from the rest of Native American identity. In one sense the history of Native American colonialism is a series of extractions, starting first with seeking to extract Native Americans from the land, either by genocide or by displacement into reservations, by extracting the people's "religion" from their lives and replacing it with another, and eventually by seeking to extract the very notion of "Indianness" from the person.[42]

Along these lines Christian missions in many ways joined in the colonial strategy of exorcising what they saw as harmful, and even demonic, rituals and conceptions out of Native American traditions, though some, including the Catholic Jesuits of Black Elk's Pine Ridge reservation, sought to nuance

---

[39] Brown, *The Sacred Pipe*, 72.

[40] Brown, *The Sacred Pipe*, 98.

[41] Brown, *The Sacred Pipe*, 99-100.

[42] As exemplified by Richard H. Pratt's infamous motto for his Indian boarding school, "kill the Indian and save the man." A motto which was taken up by many such schools across the country over the following decades.

this strategy somewhat. But in contrast, Black Elk's hybrid religiosity was an attempt to re-imagine his people's way into the future, now with the way of Christ as their pathway. In his estimation, as his Lakota traditions were reshaped around the Christian faith they could become a source of renewal for his people, even as the traditions in turn reshaped the Christian faith via a new missiological imaginary.

O. Kandaswamy Chetti: A Christ-Following Hindu Reformer

In 1914 a Hindu by the name of O. Kandaswamy Chetti (1867–1943) was invited to address a gathering of missionaries and church leaders at the Madras Missionary Conference. The missionary and Christian community knew Chetti well – he had taught English at Madras Christian College for nearly 25 years and had been involved with the Young Men's Christian Association (YMCA), as well as various initiatives for social reform. They also knew of the curious stance he took regarding religious faith. For, while Chetti clearly and publicly followed the teachings and person of Jesus, he steadfastly remained a Hindu and refused to take baptism and join the Christian church. The missionary leaders invited Chetti to speak to this. Why, they wanted to know, did he take such an unorthodox position? In light of his clear faith in Christ why was he *not* a Christian?[43] Chetti's answer, and many of his other writings and actions, point to an alternative missiological imaginary that, though misunderstood by the Christian community, presented for him new pathways for faith and identity.

To better understand this we need to briefly consider Chetti's background. Born in 1867 in Madras (Chennai), South India, Chetti grew up a part of the Chettiar caste, a traditionally well-educated community of merchants. Chetti followed his father's example of gaining education at British-established schools and, at around 20 years of age, gained entrance to Madras Christian College. He graduated from MCC in 1889 and stayed on as an assistant to the college president, William Miller. Because of his English language ability and knowledge of English literature he soon became an English teacher and remained at MCC in that capacity till his retirement in 1924.

In addition to providing accessible English- and Christian-oriented education, one of the purposes of MCC from its outset was evangelism. Indeed, numerous students from Hindu backgrounds became Christian while students at MCC, including some who went on to become prominent leaders in the Christian church. One such student, a junior of Chetti's by ten years and a fellow Chettiar, was Vengal Chakkarai Chettiar, who would go on to

[43] Chetti's speech was soon after published in *Madras Christian College Magazine*. O. Kandaswamy Chetti, "Why I Am Not a Christian: A Personal Statement," *Madras Christian College Magazine* 32 (Jan 1915).

become one of the more prominent Indian leaders and theologians of the early 20th century.

Certainly not everyone who studied at MCC were or became Christian. Chetti himself remained at MCC for nearly 40 years without ever taking baptism or identifying himself as a Christian. He did, however, identify himself as a Hindu and follower of Christ. How could he do this, and what did this mean for him?

In one of his earliest published essays related to the topic, written to a largely Christian audience via the Madras Christian College Magazine, Chetti sympathized with a missionary friend who complained about Hindus who, though possessing "culture and intelligence,"[44] were nonetheless uninterested in joining the missionary in a study about Christ. It is true, Chetti acknowledged, that this could be seen as yet another example of the evil in persons that cause them to resist the truth of Jesus. And yet, in pondering this explanation, Chetti felt it was not fully adequate. For, as he explains, "There are many thoughtful men in this country who would fain rejoice in Christ if only He were, in the first place, not presented to them as a unique phenomenon – which indeed He is – nor rooted in the life-history of one particular nation and limited by the circumstances of one particular age."[45] Rather, he goes on to explain, if certain aspects of Christ's life and teaching were presented more clearly, Christ would be very attractive to Hindus. "I cannot believe," he says, "that if Christ had appeared in India He would not have found His own among its people, of course He would then have come as the fulfilment of their peculiar aspirations and the starting point of a new and higher development of their peculiar tendencies."[46]

But how for Chetti can Christians more clearly show Christ to Hindus? First, Christians should have close discussions with Hindus so as to discover within their beliefs "something towards which your heart may leap forth as it were in recognition of a long-forgotten kinship."[47] In other words, Christians should seek out things in the Hindu tradition, as it is experienced by the Hindu friend, that Christians can affirm, however small. This, Chetti argued, should not be done for the sake of "polemical diplomacy" but for the pleasure of building and celebrating a friendship.

Second, as the friendship develops Christians can present Christ as the "light which lighteth every man that cometh into the world" (quoting John 1:9). Here Chetti suggests an overall approach by which Christians and Hindus can converse. In the broadest sense, he says, Hindus believe in a "Universal Essence" that pervades all creation and phenomena. Though

---

[44] O. Kandaswamy Chetti, "The Light that Lighteth Every Man," *Madras Christian College Magazine* 18 (July 1900), 181.
[45] Chetti, "The Light that Lighteth Every Man," 181.
[46] Chetti, "The Light that Lighteth Every Man," 182.
[47] Chetti, "The Light that Lighteth Every Man," 183.

Hindus themselves differ in opinion on the nature of this Essence, and though Christians will differ with Hindus on its specifics, they can nonetheless come together in a dialogue about the nature of this Essence. If Hindus in various ways seek to bring this Essence "down" to their level, into their experience, via various deities, gurus, etc., so the Christian can share about how this Essence "descended in flesh and blood" in order to live out and model to humanity a moral life that only God could provide. This incarnated Essence, however, paid the penalty of suffering and death "which goodness has to pay when it chooses to manifest itself for the good of others."[48] And yet, this suffering and death did not crush the Essence but only gave it a new power to attract people and allow them to identify with the Divine Being in their lives, to love others, to bear suffering, and to carry them "safely through the trails of life to the realization of their highest selves."[49]

Chetti acknowledges that this approach does not make reference to the historic presentation of Christ as described in the gospels. He senses, however, that "if the view of God herein involved appears attractive and such as the soul craves for, I feel assured that the claims of the historical Christ will be considered without prejudice."[50] Christians can and should, he suggests, allow Hindus to query, pursue, and make sense of Christ via their own framework.

But if Chetti is sympathetic to the sensitivities of his Hindu community, he is also critical of some of their own beliefs and practices. For example, in a speech given to the Young Men's Hindu Association of Madras and printed in the MCC magazine, Chetti argues that Hindu idolatry is, as his title says, a "retrogression" in the development of religions.[51] At the outset of his essay he acknowledges that he approaches the topic assuming the presence of "one Supreme Creator of the Universe" who is the "source of all power, life, and goodness," such as is common in Judaism, Christianity, and Islam.[52] He also acknowledges that these religious traditions strongly condemn idolatry. However, he is careful to state that he does not base his own critique on such pronouncements. Rather, and drawing from aspects of the evolutionary view of religion prominent in Western religious scholarship of the time, he argues that "our knowledge of God [has been] a matter of gradual evolution, of slow unfolding, of ever-dawning revelation."[53] People's understanding of God

---

[48] Chetti, "The Light that Lighteth Every Man," 186.
[49] Chetti, "The Light that Lighteth Every Man," 187.
[50] Chetti, "The Light that Lighteth Every Man," 187.
[51] O. Kandaswamy Chetti, "Idolatry: A Retrogression," *Madras Christian College Magazine* 14 (June 1897).
[52] Chetti, "Idolatry: A Retrogression," 705.
[53] Chetti, "Idolatry: A Retrogression," 706. Chetti was probably influenced, directly or indirectly, by the writings of the prominent 19th-century British anthropologist Edward Burnett Tylor whose highly influential *Primitive Culture* (1871) posited that

began in very primitive form, perceiving that nature had an order to it and was therefore animated by a "Universal Spirit." For Chetti it is this understanding of a force intricately bound up in creation that some of the earliest Vedic writings seem to reflect. After some time, though, people perceived still more about this force and, in a sense, "released" God from nature in their understanding.

But not completely. There was a stage or part of humanity that wanted to retain a physical, visible body for this invisible power, giving rise to idolatry. While perhaps understandable as a transition, Chetti argues that those who retain it and do not fully release God from the material world do a disservice to their progress in the religious life. For, "while it points to God in matter, it imprisons Him in it too and hinders men from rising to the conception that while God lives in things, He is above them as well."[54] The lesson, he says, is to learn that "an idol is whatever draws us away from a fuller and fuller touch with that Living Truth of the Universe which permeates every sphere of existence." Ultimately, it is not just images that are idols. In fact, "the man who bends the knee before an ugly stone or brazen image may often worship the living God better than one who kneels before God but refuses to give up something which… is a bar to divine purpose."[55] Examples abound, but include customs, shutting ourselves from the light of new truths, allowing intellectual pride, religious patriotism, or fear of public opinion.

The types of evolutionary theories of religion that influenced Chetti have, of course, long since been discredited, and we may excuse Chetti as being a person of his time in his use of them. But notice that what seems important for Chetti is that such an approach provided a "non-Christian" way to enter into critical dialogue with his Hindu community. Notice too that, while maintaining a monotheistic framework throughout, he does not use the common Christian objections to Hindu idols – criticisms that would have been familiar to Hindus via missionary tracts and sermons.

These early writings illustrate how Chetti's hybrid religiosity embraced biblical scripture and Christ in a way that countered certain Hindu practices but also recognized and highlighted elements in the gospel that would be "good news" to his own Hindu community. And though these were insightful and innovative, such approaches to evangelism and dialogue were not completely new nor all that controversial (at least to some Christians). Rather, as described above, it was Chetti's stance on Hindu *identity* and his choice to not "convert" to Christianity – as his friend and fellow Chettiar Vengal Chakkarai had done – that caused considerable intrigue and debate.

---

all religions evolved from primitive, largely animistic, beliefs into more and more complex systems of belief, such as Christianity.

[54] Chetti, "Idolatry: A Retrogression," 708.

[55] Chetti, "Idolatry: A Retrogression," 710.

Thus it was that Chetti accepted the invitation to explain to the attendees of the Madras missionary gathering why, as a follower of Christ, he had not taken baptism and remained "outside the Christian Church."[56] It is not, he said, because he is a secret "Christian at heart" who fears to show his commitment to others. On the contrary, he believed in Christ as *the* Savior (not one of the saviors) of the world. Jesus' particularity, his divinity, his incarnation, and his qualities were all truths that Chetti affirmed and found great hope in, and which he wanted others to know about as well. In fact, as he said, "I feel the responsibility of communicating the truth of Christ crucified for you and me to live, of communicating it through the testimony, very often silent but none the less powerful or compelling on that account, of a life and a life-work inspired by it..."[57]

Because he shared this belief with other followers of Christ, he was not sure it was accurate to describe himself as "outside the Christian church." However, he acknowledged that he had never converted and joined, nor had the intention of joining, the Christian church in the narrow sense. He affirmed that he and every other follower of Christ "is called upon to let his light shine before all the world," but he did not feel that God had called him to join the church, nor that all others were called to do this either. And while he had the utmost respect for colleagues (like Chakkarai) who converted religions he also had "nothing but contempt for those, and they are many, who, yielding to very human influence and to a call from unworthy quarters cut themselves off from those whom it is their duty to be in touch with, if for nothing else, at least in the interests of the lord whom they profess to follow."[58] After all, there was nothing "essentially sinful" in Hindu society, just as there was nothing "essentially pure" in the Christian society and church.

In the end, Chetti argued, the Christian church was largely too close-minded to the possibility of Hindu followers of Christ, such that the church often rejected them or compelled them to fully convert to Christianity. But if the church were to support such persons, trust Christ's work within them, and let them work through the various discipleship decisions such a path entails, the results could be wonderful. Such a person may not, Chetti explained, join the church, "but he will prepare the way for a movement from within Hindu society towards a Christ who shall fulfill India's highest aspirations and impart that life of freedom for which she has been panting for ages."[59]

We are uncertain of exactly how Chetti's speech was received, but two published responses, one by missionary L.P. Larson and the other by Vengal

---

[56] Chetti, "Why I am Not a Christian: A Personal Statement."
[57] Chetti, "Why I am Not a Christian: A Personal Statement," 357-58.
[58] Chetti, "Why I Am Not a Christian: A Personal Statement," 358.
[59] Chetti, "Why I Am Not a Christian: A Personal Statement," 359.

Chakkarai, were highly critical of Chetti's stance.[60] It is evident that others, however, may have had a more positive estimation of Chetti's approach, among them the Madras YMCA with which Chetti continued to partner and interact and the missionary E. Stanley Jones, who in later years partnered with Chetti in hosting a missionary conference and who invited Chetti to teach at his newly formed Sat Tal Christian Ashram.

Chetti was not a theologian per se and did not publish his beliefs very often. However, there is indication that he continued to develop and work out what it meant to be a Hindu Christ-follower throughout the rest of his life. In 1933 he began what he called the "Fellowship of the Followers of Jesus." This was a gathering of people who committed to "earnestly endeavor, whatever their communal affiliations may be, to live up to the standards, principles and ideals of Jesus, and… to understand his personality." Open to Hindus, Muslims, Christians, and any other faith, the group encouraged each other to have personal lives "of consultation and communion with God as revealed by Jesus and to cultivate the habit of active co-operation with every movement tending towards the establishment of the Kingdom of God among men."[61]

Before concluding our discussion of Chetti we need to pay attention to one additional aspect of his hybrid religiosity – Chetti's political and social activism. Chetti became involved in politics early in his life and was particularly involved in the Justice Party, a South Indian party formed in 1916 to counter the over-representation and dominance of Brahmins in the Madras Presidency.[62] By this time Chetti was already an experienced social reformer, having been the founder and editor of the *Social Reform Advocate* for several years, a paper that regularly discussed various social problems and policy debates. Chetti and other leaders helped shape the Justice Party's stance in a number of areas, including a focus on prohibition, providing education for

---

[60] L.P. Larsen, "Conversion and the Church," *Madras Christian College Magazine* 32 (Jan 1915); V. Chakkarai, "Why I Am a Christian," *The Harvest Field* 35:3 (1915).

[61] O. Kandaswamy Chetty, "Announcement Regarding the Fellowship of the Followers of Jesus," *Guardian* (April 13, 1933). The Fellowship seems to have been dissolved after Chetti's death in 1943, though in 1958 D.T. Niles seems to indicate that it was still going at that time. D.T. Niles, *The Preacher's Task and the Stone of Stumbling: The Lyman Beecher Lectures, Yale University* (New York: Harper and Row, 1958), 97.

[62] In the Indian caste system Brahmins were (and often still are) traditionally considered the highest and most privileged caste, both spiritually and socially. Other castes, such as Chetti's Vaishya Chettiar caste, were lower in historic, spiritual, and social hierarchy and privilege, though having much more of these than the lower Shudra groups and the so-called out-caste, untouchable, or *dalit* castes.

females and low-caste communities, and integrating various castes.[63] An early dispute in the party sheds light on Chetti's particular interest. In 1917 party leadership were agreed on the overall goal of empowering non-Brahmins in order to distribute power more equitably. The party became divided, however, on the strategy by which they thought this should be achieved. Chetti and some colleagues believed the way forward was through creating a broad coalition of non-Brahmin caste and Dalit Hindus as well as Muslims, Christians, and tribal communities for the purpose of social reform and education, and particularly helping non-Brahmin caste Hindus to reform their views of Dalits. Others, however, believed the party should directly challenge Brahmin political power and work to remove them from administrative and political positions. It was the latter position that ultimately won out, resulting in the party becoming more caste-specific and alienating Dalits and non-Hindus.[64]

Still, Chetti remained involved in the party and sought to influence it towards greater levels of inclusion, social reform, and justice. For instance, in 1923 he and his colleagues passed a resolution encouraging non-Brahmins to train their own Hindu priests to serve at weddings, and to arrange marriages across non-Brahmin caste lines. Doing so, they believed, would help to reduce the monopoly Brahmins had on religious leadership and break down caste divisions, at least among non-Brahmin caste Hindus.[65]

Chetti described his criticism of the Brahmin priestly caste in a particularly poignant way in an article, "The Need for Social Reconstruction in India."[66] His primary frustration with Brahmin Hindu priests was that, though his Hindu community paid and financially supported them for their services, the priests failed in their more fundamental duty. Chetti asks, "What is the service they render to us in return? Do they study the evils and weaknesses of society and help us in overcoming them? Do they rebuke our personal and social sins and follies? Do they make any appeal to our consciences? Do they inspire us with courage to do any noble deed?… They think their work is done if they chant verses and hymns."[67] The problem, Chetti says, is not that people seek after religious teachings and devotion. Rather it is that the teachings and devotion they receive from Hindu priests do not consider the moral and social needs of society, and that some teachings actually run counter to social needs and social justice. "Thus," says Chetti, "it comes about that there is so little consistency between belief and conduct

[63] Eugene F. Irschick, *Politics and Social Conflict in South India: The Non-Brahman Movement and Tamil Separatism, 1916–1929* (Bombay: Oxford University Press, 1969), 72.
[64] Irschick, *Politics and Social Conflict in South India*, 189, 75-76.
[65] Irschick, *Politics and Social Conflict in South India*, 252.
[66] O. Kandaswamy Chetti, "The Need for Social Reconstruction in India," *Madras Christian College Magazine* 32 (July 1914).
[67] Chetti, "The Need for Social Reconstruction in India," 15-16.

in our lives."[68] And all of this because "we are not properly served by those from whom one would expect us to receive guidance. We are like sheep without a shepherd."[69] Let religious traditions and the leaders who teach them, he says, not rely on past and dead practices (like child marriage) but "march forward" trusting in reason, conscience, and "God above."

Chetti was not, of course, the first nor the last Christ-follower to challenge the caste system, push for reforms, and level critique at Hindu priests and leaders. But the socio-religious location from which Chetti sought such reform *was* unique, and gave him opportunity for witness that was not available to other Christ-followers. For example, his friend and colleague Vengal Chakkarai, whom we've briefly discussed, was also very involved in the politics and social reform movements of the day. In contrast to Chetti, however, Chakkarai identified as a Christian convert. And though some of his positions were similar to those of Chetti, in the highly communal atmosphere of his context he was not allowed as a Christian to represent the interests of other communities. He was, as M.S.S. Pandian says, denied "the right to speak about and for the rest of the nation."[70] This was a "right" Chetti was allowed and which he took advantage of, speaking into areas of injustice – even those for which his own community was guilty – guided by his faith in Christ and his teachings. Chetti could, as a Hindu, challenge and seek to re-create the Hindu and wider Indian society, and do so from *within* the Hindu community.

Conclusion

Black Elk and Chetti, though coming from very different contexts, share some similarities in the alternative missiological imaginaries they present. Both were convinced of the Lordship of Christ for them and their community and sought to follow Christ's example and teachings. Both were appreciative of the Western Christian influences and persons that had brought them to that faith. But both were also critical, each in their own way, of the colonial and structural powers of their day and the ways in which these had subjected and caused hardships for their people, as well as the dominance of the Western interpretation of the gospel. In response, Black Elk and Chetti challenged some of the Western dichotomist understandings of religion and religious tradition, asserting that Christ could work within and *through* their religious tradition and communities to bring healing and wholeness to their people.

We don't know the response of everyone in their respective communities to their approach. It is probable that some of their Native American and

[68] Chetti, "The Need for Social Reconstruction in India," 16.
[69] Chetti, "The Need for Social Reconstruction in India," 17.
[70] M.S.S. Pandian, "Nation as Nostalgia: Ambiguous Spiritual Journeys of Vengal Chakkarai," *Economic and Political Weekly* 38:51/52 (2003), 5363.

Hindu co-religionists rejected their stance as being too unorthodox or untraditional. But even if this is the case, we know that there were many others who accepted their stances and gave them voice and leadership within their communities. It may even be the case, though we do not (yet) have record of it, that there were some Native Americans and Hindus who, in their own quiet ways, were influenced by Black Elk's and Chetti's alternative Christ-following imaginary and sought to follow Christ in a similar way. But though we do not know this to be the case, we do know that in recent decades many thousands of persons from Native American, Hindu, Muslim, Buddhist, and other religious traditions have discovered and developed insider imaginaries that reflect those of Black Elk and Chetti. It is some of these from whom we now want to hear.

5: Insider Christ-Followers Today

In this chapter I want to continue introducing us to the stories of insider Christ-followers, now turning to more contemporary examples. Some of these come via the stories and reflections of insiders themselves, and some from the writings of "alongsiders," or those (often Westerners) who have intimate knowledge of these people and their faith, as well as their trust. My method in this chapter is not primarily empirical; more work can and needs to be done – as timing, security, and trust allows – to more systematically account for the variety of experiences, theologies, and approaches of insiders. Rather, these qualitative case studies, along with the historical examples from the previous chapter and others to come throughout this book, provide for us insights into the actual lived stories of some of these followers of Christ, along with the hopes, joys, and challenges they encounter in following Christ in their own religious communities.

"Bhaktas in the Lord" in Northeast India

In the northeast of India, a small network of Hindu followers of Christ has been slowly and quietly developing. This has occurred around one particular individual – Vijay – and his family.[1] Vijay is part of a Hindu Brahmin family in a large city in Northeast India. This region, though politically united with India and sharing similar religious traditions, nonetheless has very distinct languages and cultural histories.[2] In terms of religion, too, the northeast has differed from the rest of North India in particular ways. For instance, the region was highly influenced in the 15th–16th centuries by the Hindu poet-saint Sankardeva, who started a religious movement focused on the Hindu god Vishnu. This movement, called *ek sarana dharma* (the way of taking shelter in the One), had several distinct teachings and practices that

[1] A pseudonym. The following information is from personal interviews conducted with Vijay.

[2] These differences helped to spur successful movements to create separate states and unsuccessful movements to create separate nations. Following independence in 1947 the Northeast was comprised of one state – Assam – but in the 1960s–80s was subdivided into four additional states – Arunachal Pradesh, Nagaland, Meghalaya, and Mizoram.

permeated many of the other Hindu traditions of the area, including a de-emphasis (though not an elimination) of caste divisions. Another religiously distinct characteristic of the area is that, in more recent decades, several tribes of the northeast responded favorably to and converted to Christianity such that the states of Mizoram and Nagaland are now 87% and 88% Christian respectively.[3]

Vijay's region, however, remains highly Hindu. As a young boy he was drawn to spiritual questions and even considered taking the vows of a *sanyasi* (Hindu monk). He began to learn about Christ, however, through reading a Bible storybook that he obtained as a teenager and that sparked an interest in Christ. Three years later he attended a church at the invitation of a friend. After attending for a time and finding the teaching compelling Vijay decided to take baptism. He became more involved in the church and was eventually trained and sent by his church to other regions for evangelism. As he sought to explain and convince others of his Christian faith, however, he began to realize more and more just how "foreign" the Christian teachings, worship, and buildings felt to his Hindu family and community. Christians' strong rejection of anything associated with Hindu religion, including all structures, rituals, and most anything else that somehow reflected positively on Hinduism, caused most Hindus to reject any invitation to imagine a life shaped by Jesus and the gospel.

Over the course of ten years two experiences created within him a new imaginary for how to understand and express his faith in Christ. The first was the teaching he received on developing "house churches." This, he says, freed him from "traditional church" by untying notions of faith from the structural/institutional church. Persons like his Hindu father, he reflected, would never enter a church but would gladly have spiritual conversations in a family home. The second experience was a seminar on contextual Christianity that explored biblical and cultural continuities between his faith in Christ and his Hindu community and tradition. This teaching, provided by Indian Christ-followers who themselves had grown frustrated by the approaches of some Christians, gave voice to the discomfort he felt about the discontinuity between the two communities and traditions. Though there were no models in his area for him to follow, he felt the desire, and need, to re-enter his Hindu community and begin following Christ from within it.

What he did next shocked both his Hindu family and his Christian community: he submitted a letter of resignation to his church denomination and hosted his own ceremony to re-enter his Hindu community. 250 people attended his ceremony, including his family, and watched as he followed a ritual developed by other Hindu followers of Christ. As Vijay spoke to his community, he repented for leaving them and shared that he now realized

[3] Census of India. "Religious Census 2011", https://www.census2011.co.in/religion.php. Accessed July 12, 2022.

that his God and faith hadn't actually required that of him. He asked them for forgiveness and permission to re-enter the life of the community, and to do so as one who follows Jesus. His father responded, saying that Vijay could follow whatever god he wanted, but that as a father he was very pleased that Vijay was returning to the family. Vijay says, "I felt God's favor was on me that day."

Vijay had to reorient himself in some significant ways after this. On a practical level he had to find a new source of income apart from the Christian denomination that had provided his salary. He was able to do this by starting a small business. He also had to re-negotiate his relationship with his former church. In his letter of resignation, he requested their blessing, but did not receive a response. He has heard various rumors circulating about him among the Christian community, many which he feels are slanderous. This has been difficult for him, but it has also affirmed for him his commitment to be in greater relationship and interaction with his Hindu community.

Vijay is still involved in meeting with people and sharing his faith with them, but this happens in a very different way now. His principal way of interacting is to gather with friends and families during the week, as they are able, and to discuss issues in life, share from the Bible, and to pray together. Occasionally he will host or help lead a *puja* or *satsang*[4] that is focused on Jesus. He does not host these weekly but rather, as is common in his Hindu community, does so for special or life events or festivals. For him it is not necessary to make worship gatherings a weekly event since this would not reflect the normal rhythm and pattern of Hindu worship.

No doubt many Christians will find Vijay's return journey to Hinduism perplexing, if not disturbing. But notice that for Vijay this was and is part of a quest of what it means to be a faithful follower of Christ within his context. The return to his family was not, as some might wonder, an escape from persecution or a search for acceptance. If anything, he had gained a system of support and acceptance within the church structure that he had joined but then voluntarily left in order to reconcile with his family. As a result, his community, he says, have "open hearts and homes" and his people have a "better understanding of the gospel." Various family members have become followers of or have started a journey towards Christ. As Vijay expresses it, "The greatest reward of my coming back to my community was a clear conscience towards God and my community that resulted into having boldness in witnessing Him to my people."

---

[4] *Satsangs* are a common type of worship gathering for Hindus that include prayers and other acts of devotion, often to particular deities. In this case the *satsangs* are focused on Jesus and adapted Hindu songs and rituals to express devotion to him. See also Darren Duerksen, *Ecclesial Identities in a Multi-Faith Context*.

Vijay continues to meet with various other Hindus who are at different places on the spectrum of their understanding and commitment to Christ.[5] As and when someone wants to commit themselves in a more formal way to follow Christ he offers them what Hindus in his region call *saran*, which literally means "taking refuge."[6] This is a form of initiation common among the Vaishnava (devotees of Vishnu) Hindus of his region and which Vijay adapts towards following Jesus. For instance, Vijay incorporates into the ceremony the use of water, even though the *saran* does not traditionally use water as part of the ritual,[7] and biblical passages regarding baptism.

Vijay and his growing community of Hindu Christ-followers are on a continual journey. For him and others it is important at this stage to show solidarity with his Hindu family and find ways to follow Christ from within this community. True, the New Testament calls Christ-followers to "die" to themselves, a teaching that some will apply to people's Hindu religiosity and religious identity. And for his part Vijay, reflecting on John 12:24-25,[8] agrees with the idea that followers of Christ need to humble themselves in submission to Christ. But, he reflects, a mango seed that falls to the ground and dies will become a beautiful mango tree, bearing mango fruit. It will not be an apple tree. His hope is to bear fruit as a Hindu that draws people to Christ. The mango tree of the Hindu community is reimagined, not as a different tree, but one that brings true health and blessing to his people.

Sufi Christ-Followers in South Asia

In 1969, by the time he was 17 years old, a Muslim boy by the name of Yussef had spent a majority of his life in a Muslim madrasa (school) in south Asia. Here he learned the Qur'an and prepared himself to someday take his father's place as imam (leader) in the local mosque and teacher in the madrasa.[9] Yussef had an enquiring mind, asking probing questions about the Qur'an.

---

[5] He also meets with Christians who are at various stages in their faith journey.

[6] Audrey Chantlie, *The Assamese: Religion, Caste, and Sect in an Indian Village* (London: Curzon Press, 1984), 157-161.

[7] Water, however, is widely used in other Hindu rituals and viewed as an important element for cleansing spiritual impurities.

[8] "Truly, truly, I tell you, unless a kernel of wheat falls to the ground and dies, it remains only a seed; but if it dies, it bears much fruit. Whoever loves his life will lose it, but whoever hates his life in this world will keep it for eternal life."

[9] The details for Yussef's story, which has been told in several places, are drawn from the following sources: personal correspondence (2019); unpublished video footage (2020); Rick Brown, "Brother Jacob and Master Isaac: How One Insider Movement Began," *International Journal of Frontier Missiology* 24:1 (2007), 41-42; David Garrison, *A Wind in the House of Islam: How God is Drawing Muslims around the World to Faith in Jesus Christ* (Monument, CO: WIGTake Resources, 2014); Jan Hendriik Prenger, "Muslim Insider Christ Followers: A Grounded Theory" (Doctor of Missiology thesis, Biola University, 2014).

In particular, the person of *Isa al-Masih* (Jesus Christ) stood out to him. He asked his teachers numerous questions about the title of Messiah/Christ and his particular message but did not receive what he felt were adequate answers. Yussef wondered, "What was Allah trying to say through the Messiah Jesus?" After thinking over this for a time he resolved to pray that Allah would help him know more.

Shortly after this he was one day walking through his town when he paused at a local Christian mission compound. Though he, like most of his village, had normally avoided the place and its people, he now wondered if or how they might respond to his questions. He went in and was introduced to an older Norwegian missionary, to whom he posed his question, "Why is Isa called the Messiah in the Qur'an? What do *you* say"? The missionary responded saying "The Qur'an is satanic and we don't believe in it, but I have the Bible here and I can show you." Though Yussef found this response quite offensive he just "digested" it to show good manners and hear the missionary's opinions.

Yussef was intrigued by the missionary's description of sin, the need for forgiveness, and the fact that the Messiah was sent to provide this. All of Yussef's actions, explained the missionary, though done to satisfy Allah, could not satisfy Allah for the purposes of salvation. Forgiveness could only come through Isa and his sacrifice. After some time the missionary challenged Yussef; if he believed this message he needed to accept Jesus as Lord and follow him. This was something Yussef felt drawn to do except for two things: his father and his future.

Yussef's father knew of his visits to the missionary, and Yussef finally told his father about his interest in following Jesus. His father took this in and then responded, "If you believe this is what you are looking for, and this is what you want, you can go. You can go and become a Christian. But you must leave the house. I will not tell anyone as long as you are here. But I will tell everyone when you leave. Never come back. Because they will kill you. I cannot stop them." With this Yussef knew he would also lose his father's inheritance and any association with the family.

Yussef left for a city, found work as a rickshaw puller, and eventually found and was cared for by a missionary there. The missionary taught Yussef from the Bible for over a year, an experience Yussef says changed his life. He was baptized in the local church and, with that, felt "now I am one of them, the Christians."

And yet there existed a gulf between him and the Christian community, most of whom had been Christian for at least two generations and whose ancestors were converts from lower-caste Hindu or tribal families. At that time, they had no experience of a Muslim converting to Christianity. But despite this, missionaries saw Yussef's growing desire to share his faith with anyone, including Muslims, and challenged him to return to his home region to share with the Muslim communities there. After some further training

Yussef did so, joining a Presbyterian mission in that area. He started to work in a local church and gained acceptance with the Christians as a prominent preacher, teacher, literature translator, and leader in his denomination. But though he had gained a good reputation in the Christian community he found little such acceptance among the Muslims he tried to evangelize. Knowing that Yussef had converted from Islam, the Muslims of his area viewed him as a traitor. Yussef grew discouraged about this part of his ministry, wondering why God had called him to become a Christian only to have no influence or impact on his own Muslim community.

One day in 1976 a Christian associate brought six Muslim young men to Yussef. These men had read some Christian literature and listened to preaching brought to their village by a team from the missionary group Operation Mobilization. They were now interested in taking the steps to follow Christ and become Christian. Knowing that Yussef was from a Muslim background, the associate brought the men to him so that he could ascertain their sincerity and give them further guidance.

As Yussef talked with the men he grew convinced that, in their hearts, they had indeed accepted Jesus as their Lord and Savior. However, the men assumed that they also needed to be recognized by and have full acceptance in a church and would need to change their religion and become "Christian" in order to do so. Reflecting on the way his own decision to become a Christian had severed his relationships with his Muslim family and community, Yussef took a bold step. He advised, "No, you don't want to become Christian. You don't need to become Christian. You are believing Jesus' sacrifice and that he is your Messiah. You are just fine. Don't call yourself 'Christian,' don't come out from your home. Don't tell anyone in your home what you are believing. Just remain silent, follow Jesus, and go home." This did not match the advice the men had been getting and they questioned Yussef further. Wasn't it true that they needed to become baptized Christians right away? Yussef replied that if they really wanted to tell someone, they should share about their faith in Isa al-Masih to some close friends, privately. There was not, he insisted, any need to "come under the signboard of 'Christian.'"

After the men left Yussef told his associate and other Christians in the mission about the advice he had given. They were perplexed. And even Yussef himself was not totally sure why he did it – there was no precedent that he knew of for someone to follow Jesus without declaring themselves to be "Christian." After a week, however, the six men came back with 15 family elders with whom they had told Yussef's words of advice. They asked Yussef to share with their uncles what he had shared with them and, for the next four to five days, listened to Yussef explain the truths about Isa. At the end of this time they went back to their villages, only to return the next month with several more people. This process continued for nearly a year, and a small movement of Muslim Christ-followers began to develop. For their part, the

Presbyterian missionaries were unsure of what to do with the developing movement; it was growing larger than the local church, and they knew that the local Christians would not be able to accept these new Christ-followers as fellow believers. They did, however, provide training for the groups, which helped it continue to grow.

Yussef was encouraged by the fruit of this approach and grew more and more convinced that Muslims could follow Christ as Muslims. But what did this mean for him and his identity? He still identified firmly as a Christian and had sacrificed a lot to do so. But if others could remain Muslim and follow Christ, could and should he re-adopt his own Muslim identity? After several years of difficult, personal deliberation, Yussef decided to make a change. He moved away from the mission compound that was his home and back into his own community. He decided to re-adopt Muslim vocabulary for worship and for describing his faith. He went to his extended family and apologized, explaining, "I am a Muslim but I follow Isa al-Masih. He's my Savior. That's all. Otherwise I am a Muslim. I am born Muslim. It was wrong to say that I am a Christian. I apologize to you."

To this day Yussef considers himself a Muslim follower of Christ and is one of several leaders instrumental in starting and leading insider movements throughout the region. It is difficult to quantify the number of groups and Muslim Christ-followers because of the nature of their faith identities, though the World Christian Database estimates that as of 2015 the majority of Muslim-background believers in this region were members of insider movements – 100,000 out of 180,000.[10] However, for their part, the leaders of these movements do not generally try to count or verify numbers and statistics, nor explain or defend the various ways in which insiders characterize their Muslim identities in relation to their commitment to Christ. Each group and movement are unique, and there is a sense that the Holy Spirit is shaping new imaginaries among each group in ways that pertain to their own communities.

Buddhist Followers of Christ

Similar to others in the Southeast Asian Mekong River countries of Myanmar, Laos, Thailand, and Cambodia, Vichika grew up Buddhist. In addition, and again similar to others in his society, he understood his Buddhism to be closely connected to his national and ethnic identity, as

---

[10] Todd M. Johnson and Gina A. Zurlo (eds), *World Christian Database* (Leiden/Boston: Brill, 2018). The World Religion Database estimates that in 2020 there were approximately 900,000 Christians, making insiders comprise perhaps 10–15% of all Christ-followers of the region. Todd M. Johnson and Brian J. Grimm (eds), *World Religion Database* (Leiden/Boston: Brill, 2020).

expressed in the common feeling and saying, "To be Burmese/Lao/Thai/Cambodian is to be Buddhist."[11]

This deep integration reflects the way the Buddhism of Vichika's region has, over the centuries, hybridized to local cultural elements. One such element is a common belief in a god or gods, reflecting earlier influences of Hinduism. Another is that these gods, as well as spirits and ancestors, are very immanent and involved with people's lives, an influence of the local animistic beliefs in spirits. Because of this it was common for Vichika and others to go to local shrines and pray to spirits for protection over the immediate circumstances of life. They would also participate in the rituals at the local *pagodas* (temples) and request the Buddhist monks to present offerings and chants to be sent to their ancestors to benefit both the ancestors' and their own karma.[12]

Vichika was familiar with Christianity. Most people in this region knew and know of Christianity by its general reputation of being somehow "foreign" and non- Burmese/Lao/Thai/Cambodian. Part of this reputation has stemmed from its history. For though Buddhism, like Christianity, originated outside of the region and was gradually introduced by foreigners, Buddhism was eventually able to shed its "foreign" identity and integrate with the social imaginary. Christianity, however, on the whole has not succeeded in doing so.[13] Of course, there can be little doubt that one of the main reasons for this has been the power dynamics associated with colonialism. During the 19th and early 20th centuries, and alongside the increased activity of colonization,

---

[11] Buddhism first entered this area nearly 2,000 years ago. In the 11th century Buddhism experienced a reform movement influenced by Theravada monks. Since then the majority population in all of these countries have identified as Buddhist, and Buddhism has deeply shaped cultural practices and values. Donald K. Swearer, "Buddhism in Southeast Asia," in Joseph Kitagawa (ed.), *The Religious Traditions of Asia: Religion, History, and Culture* (Oxford: Routledge, 2002), 119, 26-27.

[12] As Paul De Neui notes, popular "folk" Buddhism incorporates what many might think of as many "non-Buddhist" elements. "To outsiders the accommodation of primal (and other) religious traditions, practices, and beliefs may appear contradictory but is perfectly acceptable to all but a handful of elite Buddhist monks who seek purification of the religion." Paul H. De Neui, "Appropriate Typologies for Thai Folk Buddhists," in Paul H. De Neui (ed.), *Becoming the People of God: Creating Christ-Centered Communities in Buddhist Asia* (Pasadena, California: William Carey Library, 2015, kindle edition), paragraph 3.

[13] Christian missionaries first came to modern-day Vietnam in the 1300s, and evangelistic missions in the wider Mekong River region by both European and Vietnamese missionaries started in the 1500s. Thus, as Munson points out, Christianity in these countries was seen as foreign "because it came from two groups of outsiders: the European colonizers and missionaries, and the Vietnamese who spread it further into Indochina." Tara Villalba Munson, "Christian Communities in Southeast Asia," in Mark Juergensmeyer (ed.), *The Oxford Handbook of Global Religions* (Oxford; New York: Oxford University Press, 2006), 379.

a growing number of Catholic and Protestant missionaries settled in the Mekong region, seeking to establish churches as well as various educational and medical institutions.[14] And though many of these missionaries sought to distance themselves from the colonialist umbrella, their work was and continues to be inextricably tied to foreign identity and interests, even contributing to terrible persecutions and killings in recent decades by groups and regimes like the Khmer Rouge.[15]

In addition to knowing Christianity's general reputation, Vichika had also observed some Christians in his local area. Starting in approximately 2005 missionaries began to evangelize in a nearby village and several families converted to Christianity. As has been common among churches across the region, the new Christians were discipled to distance themselves from Buddhist festivals, rituals, and practices. In addition, the missionaries modeled the practices of Western churches. This had the unfortunate consequence of making the Christians a distinct social community and religion, straining the Christians' relationships with family and friends, and further reinforcing the foreign reputation of Christianity.[16]

---

[14] Local leaders and communities grew adept at accepting the educational and medical contributions of these missionaries while, on the whole, resisting the pressure to change religious identities. Parts of a 1928 speech by Prince Damrong, the King of Thailand, would express the prevailing assessment of Christian missions in this region during this period of time. In it he expressed appreciation for the missionary's medical and educational efforts of the past century while recognizing that the missionaries came primarily to spread the knowledge of Christ. He stated, "The medical and educational services are a means to an end, of course, but the means has been widely appreciated apart from the end itself… To them are due the grateful thanks of the communities among whom they work, even if the major part of such communities do not accept the path which is pointed out to them." George Bradley McFarland, *Historical Sketch of Protestant Missions in Siam, 1828–1928* (Bangkok: Bangkok Times Press, 1928), 14.

[15] Robbie B.H. Goh, *Christianity in Southeast Asia* (Southeast Asia Background Series, Singapore: Institute of Southeast Asian Studies, 2005), 74.

[16] As Peter Thein Nyunt, a Christ-follower in Myanmar, notes, the church there has adopted "models of ministries manufactured in Western mission" and, as a result "are just the replicas and potted plants of Western churches." Peter Thein Nyunt, "Emerging Indigenous Leaders for Jesus Movements in the Myanmar Buddhist Context," in Paul H. De Neui (ed.), *Developing Indigenous Leaders: Lessons in Mission from Buddhist Asia* (Pasadena, CA: William Carey Library, 2013, kindle edition), paragraph 3. See also related insights from G.P.V. Somaratna's study of Buddhist visitors to Evangelical churches in Sri Lanka. These visitors were confused and bewildered by several features, including lack of reverence (as symbolized by the loud worship, not taking off shoes, chairs instead of mats, and chaotic raising of hands), the long times of singing, being asked to stand as newcomers, and use of strange words such as "sin," "dedication," and "offering." They did, however, appreciate being welcomed by church members and the approachability of the pastor (in contrast to the social detachment of Buddhist priests). G.P.V. Somaratna, "From Becoming the People of God: Creating Christ-

Vichika observed all of this, including how many of these Christian families, having grown tired and frustrated with their growing isolation and the divide that was deepening between them and their families, turned back to Buddhism. All this seemed to reaffirm for Vichika the notion that Christianity was unnecessary, if not in some ways harmful, and caused him to feel sorry for the new Christians. In his opinion they were sadly and needlessly misled to turn their back on aspects of their culture and identity.

But Vichika faced plenty of his own challenges. His relationship with his wife had become strained due in large part because of his own bad decisions, and he found it hard to get good work. He was quite discouraged when, one day, he met Surya, a Christian missionary. Surya had lived and worked in Vichika's country for several years and, for her own part, had grown increasingly frustrated with the disconnect between Christian churches and the wider culture. As a result, she had recently begun exploring Buddhist insider approaches to following Christ and discussing with her friends the ways in which they and other Buddhists could follow Christ without converting to a Christian religion. One teaching she learned and was developing regarded the well-known four noble truths of the Buddha, and how Jesus' teachings could be understood as providing the desired pathway to Nirvana for those who depend on Jesus and his grace.[17]

Surya had heard of Vichika from his family members and knew that he was dedicated to regular prayers and other practices at the local Buddhist shrines and temples. As they talked, she shared with Vichika her thoughts on how Jesus taught a form of Buddha's four noble truths. For Vichika this was a very new and different way of thinking about Jesus and Buddhism. His questions began to pour out. How could this be? Wasn't Jesus the god of the Christian religion? Wasn't it true that the Christian god requires them to attend foreign-looking religious ceremonies (worship services) on a weekly basis? And, if it was true that Jesus was also somehow a god for Buddhists, would he allow them to burn incense in their prayers? Surya was able to assure him that it was not necessary to join the Christian religion to follow Christ. Neither was God concerned about things like lighting or not lighting

---

Centered Communities in Buddhist Asia," in Paul H. De Neui (ed.) *Becoming the People of God: Creating Christ-Centered Communities in Buddhist Asia* (Pasadena, California: William Carey Library, 2015).

[17] This approach, known among Christ-followers as "The Four Noble Truths of Christ," was developed in Myanmar by a Burmese Christ-follower to present Christ to his Buddhist neighbors in a way they could understand. For a description of the approach and its development see Jay Judson, "Longing for the Golden City," *Mission Frontiers* (Nov/Dec 2014). For a discussion of the ways in which this approach speaks to, and differs from, common Buddhist worldviews see David S. Lim, "Contextualization of Merit-Making and Grace for Christward Movements in the Karmic World," in Paul H. De Neui (ed.), *Gift and Duty: Where Grace and Merit Meet* (Eugene, OR: Wipf & Stock, 2017).

incense in prayer. The important question, she explained, was *to whom* the prayer and incense were directed. At the end of a lengthy conversation, Vichika decided he wanted to start depending on God through Jesus and, in this way, to allow God to give him "merit" and free him from the effects of his bad decisions (bad karma and sin).[18]

Vichika began to pray to and learn about Jesus, and as he did so, felt a great peace. He also found encouragement from Jesus' words to his disciples, and him, that Jesus would be with him always. After two weeks he told Surya that Jesus had become for him more significant than Buddha, and that he felt he was being released from hundreds of chains – the effects of all his bad decisions – that had accumulated and held him down. He also started to share with others around him, including some of the monks in local temples, that God through Jesus could release them from the effects of their karma, but without having to join the Christian community and church.

Vichika related to Jesus in ways he knew and with which he was familiar. He prayed to Jesus at the local shrines, as these were now for him infused with a sense of Jesus' presence. He also attended the main Buddhist festivals, including going into the temples. Though these were all practices which Christian followers of Jesus would preach against, Vichika reasoned that, if Jesus was indeed the creator and Lord over all of creation and owner of everything, this also included temples, shrines, and incense. For him, following God through Jesus changed the narrative – of both Buddhists and Christians – of why and how such places and rituals were significant. Vichika's hybrid religiosity was, and continues to be, a continual journey of exploration and development.

Native North American Christ-Followers

Our final contemporary case study shifts our focus to Native North American Christ-followers, specifically in Canada and the United States. However, before discussing our story, it is perhaps important to briefly describe the ways in which Christianity has interacted with Native American religious culture and the different types of Christianities that have emerged among Native Americans.

A Doctrine of Discovery and Destruction

As has often been documented, Christian mission among indigenous American groups was frequently complicit with policies that sought to take the land of indigenous communities, subjugate them under the dominant rule

[18] For Lim's explanation of this idea see Lim, "Contextualization of Merit-Making," 70-73.

of the colonizers, and eliminate their culture and physical presence.[19] Mark Charles and Soong-Chan Rah explain that the theological and legal premise for this was a set of principles that became known as the Doctrine of Discovery.[20] The initial framing of this doctrine stemmed from a series of papal bulls in the 15th century that gave the king of Portugal permission to invade new lands and completely dominate its inhabitants. But in addition to its legal authority, the Doctrine of Discovery provided European settlers, and eventually the White dominant structures of Canada and the US, with what Charles and Rah call a "dysfunctional theological imagination" with which to dominate indigenous communities in the name of Christianity and its God.[21]

It is true that many – though not all or even most – Christian mission workers disagreed with and sometimes even challenged the explicit selfish economic motivations and policies of colonial settlers and powers. However, most did not challenge the implicit animosity they felt for Native American identity and culture. Richard Pratt's infamous motto, "kill the Indian and save the man,"[22] could be said to characterize most mission efforts of the colonial era, leading to the elimination of indigenous language, culture, beliefs, stories, and identity. Even later missionaries who were more benign in their judgements of Native American culture and identity still often viewed indigenous *religious* traditions as harmful and dangerous superstitions that needed to be replaced with the message and practices of Christianity.

Types of Christianities Among Native Americans

And yet, many Native Americans became Christian. And as was common in many other countries, the churches that initially emerged out of this milieu largely adopted the theologies and rituals of the White dominant missionaries and church denominations with which they were most closely associated. This often included the White colonial antipathy towards Native religious traditions. Practices such as traditional dances and instruments were often discouraged in church services, even when adapted to a Christian meaning or use. And church leaders strongly condemned any attendance at traditional rituals and events that contained what were felt to have religious components

---

[19] For a poignant discussion of this see George E. Tinker, *Missionary Conquest: The Gospel and Native American Cultural Genocide* (Minneapolis: Fortress Press, 1993).

[20] Mark Charles and Soong-Chan Rah, *Unsettling Truths: The Ongoing, Dehumanizing Legacy of the Doctrine of Discovery* (Downers Grove, IL: IVP, 2019), 14-23.

[21] Charles and Rah, *Unsettling Truths*, 15.

[22] Pratt's 1879 motto for his newly established Carlisle Indian Industrial School.

to them.[23] Such ceremonies were seen to be "evil," deceptive, or otherwise antithetical to God's intention for Christians.[24]

In recent decades, as Native American churches have become autonomous and developed their own leadership they have developed various ways of relating to, or not relating to, their cultural and religious heritages and identities. Jessica Blanchard suggests that these diverse responses can be summarized into three general categories.[25] The first are Native American Christians who regard traditional tribal practices as irrelevant and old-fashioned. Such rituals and practices, in their estimation, belong to a past non-Christian generation and have no relevance to contemporary Native Christians. Such assessments, however, often reflect the Christian's overall unfamiliarity with the rituals and practices; most Christians in this group did not grow up with the practices, either because their families were already Christian, or they were disconnected from that part of their cultural heritage for other reasons.[26]

The second group are those who themselves converted to Christianity and strongly repudiate the rituals and practices of their tribe. For these believers the rituals and practices of their tribe represent a way of life, and a part of their community, from which they have turned away. These Christians often have a contentious relationship to the tribe and its way of life.[27] However, it is important to note that for many this contentious relationship, and the process of turning away or being turned away from parts of the community and its practices, often began well *before* their turn to Christ.[28] Persons who

---

[23] Anthropologist Jessica Blanchard found that such negative assessments are still common among various Native American Baptist churches in Oklahoma. As one person told her, referring to a traditional ceremonial dance, "[if] I'm seen at a stomp dance, that would be really, really bad. I mean it just wouldn't be right." Jessica Walker Blanchard, "'They Came One at a Time': Native-Led Church Planting and Growing the Body of Christ From the Margins of Culture" (PhD thesis, University of Oklahoma Graduate College, 2010), 37.

[24] As a Christian church-planter told Blanchard, a new church was needed among an Oklahoma tribal community because "they were really involved in other things, traditional things" such as traditional dances. Blanchard, "'They Came One at a Time,'" 85.

[25] Blanchard, "'They Came One at a Time'," 274-279.

[26] Blanchard found that some in this group may be interested in traditional practices that are contextualized for Christianity, so long as they are not seen as having any "religious" or "spiritual" significance.

[27] Blanchard, "'They Came One at a Time'," 278.

[28] Blanchard finds in her research that in fact there are many native people who "do not participate in tribally specific cultural practices" and remain connected to the community. Thus the perception that born-again Christians are disconnected from and even live against their culture cannot be explained simply by their lack of participation in tribal practices, but suggests that many already lived at the periphery for a variety of reasons. Blanchard, "'They Came One at a Time'," 280.

were *already* living at the margins of their tribe found within Christianity a discourse that helped explain, provide a fuller meaning to, and perhaps even alleviated some of the shame associated with being on the periphery of the dominant tribal culture.[29]

These two groups – those ignorant and indifferent and those opposed to traditional religious ways – make up a large part of the existing Christian churches. Thus, despite the use of local language and other cultural components in some churches, and the fact that many of their churches have long since been led by Native American Christians, Native American non-Christians often do not regard these churches to be truly indigenous, at least not in the way that the traditional ceremonial rituals and spaces are.[30]

In recent decades, however, a third group of Native American Christ-followers have begun to seek out pathways for following Jesus that do not require them to embrace what they see as the Christian religion of the colonizers. Though many of these Christ-followers continue to call themselves Christian and to associate with other Christian churches in various ways they, similar to persons like Black Elk, have a much more positive assessment of their tribe's religious and cultural rituals, practices, stories, and heritages. Their hybrid religiosity is often criticized by Native American non-Christian traditionalists, Native American Christians, and dominant culture Christians.[31] Despite this, many have persevered and charted pathways and fostered communities whereby they can more deeply hybridize their traditional religiosity and faith in Christ.[32] As an example we

---

[29] "The contest for many native Christians is not between being native and being Christian. Rather, the contest… is reconciling the local and historical conditions that bring some individuals to live comfortably within the confines of native culture, while others come to live against it." Blanchard, "'They Came One at a Time'," 336-337.

[30] Blanchard, "'They Came One at a Time'," 124. Some more "contemporary" Native American churches have sought to, overall, be more culturally "flexible," but by this they usually mean they seek to reflect a more universal culture that is not just Native American, White, or any other specific cultural form. As one church member expressed it to Blanchard, "I think our main focus should be about the Lord. So whether you're Indian or white or black… I think it's important to keep your heritage but I don't think that should determine how a church is set up. As long as your main focus is on God and going to Heaven and saving people and all that…" Blanchard, "'They Came One at a Time'," 227.

[31] Blanchard notes that, in her assessment, few are able to "maintain uninterrupted commitments to both an active church life and a traditional way of life that includes ceremonial ground activities (such as ceremony participation, social dances, football games, and camp maintenance), family feasts, traditional funerals, and other extensive commitments." Blanchard, "'They Came One at a Time'," 278.

[32] These Christ-followers come from diverse native communities and have networked and worked together over the last 10–20 years in various ways. Many have formed collectives and ministries, some of which are now a part of Indigenous Pathways, an organization and network which seeks to be "rooted in Indigenous life

can consider the experience of one particular leader and the way his work is shaping an alternative missiological imaginary not unlike other insider Christ-followers.

Casey (Leonard) Church

Growing up as a Native American Christian in Southwest Michigan, Casey Church recalls attending his family's Native American church as well as attending and selling food at their Pokagon-Potawatomi tribe's pow-wows. In their own home his family valued the tribe's traditions and heritage; they "were very Native at home."[33] Their church, however, was a very different space from home and his tribe's gatherings. Though it had been established for and was led by Native people, "It was like when you stepped through the doors of the church, you had to leave all that [Native heritage] behind." If someone were to close their eyes and pay attention only to the sounds and style of the church, "there was nothing that would make you think it wasn't a white church."[34] In addition, the church leadership discouraged their members from attending tribal events. When Church's mother one time informed the pastor that they would be away on a Sunday to sell food at a pow-wow the pastor remarked, "If you go to that event next week, don't bother coming back to this church again."[35]

Church thus grew up living in two worlds, caught between his tribe's cultural traditions and a church community that rejected that tradition. It created a gap in his life and an "unrest" of his soul.[36] This unrest grew even stronger as he trained for church ministry and developed a passion to see his people find wholeness through faith in Christ. However, while in college in 1992, Church had two pivotal experiences that began to address his unrest and questions. The first was an English class assignment for which he reflected deeply on his struggle to understand why his two worlds were so separated. This was perhaps the first time he articulated and clarified in himself the deep discomfort and questions he was facing.

---

and values… [and] simultaneously framed by [their] faith as followers of the Jesus Way" and includes the Native American Institute for Indigenous Theological Education (NAIITS). The persons of this collective "offer [their] own stories of this experience as a way for others to find their way as well." Indigenous Pathways. https://indigenouspathways.com/aboutus/. Accessed July 12, 2022. Prominent leaders and spokespersons have included Terry LeBlanc, Casey Church, Richard Twiss, Randy Woodley, Ray Aldred, Cheryl Bear-Barnetson, Andrea Smith, Siouxsan Robinson, Wendy Peterson, and many others.

[33] Nate Harrison, "Native Expression," *Fuller Magazine*, 2020, 13.

[34] Harrison, "Native Expression," 13.

[35] Harrison, "Native Expression," 13.

[36] Casey Church, *Holy Smoke: The Contextual Use of Native American Ritual and Ceremony* (Centre for Pentecostal Theology Native North American Contextual Movement Series: Cleveland, TN: Cherohala Press, 2017), 112.

The second, and perhaps more profound experience, was a subsequent vision. In this vision Church watched a young Native boy engage in a vision quest – an experience Church was never able or allowed to have. The vision quest of the boy was unique, however, in that he had an encounter with Christ. In particular, the boy saw Christ dying on a pole and, without knowing Christ's name or identity, knew that this was being done for him and his people. The boy responded by raising a piece of roasted rabbit and bowl of water to the sky and eating it in remembrance of the man on the pole. When Church emerged from the vision, he realized that the Holy Spirit was beginning to lead him on a journey of being both a follower of Christ *and* fully Native.[37]

As he started to lead and plant churches Church experimented with and adapted various Native practices, such as Native drums, dancing, and smudging (incense burning) into the worship services. Some Christians resisted this, but many others – both Christian and non-Christian – found hope and healing in the integration. Eventually Church's journey connected him with other Native Christ-followers who were also seeking, as one of Church's friends and colleagues stated it, "to follow Creator-Jesus within our Indigenous cultural ways without submitting to the hegemonic cultural assumptions" of the wider Christian (and particularly conservative evangelical) church.[38]

Church has helped to start and lead Good Medicine Way, a new Native gathering that seeks to honor "Creator and his son" in a Native American cultural context. He is also the director of Wiconi International, an indigenous organization that seeks to bring about a "preferred future for our Native people" by spurring a "contextual movement" of Native Christ-followers.[39] One of the ways it does this is to host gatherings and events, such an annual "family camp," in which Christ-followers dialogue, learn, and "retraditionalize" various Native practices and teachings in light of their commitment to Christ.[40] These camps attract persons who have experienced the conflict that Church himself felt and provides for them "the opportunity to enter into a new internal wholeness" that integrates their cultural identity as Christ-followers.[41]

A brief description of one of Church's practices in this camp – the sweat lodge – provides a glimpse into how such practices provide profound

---

[37] Church, *Holy Smoke*, 12-13.

[38] Richard Twiss, *Rescuing the Gospel From the Cowboys: A Native American Expression of the Jesus Way* (Downers Grove, IL: InterVarsity Press, 2015), 17.

[39] Leonard Church, "Rites of Passage: Implications of the Change Process at Overcomers Alcohol Treatment Program and its Relation to the Change and Transition with the Wiconi Organization" (Doctor of Intercultural Studies thesis, Fuller Theological Seminary, 2015), 4.

[40] Church, "Rites of Passage," 133.

[41] Church, "Rites of Passage," 58.

moments of insight and healing to participants, as well as the alternative imaginary Church and other Native American Christ-followers are developing. After together constructing the dome-shaped sweat lodge, community members enter and sit in the hot, humid setting. Both before and during the actual "sweat" Church blesses and "cleanses" the space and community with the incense of a smudge mixture.[42] The space, time, and persons of the sweat lodge are recognized as sacred and prepared for transformation. Church then leads the community to sing and pray to, reflect on, and receive spiritual cleansing from Christ, who inhabits the space and traditions of that space. He concludes the time by celebrating the Lord's Supper, utilizing indigenous fried bread and steam that emanates from the water poured on the heated rocks. When the community emerges from the lodge, they do so "as a new creature like a baby wet from the amniotic fluid of the womb."[43]

Notice how Church's practice and language reflects a sense of baptismal transformation; persons who were separated from Christ and/or their Native traditions are immersed in Christ *and* tradition, only to re-emerge as new, transformed, and integrated beings. But Church's vision, and that of other Native Christ-follower leaders, indicates that this is a microcosm of the larger transformative work that the Holy Spirit is doing and wants to do among his people. That is, Christ desires to take a people oppressed by neo-colonialism and discipled under colonial mission visions of the Christ-life, immerse them in the Spirit's "steam" of Christ's purifying work (via their own traditions), and be transformed, not into a separate Christianity defined and shaped by colonial whiteness, but one that reflects the move of the Spirit in their own tradition and community.

Gatherings such as these are spurring small and growing communities of Native Christ-followers, such as Church's Good Medicine Way. Each hybridizes its religiosity in unique ways, according to the particular traditions and settings of their communities. Each, in their own way, seeks to provide visions of the "preferred future" that Christ has for them and their people.

Conclusion

Our contemporary case studies of Hindu, Muslim, Buddhist, and Native American Christ-followers have been necessarily brief. But these begin to highlight several characteristics of the hybridized religiosity of insider groups in various contexts. Often these leaders have sought to follow what they feel is the Spirit's leading to repair the gap that missionaries and Christians in their context created between Christ and their identities and communities.

---

[42] Church follows some tribal traditions by mixing and smoldering sage, sweet grass, cedar, and tobacco in an abalone shell.

[43] Church, "Rites of Passage," 71.

Such a split created not only painful relational separation between the Christ-followers and their communities, but also a separation within their own identities. In various ways the Spirit sought to help them correct this, finding that the work of Christ was one that could very much flow through, not be apart from, their religious traditions and practices.

They thus sought to re-integrate, or stay integrated, within the nexus of relationships and the community of tradition that those relationships practiced and embodied. Similar to the process envisioned by Casey Church's sweat lodge, Christ-followers in each of these contexts journeyed, emerged, and continue to emerge from the transforming work of the Spirit with new missiological imaginaries that re-envision a new future for themselves and their community. These new imaginaries and the practices that embody them, they might say, are the Spirit's gifts to them. But though these sacred gifts of imaginary are forged in their contexts, they can also be gifts to the wider body of Christ, if we will continue to listen and consider what they may teach us about various aspects of God's work of re-creation. It is to these various learnings that we now turn.

Section Three

Insider Missiological Imaginaries in Practice

6: Insider Imaginaries and Religious Revelations Part 1

In arguing that insider Christ-followers have alternative missiological imaginaries from which Christians can learn, I have sought in previous chapters to make two main points. First, the faith of all Christ-followers, particularly insiders, emerges through a process of religiosity – an interaction with various cultural and religious influences. Second, though this process can and does sometimes lead to unhelpful, and even evil, distortions of the gospel, it can also reflect the work of the Spirit in and through communities, including other religious communities and traditions. In the last two chapters we have illustrated some of the ways in which the Spirit has led various insider Christ-followers to serve and reflect Christ within their religious communities. Their stories have touched on aspects of their missiological imaginaries, or the diverse ways in which they make sense of God's mission in and for their context. Each imaginary is unique, as would make sense given the diverse religious traditions our examples represent. But each also has the common theme of prioritizing and following Christ from within the framework of their own community and tradition and in turn reshaping the hope and the *telos* provided by those traditions.

In this and the following chapters we will more closely examine some of the particular components of such imaginaries. For insiders, what does it mean to read the scriptures of their traditions and hybridize these with their reading of the biblical scriptures? What is "good news" and salvation in their contexts, and in what ways does Christ offer this? What does it mean to "convert" to Christ? And what is the interpretive function and importance of family? Each of these form pieces of the new missiological imaginaries that insider Christ-followers are developing through their lived practices.

As we continue in these discussions it is once again imperative to recognize that a) these are *our* questions, not those of insiders, and b) insider Christ-followers are often not analyzing and articulating their faith in systematic and written ways, at least not in the ways to which Western Christian scholars are accustomed. Rather, these are theologies of practice flowing from missiological imaginaries. We can again recall Charles Taylor's description from chapter 1 that imaginaries are "the deeper normative notions and images,"[1] or the unarticulated knowledge informing people's practices, identities, and beliefs.

With this in mind, I will focus in this and the next chapter on the first of our specific enquiries: the question of religious revelation, including written scripture, oral stories, and various other artistic and liturgical expressions. To what degree do insider Christ-followers value their religious community's scriptures and other forms of revelation? What does it mean that they give "authority" to biblical scripture, and how does this relate to their community's sources for religious revelation? We will begin with two brief examples of insiders and their approach to non-biblical revelation and consider the ways in which religionists, including insiders such as these, often affirm a "canon" or "canons" of revelation, but also interact with it in dynamic ways. In the next chapter I will continue this discussion by considering the various strategies and methods that Christ-followers use when engaging non-biblical scriptures, and how insiders evaluate and use some of these.

Christ-Followers (Re)Encountering Non-Christian Scripture

Growing up, Dayanand Bharati occasionally recited Hindu scriptures and heard them recited as part of his Hindu community's rituals. And, as was common for most Hindus, he focused primarily on the sounds and immediate devotional meanings of the words rather than analyzing or interpreting them. However, when he began following Christ as a young man he was introduced to a different approach to scripture. With the help and example of Christian friends he began to eagerly read biblical scripture on a daily basis and use commentaries and other guides for scriptural study.[2]

Unsurprisingly, the enthusiasm that Bharati's Christian friends had for Bible study did not extend to Hindu scriptures. The only exception to this was when they sought to answer the question, "What does Hinduism lack?" As a new Christ-follower Bharati felt this was certainly a legitimate question, but he was surprised at the shallow understanding his friends had of Hindu scripture and their offensive attempts to discredit Hinduism.

Though he had not previously studied Hindu scriptures in any great depth, he now felt compelled to read and study them on their own terms, even using Hindu commentaries. Initially his studies helped him find ways to share the gospel with other Hindus in convincing but sensitive ways. His studies also helped to reinforce his sense that the biblical scriptures provide an important and unique perspective on how to have a relationship with God and salvation.

[1] Taylor, *A Secular Age*, 171.

[2] This and the following paragraphs are from Bharati's unpublished manuscript called "Faith and Hindu Scriptures." I use it with his permission and am grateful for the conversations we have had around these topics.

Eventually, however, Bharati felt that God was using these studies and other experiences for something more – to reconnect him with his Hindu identity. Through several circumstances and what he felt was God's calling he re-embraced his Hindu identity and community, even taking the vow to become a *swami* (Hindu monk).[3] Through this process he has found that his studies of biblical and Hindu scriptures have focused less and less on identifying what is missing in Hinduism. Instead, he says, it has become more about "how my faith in the Lord helps me to integrate the valuable things in Hinduism both for my private spiritual life and [to] apply it in my relationship with others. The best of Hinduism enriches my new faith in the Lord."

But this does not mean that biblical and Hindu scriptures easily harmonize, or that everything about Hindu scriptures enriches his faith. Bharati continues to acknowledge and grapple with the differences between Hindu and biblical texts. He does not want to ignore a Hindu scripture if it seems to contradict his faith, but neither does he want to reinterpret it in ways that his Hindu community would not recognize and would therefore reject. Rather his hope is to model for other Hindu Christ-followers a willingness to "remain faithful" to the meaning of both biblical and Hindu scriptures "without compromising one with the other" – to perhaps allow for some tension, even as they prioritize the biblical scripture's witness to Christ.

In a similar way to Bharati, though in a very different context, Mazhar Mallouhi had a gradual transformation in his understanding of the scripture of his Muslim tradition, the Qur'an. As a 24-year-old in the Syrian military he became a Christian through his friendship with a fellow soldier and his own readings in the New Testament.[4] Sometime later he left for Lebanon, attended a Bible college, and worked for a Christian publisher. At first, he turned against most everything about Islam and its scripture and criticized any Christian that sought to read the Qur'an or even use it in evangelism. "There is a lot of honey in the Qur'an," he would say, "but there is also a lot of poison."[5]

But over the following years Mallouhi underwent a gradual change of perspective. He found himself less and less comfortable with the harsh approaches and proclamations he himself and other Christians made against Muslims and the Qur'an, and he became more sensitive to the pain and distance such approaches created in his relationships with Muslims. He began to learn from persons with more "generous" approaches and started viewing

---

[3] This was a vow he had made earlier in his life and laid aside when becoming a Christ-follower. Now, however, he found the pathway by which to renew this vow as an expression of his devotion to Christ.

[4] Paul-Gordon Chandler, *Pilgrims of Christ on the Muslim Road: Exploring a New Path Between Two Faiths* (New York: Rowman & Littlefield Publishers, 2007), 21-23.

[5] Chandler, *Pilgrims of Christ*, 77.

Muhammad and the Qur'an as "potential signposts point[ing] toward Christ."[6] He eventually shifted in his self-understanding and his approach to be a Muslim follower of Christ. He now says,

> Islam is the blanket with which my mother wrapped me when she nursed me and sang to me and prayed over me… I inherited Islam from my parents, and it was the cradle which held me until I found Christ. Islam is my mother. You don't engage a man by telling him his mother is ugly… I have an emotional attachment to my culture which I imbibed along with my mother's milk.[7]

Notice how, for Mallouhi, Islam has a nurturing quality that, though superseded by Christ, still holds a special place in his heart and journey. In a similar way the Qur'an, when he now hears it read, has a beauty in its language that brings "chills" down his spine.[8] But also notice that Islam and the Qur'an are superseded, not by another religious system or another set of scriptures, but by a person. This is an important point for Mallouhi. For though the Qur'an and other aspects of Islam are of value, they are transvalued only by some*one* else, by Christ. He explains this through an illustration. "When one feels like they are drowning, do you reach for a book on how to swim, or a hand? The prophets it seems to me gave me a book, whether it is the Qur'an or the Christian Scriptures, but Jesus gave me a hand."[9]

For Mallouhi this helps address the centuries-old framing of Christianity and Islam as religious competitors. He wants, as much as possible, to not pit religions and scriptures against each other, but to make Christ the supreme authority over all and interpretive key for all.

The Bible and Other Scriptures

It is evident that Bharati and Mallouhi implicitly sense that God is not absent from their respective traditions and scriptures. Recall our discussion of Robert Johnston in chapter 3 – the Spirit has been at work throughout all of creation, including in religious traditions and their written and oral scriptures, stories, prayers, songs, and other expressions. These are indications of God's "footprints" – evidence that the Spirit moved in and through those spaces. But the revelatory work of the Spirit is always and everywhere an event that happens in the present. So, if and when we discern the past presence or "footprints" of the Spirit in those traditions, it is only because the Spirit in

---

[6] Chandler, *Pilgrims of Christ on the Muslim Road*, 78.

[7] Mazhar Mallouhi, "Comments on the Insider Movement," in Harley Talman and John Jay Travis (eds), *Understanding Insider Movements: Disciples of Jesus Within Diverse Religous Communities* (Pasadena, CA: William Carey Library, 2015), 111.

[8] Chandler, *Pilgrims of Christ on the Muslim Road*, 82.

[9] Chandler, *Pilgrims of Christ on the Muslim Road*, 170.

and through us *now* is helping us see and understand it as such. Though they do not state it in these terms, Bharati and Mallouhi are seeking the Spirit's understanding of how the Spirit was and is at work in the scriptural traditions of their communities.

But what does this mean for the biblical scriptures? How do insiders regard the Bible in relation to other scriptures? And what might this suggest about the revelation of the Spirit and if/how other scriptures and sources are a part of God's mission? First, many insiders that have been interviewed around this topic regard biblical scripture as authoritative for their faith and lives. In his study of 26 leaders of Muslim Christ-follower groups from around the world, for example, Jan Hendrik Prenger found that, when asked "How would you describe the status of the (biblical) Scriptures?", most responded by describing it as "the Word of God" and a "guide for right living on a right path."[10] Three described the Scripture using the phrase "breathed out by God." As one respondent put it, "The holy book, or books, is a book of which its [sic] content is revealed and breathed out by God."[11] Of course, the language of "breathed out by God" likely refers to the description of scripture in 2 Timothy 3:16 ("All scripture is God-breathed and useful for teaching…). However, these Muslim Christ-followers are also using creation language, echoing both the Qur'an (Surah 15:28-29) and the Bible (Gen. 2:7) to evoke an image of God breathing life into humanity. Note also that this revealing is not past tense, but somehow present tense. It is as if, for these Christ-followers at least, the biblical scripture is an object that has been crafted by God and has much value, much like Adam's body was crafted from the dirt and could be valued because of this handiwork alone. But Scripture, just like humanity, is then also animated by God's breath and Spirit, certainly at an initial point, but also continually.

Second, though for insiders this animation or revelation of the Spirit occurs first and foremost through biblical scriptures, this does not negate the value of other religious sources or the revelation that the Spirit can provide through them. Perhaps it is most accurate to say that many, or even most, insiders prioritize biblical scripture above other scriptures, but also value the ways in which God by his Spirit may provide blessing, truth, and goodness through other scriptures, prayers, stories, etc. Recall how Mallouhi came to the conviction that the Qur'an could provide a "signpost" towards Christ. In a similar way, in Prenger's study of Muslim insider leaders, most of the leaders value parts of the Qur'an for the "pointers" it provides towards Christ.[12] Some go further than this, indicating that the Qur'an provides the "amen" to the biblical scriptures that came before and that, when "properly

[10] Jan Hendrik Prenger, *Muslim Insider Christ Followers: The Theological and Missional Frames* (Pasadena, CA: William Carey Library, 2017), 71.

[11] Prenger, *Muslim Insider Christ Followers*, 72.

[12] Prenger, *Muslim Insider Christ Followers*, 74-76.

interpreted," can affirm the biblical truths about Jesus Christ and "help people better understand the grace and mercy of God."[13] In this way most of these insider leaders either believe the Qur'an "records part of an ongoing conversation between God and (humans)" or that it at least contains "many truths."[14]

But what about traditions, such as Native American traditions, that do not prioritize a "text"? For these, revelation is most often understood and conveyed through experience and stories. It is often oral stories that describe the creation of the world and tribe, make sense of a tribe's context and history, and ponder the complex and interesting patterns of the created order. Tribes regard these stories as sacred and carefully curate them accordingly. As Richard Twiss explains, because of their sacredness some stories "are not meant to be told to others, and some not fully explained."[15] In addition, some stories should not be told to outsiders, and some should only be told at certain times of the year lest the inappropriate telling of them diminish their power.

As we saw in chapter 5, Native American Christians have often been taught that the traditional stories of their tribes, along with accompanying rituals, are not of God and thus dangerous.[16] Many Native American insider Christ-followers, though, have come to relate to their tribes' traditions and sacred stories differently. Rather than dismissing these stories, insiders instead listen for the parallels that they have with the stories, songs, and truths found in the biblical scriptures. They find that their own stories and teachings often parallel biblical stories such as those about creation and the flood, or teachings such as those by Jesus. These parallels indicate to them that God was at work revealing himself to them through their culture "before we even knew about Christ."[17] As we have seen, this impulse – this Spirit-inspired ability to discern godly wisdom in other traditions – is not new. Recall how the writers of our Jewish and Christian scriptures included the wisdom of other (Babylonian, Egyptian, later Greco-Roman) traditions. It is thus not at all surprising that indigenous insiders too read biblical scriptures in the light of the wisdoms of their communities and traditions.

---

[13] Muslim insider as quoted in Prenger, *Muslim Insider Christ Followers*, 76.

[14] Prenger, *Muslim Insider Christ Followers*, 223. It should be noted that not all insider leaders agree on this point. About 5 of the 26 of Prenger's respondents place little value in the Qur'an aside from being a means by which to "reach" fellow Muslims. Even these opinions, however, were more positive – or less negative – than those of many Christians. Prenger, *Muslim Insider Christ Followers*, 77, 223.

[15] Twiss, *Rescuing the Gospel From the Cowboys*, 94.

[16] Cheryl Bear, "The Smudge Ceremony: Inspiring Faith in Indigenous North Americans," in R. Daniel Shaw and William R. Burrows (eds), *Traditional Ritual as Christian Worship: Dangerous Syncretism or Necessary Hybrid?* (Maryknoll, NY: Orbis Books, 2018), 194.

[17] Twiss, *Rescuing the Gospel from the Cowboys*, 117.

In addition, as they do so, indigenous insiders sometimes even highlight and sharpen the prophetic edge of certain biblical teachings. For instance, Cheryl Bear, a Native American Christ-follower from the Dakelh people, tells how an elder from her tribe once shared their creation story and indicated from it that "Creator is going to come back and look at how we have taken care of the land that was loaned to us." This story and interpretation challenges Bear, who concludes that her tribe's story, similar to the biblical narrative, indicates that "there is always a reckoning" in relation to our actions.[18] In such cases the Spirit can use the wisdom of other religious traditions to accentuate the radical teachings of biblical scripture, teachings which may have been softened or overlooked.

The Spirit in Canon and Charisma

The above indicates that insiders often prioritize the Bible, regarding it as having unique revelatory status, but that they also see evidence of God's presence and work in their tradition's scriptures, oral and written. God has spoken and continues to speak through the Bible in a unique way, they would affirm, but God is not and has never been confined to biblical scripture. God's "footprints" can be found in the scriptures and prayers of others, and the Spirit continues to reveal himself to Christ-followers through these. The missiological imaginary of many insiders thus seems to be comfortable with a dynamism, perhaps we could say a fluidity, to the work of the Spirit across scriptures and revelatory sources. It is this sense of fluidity that makes some Christians anxious, and central to this anxiety is the concept and function of the biblical canon. Are not insiders essentially adding their community's scriptures and stories to the canon of biblical scripture, at least in practice?

To unpack and bring focus to what could otherwise be a long and complex discussion, we can begin by highlighting that insider Christ-followers are not alone, and not the first, to read scriptures in dynamic ways. What do I mean by this? Heinrich von Stietencron has shown how, in many religious traditions, there are often two dynamics working at the same time – canon and charisma. Scriptural canons, like that of the Qur'an, Bible, Vedas, or, in some cases, sacred stories, are the result of "a deliberate attempt to collect, arrange and preserve the original message of a religious community, and to protect it against all corruption." In the midst of an ever-changing world, a canon of scripture becomes "a device to arrest time, or rather to pick out and separate from the change-inducing flow of time a selected set of elements that are considered essential and eternally valued… [and that] provide lasting orientation to the community."[19]

---

[18] Bear, "The Smudge Ceremony," 201.

[19] Heinrich von Stietencron, "Charisma and Canon: The Dynamics of Legitimization and Innovation in Indian Religions," in Vasudha Dalmia, Angelika Malinar, and

Charisma on the other hand seeks to ensure that a canon is vital, that the fixedness of a canon does not render it obsolete. It is a power that operates in the present moment. As Stietencron describes, “It is not the rule, but the exception: a spark of divine presence flashing into ordinary life and legitimizing leadership and change. It is divine agency operating through [humanity], a power temporarily conferred on [them] which creates extraordinary authority.”[20] The dynamic work of charisma can lead to various outcomes: sometimes it gives birth to new religious movements and at other times it brings reinterpretation and renewal to meaning and authority in an existing tradition.

While Stietencron applies this framework across religious traditions, we can note the ways this connects theologically to the Christ-following tradition. Canon has historically provided stability within Christ-following communities, as well as helping to form a unique sense of identity. Charisma, on the other hand, via the work and presence of the Spirit, has provided innovation, inspiring new interpretations, meanings, and motivations within these communities. These two operate as opposing but also interacting principles. When scriptural canon and its interpretation, historically and contextually oriented as they are, have become too disconnected from a new era or context, an influx of charisma via the Spirit has revitalized the canon’s relevance. Without the Spirit’s charisma, canon can stagnate and lose some of its power and importance.

Insider Christ-followers, as we saw from some of the earlier examples, affirm the need to prioritize the biblical canon over others. However, they also seek to resist two implications made by Christians, and sometimes their co-religionists. One is the implication that the biblical canon is the scripture of Christians. Indeed, as Stietencron indicates, canons are not only repositories of established teachings and narratives but are also “one of the strongest possible forms of defining and securing a special religious identity.”[21] Canons provide a source for self-awareness and self-definition, and also become an identity boundary marker. Christians, for example, are people who revere the Bible, not the Qur’an. If and when persons prioritize the teaching of another scripture over that of their community, such a shift is usually associated with a person’s conversion of religion and religious community.[22] But this is something that insiders seek to resist. While they

---

Martin Christof (eds), *Charisma and Canon: Essays on the Religious History of the Indian Subcontinent* (New Delhi: Oxford University Press, 2001), 14-15.

[20] Stietencron, “Charisma and Canon,” 15.

[21] Stietencron, “Charisma and Canon,” 14.

[22] Though this is often the case for many religious traditions it does not hold true for all. Dayanand Bharati notes that, for many Hindus, it is possible to “give priority to all Scriptures while continuing to remain within their sampradaya [Hindu sect and community] [while] not converting to another one. For most Hindus no particular

acknowledge that biblical scripture has been central to the development of Christian cultures and identity, they deny that this makes biblical scripture the property of Christians. Rather, they assert that they as Hindus, Buddhist, Muslims, etc. can incorporate, and even prioritize, the biblical scripture, embracing the biblical canon while retaining their religious community's identity.

How can insiders embrace the biblical scriptures while not allowing it to define them as a set-apart group? One method used by many insiders is to rename the biblical scriptures. For instance, in the Muslim context, Christians commonly refer to the Bible as *al-Kitāb al-Muqaddas* (the Holy Book). Muslim followers of Christ, however, retain the Muslim titles for the biblical scriptures: the *Tawrat* (Torah), the *Zabur* (Psalms), and the *Injil* (Gospel). As another example, while Christians in India use the English word "Bible" to describe biblical scriptures, Bharati and his group refer to them as *muktiveda* (freedom/salvation scriptures). This title is an Indian term that, as he explains, "looks familiar to me (and) in which I feel comfortable." He recognizes that, though Hindus (like any religionist) could sometimes be sensitive about someone piecing together and creating new words from their religious tradition, "as an Indian I have my right to use those terms (while) at the same time not hurting the religious sentiments of our own people."

Another strategy important to insiders is to translate or paraphrase biblical scripture, as they are able, into their own languages using terminology that is both faithful to the biblical meaning and that resonates with their community.[23] As is well-known, missionary Bible translators past and present regularly deliberate on the best way to translate biblical words such as "God," "baptism," "Son of God," etc. Their preference has often been to use terms that already exist in the language as much as possible so that the community would feel that the Bible was "their" scripture. If, however, translators determine that a certain word has too many unbiblical connotations they may seek for an alternative term, sometimes even creating new words derived from the biblical term. Many insiders have sought to retranslate these terms, either by simply re-inserting a term they feel is more appropriate, paraphrasing scriptures, or developing a whole new translation.[24]

Scripture holds the final authority on her faith but mostly family tradition." Dayanand Bharati, email message to author, August 11, 2020.

[23] This reflects the sense of many insiders that the existing translations often use loan words or Christianized words that reinforce the perception that the biblical scriptures are the Christian scriptures.

[24] For example, some Hindu followers of Christ prefer to refer to "baptism" as *Yeshu diksha* rather than *baptisma* and to call "Jesus" *Muktinath* instead of *Yesu Mesiha*. An example of a paraphrase, again from the Hindu context, is Dhanjibhai Fakirbhai's paraphrase of the Gospels in the style of the *Bhagavad Gita*. A translation of this into English is *Immortal Life: The Mukti Marg of Sri Jesus* (New Delhi: BR Publishing Corporation, 2020). For an example of a contextual translation

Though such linguistic work certainly helps insiders and their communities better understand biblical scriptures, it also signals to themselves and, by extension, to the Western Christian translation tradition, something important; Western Christians do not own or control God's word. Rather, it is meant for all persons, of all religious communities.

A second approach used by some insiders is to counter the belief, often held by Christians, that God only reveals himself through the Bible and the Christian tradition. It is here that the idea of the charisma of God's Spirit is particularly important. If God's Spirit provides revelation through non-biblical scriptures and sources, as some insiders' statements and practices indicate, this suggests a charisma that resists, not the fixedness of the biblical canon, but the implications that God's revelation is solely concentrated in the Christian tradition that stems from it. Thus, the charisma of the Spirit brings innovation, not by undermining the biblical canon, but by instead revitalizing it with insights from other religious traditions.

But notice the dynamic interaction of canon and charisma that this suggests: the Spirit uses the canon of biblical scripture to help reveal truth in other scriptures and also uses other scriptures to illuminate biblical truths sometimes obscured by Western colonialism and cultural influences. That is, as insider Christ-followers read their religious tradition's scriptures, the Spirit now uses both biblical and non-biblical scriptures as mutual hermeneutical keys through which they can gain new insights. Recall the cyclical way in which Black Elk's Native American and Catholic identities created the meaning of his vision. In a similar way, Native American insiders such as Richard Twiss discern ways that their indigenous stories and teachings parallel and resonate with the biblical stories and teachings while also highlighting key themes not taught to them by Western Christians. Likewise, Muslim followers of Christ sense that the Spirit uses biblical scripture and Christ to reveal God's past work and testimony in the Qur'an, and also uses the Qur'an to highlight and affirm certain understandings of God. To echo the classic insights of philosopher Hans-Georg Gadamer, biblical scripture becomes a new way, a new location by which to frame the "horizon" of their community's scripture, and vice versa.[25]

But though insiders present a dynamic, even dialectical, relationship between the Spirit-inspired canon of biblical scripture and Spirit-inspired charisma of other traditions, this dialectic nonetheless presupposes the special status of biblical scripture as authoritative for their faith and lives. Many or most do not, of course, know or articulate a "theology" of revelation and inspiration, but would perhaps agree with Sandra M. Schneiders' summary that "the Bible enjoys a privileged position among the multiple

---

from the Muslim context see Mazhar Mallouhi (ed.), *The True Meaning of the Gospel of Christ*, 2nd ed. (Beirut: Dar al-Farabi, 2016).

[25] Hans-Georg Gadamer, *Truth and Method*, 2nd ed. (New York: Continuum, 2002).

actualizations of revelation."[26] This because it uniquely witnesses to the encounter and intervention of God in history (with Israel, and all of humanity), and ultimately through Christ. It is in and through the biblical scriptures that God self-discloses his character, interaction, and work of new creation in ways that are not revealed anywhere else.[27]

In addition, insiders understand the power of biblical scripture, and *any* scripture or narrative, for creating community. Narratives, written or oral, do not simply convey information; they shape a people. In this insiders would not deny the way in which the biblical scripture has shaped, and developed through the tradition of, Christ-following communities (the Christian church). Though they would perhaps challenge some of the colonially tainted ways in which Christians have translated and interpreted the Bible, and the ways the Bible has become associated with Western Christianity, they nonetheless often embrace the importance of small groups of followers gathering together to read, pray, and learn from biblical scriptures – to be shaped by them.[28]

Thus, the missiological imaginary of insiders suggests a faith in the Spirit's ability to reorient believers to the canonical witness of biblical scripture and to use this as a means to transform their understanding of the revelations of their own traditions. But they also affirm the way the charisma of the Spirit can use those same traditions to enrich their understanding of biblical scripture. As one Muslim insider leader states, "We never ask [Muslim Christ-followers] not to read the Qur'an, but we know that the [biblical] Scriptures have more power and will shift the people's attention away from the Qur'an to the Scriptures." The Spirit, he is asserting, will draw people to prioritize the biblical canon of scripture. But at the same time, he can affirm, "The Qur'an has some passages here and there that are the Word of God, [though] as a whole it does not have the same status as the other books."[29]

Again, this applies to those traditions that prioritize the reading and interpretation of fixed texts, such as Islam and Christianity, as well as those that do not. For example, though Hindus are rarely taught to read and study

---

[26] Sandra M. Schneiders, *The Revelatory Text: Interpreting the New Testament as Sacred Scripture*, 2nd ed. (Collegeville, MN: The Liturgical Press, 1999), 45.
[27] Stanley J. Grenz, *Theology For the Community of God* (Grand Rapids, MI: Eerdmans, 2000), 396-397.
[28] Stanley Grenz argues that the Bible is a "paradigmatic narrative" that not only records God's revelation and work in past history, but through the Spirit "shapes the community's way of conceiving the totality of reality as well as the community's understanding of its ongoing experience of reality." Stanley J. Grenz, "How Do We Know What to Believe? Revelation and Authority," in William C. Placher (ed.), *Essentials of Christian Theology* (Louisville, KY: Westminster John Knox Press), 25.
[29] Prenger, *Muslim Insider Christ Followers*, 259, 165.

their religious scriptures, they are nonetheless surrounded by and immersed in the stories and images of their religious traditions. Many, if not most, Hindu children learn some of the stories of Krishna through school, cartoons, or comic books. Around popular festival times like Diwali or Navaratri they hear stories and fragments of stories regarding the exploits and intrigues of deities, heroes, and villains that mark the occasions. Though these do not form a clear and defined "canon," nor are studied or exegeted as such, they nonetheless invite people to inhabit and live in a particular way of understanding and living in the world. These narratives operate as revelation, or authoritative "texts" for Hindus, ones which many Christians reject as unhelpful, or even evil. Insider Christ-followers, however, would see their study of biblical scripture as providing them with new lenses through which to "read," understand, and even revitalize some of the meaning of these narratives.

But what more can we say and learn about these "lenses," these ways of interpreting their tradition, scriptures, and stories? For this we can consider an important insight from biblical and literary studies that sheds light on the various ways that any person, including insiders, integrate prior texts, speech, music, and art into their own.

7: Insider Imaginaries and Religious Revelations Part 2

In the previous chapter I explored how, for insiders, biblical scripture becomes an interpretive key by which to understand their own community's scripture and tradition.[1] As they do so the charisma of the Spirit uses these insights to close cultural and historical gaps between the biblical canon and their own religious tradition and location. This is, of course, not new. Christ-followers since the 1st century have implicitly and explicitly interpreted extra-biblical ideas and "common-grace" revelation (whether scriptures, stories, philosophies, experiences, etc.) in light of biblical scripture. In what ways have Christians historically done so, and how does this help us understand the interpretive choices of insiders? This chapter forms a second part to our discussion on scripture and revelation. In it I will consider some of the theoretical work on *intertextuality* and how this, combined with an understanding of the Spirit's work through canon and charisma, can help us better understand the interpretive strategies of Christ-followers in general, and insiders in particular.

Intertextual Strategies

Over the last 40 years literary scholars have increasingly theorized how *intertextuality*, or the "imbedding of fragments of an earlier text within a later one,"[2] can help conceptualize the way people produce or interpret a text via other texts. When we write or speak, these scholars point out, we commonly use past speech to help construct our own. However, we do not refer to past texts arbitrarily. Rather, and this is a key aspect of intertextuality, we choose texts mindful of their meanings and associations and weave these together

---

[1] What, as mentioned in chapter 2, I and William Dyrness discuss as the "reverse hermeneutic." Duerksen and Dyrness, *Seeking Church: Emerging Witnesses to the Kingdom.*

[2] Richard B. Hays, *Echoes of Scripture in the Letters of Paul* (New Haven: Yale University Press, 1989), 14. For an overview of the history of intertextuality in literary studies see Graham Allen, *Intertextuality*, 2nd ed. (The New Critical Idiom: Abingdon, Oxon.; New York: Routledge, 2011).

into sentences or utterances with new or renewed sets of meanings and associations.

It is important to point out that, though intertextuality has been developed in literary circles with a focus on *text*, scholars have also applied this as a framework for communication in general. Thus, *any* form of communication, whether textual, oral, paralinguistic, musical, artistic, etc., regularly make intertextual references to past communications. This is certainly crucial to our discussion of insider groups, whose religious traditions communicate truths and revelation in a wide range of forms. Thus, though our discussion here will often refer to "texts," this includes the wide range of communication forms by which meaning is made.

It is also important to point out that, though intertextuality focuses on the interaction between particular texts or communications, for Christ-followers the ultimate hermeneutical key, or interpretive framework, is the Christ event. That is, all intertextual interactions have Christ as an ultimate referent point, whether the specific texts refer to Christ or not. Steve Moyise reflects on how this same dynamic guided the NT authors and their interactions with the Hebrew scriptures. "The New Testament authors," he says, "were involved in a dynamic process whereby the Christ event affects the interpretation of the ancient texts, and ancient texts affect the interpretation of the Christ event."[3] As we will see, in their intertextual work, insiders, just like Christians historically, often reflect and presuppose a commitment to the lordship of Christ.

What then are the various methods and strategies that people in general use when using and/or engaging a past text? In 1982 poetry scholar Thomas Greene outlined four different intertextual strategies used by Renaissance poets. Shortly thereafter Greene's framework was adopted and applied by biblical scholars such as Richard Hays and Steve Moyise and religious studies scholar Mark Swanson. It was, of course, already obvious that writers regularly referred to past poets/writers/texts, whether explicitly or implicitly. But of particular interest to these scholars was, as Hays says, the writers' "posture" toward the past as it was expressed in the symbolic world of the text.[4] How and to what degree did they engage the meaning and feeling of a text? Did they selectively pick and choose from small parts of the text's symbolic world, or accept larger parts of that world without question? Did they seek to update the text's world and message, or let it freely speak to their

---

[3] Steve Moyise, "Intertextuality and Historical Approaches to the Use of Scripture in the New Testament," in Richard B. Hays, Stefan Alkier, and Leroy A. Huizenga (eds), *Reading the Bible Intertextually* (Waco, TX: Baylor University Press, 2009), 28.

[4] Hays, *Echoes of Scripture*, 174.

present context?[5] The four strategies outlined by Greene – *eclectic* (or what I will call *extraction*), *reproduction*, *heuristic*, and *dialectical* – represent four different postures towards and engagement with a previous text's world and meaning. I will outline each of these in turn and consider how they may help us understand the choices that insider Christ-followers, and all Christ-followers, make when interpreting extra-biblical "texts."

Extraction

Greene's first intertextual strategy is what he called *eclectic* and, for our purposes, I will develop and call *extraction.* With this strategy a person references a past text (whether a written or spoken phrase, part of a story, music, practice, etc.) with little reference or commitment to that text's context and traditions of interpretation. This can take two forms, depending on the person's posture towards the text's tradition. In *evocative extraction* persons seek to evoke a prior text's general idea in order to reinforce a truth or point, even though they may have little or no commitment to a text's original context.[6] By contrast, in *exploitative extraction* persons do not want to allow the text's general idea to be felt at all. Instead, they reference the prior text in order to reinterpret it, and sometimes to say something very different (and even opposite!) from what that text's tradition has often understood it to say.

We can see many examples of how religious writers have used both forms of intertextual extraction. As an example of evocative extraction, in the New Testament Matthew tells us that the journey of Jesus' family to Egypt is a fulfillment of the words "Out of Egypt have I called my son" (Matt. 2:15). Of course, it only takes a quick look at this verse's original context in Hosea 11:1-2 to see that the "son" God is talking about is not a person, much less the Christ, but rather the wayward nation of Israel.[7] In one sense Matthew uses the verse quite out of context and with little regard for its original meaning. And yet, as Steve Moyise has shown, for Matthew the words draw on a rich and important set of associations from Exodus onwards. As Moyise explains,

> The words are highly charged. They speak of deliverance, calling, and adoption and hence set a context for the reader to interpret the life of Christ. The point is

---

[5] Mark N. Swanson, "Beyond Prooftexting: Approaches to the Qur'an in Some Early Arabic Christian Apologies," *The Muslim World* 88:3-4 (1998), 315.

[6] This is similar to Hays' description of "echoes." This technique, he says, "may involve the inclusion of only a word or phrase that evokes, for the alert reader, a reminiscence of an earlier text. Readers who hear the echo will discern some semantic nuance that carries a surplus of significance beyond the literal sense of the text in which the echo occurs."

[7] The passage reads, "When Israel was a child, I loved him, and out of Egypt I called my son. But the more they were called, the more they went away from me. They sacrificed to the Baals and they burned incense to images."

> not argued didactically but when we go on to read of Herod's decree to kill the young (2:16), Jesus going up the mountain (5:1), his transfigured face (17:2) and the words 'This is my beloved son' (17:5), the 'voices' are becoming a veritable chorus. By quotation and allusion, Matthew makes his point with (what Thomas Greene calls) a "keyboard of richer harmonies."[8]

Though Matthew in a sense extracts the verse out of its literary and interpretive context, he does so with a sensitivity to its original reference to Israel and the exodus. But his new use of the text makes new associations and evokes the sense that Jesus embodies God's work as a renewed Israel.

Some insider Christ-followers practice a form of evocative extraction when they draw on a phrase from non-biblical scripture with appreciation for its tradition and the associations and feelings it evokes in its community, but with little reference to its specific context of origin. For example, some Muslim Christ-followers sometimes use the phrase *inshallah* (if Allah/God wills it) in their conversation with Muslim friends to evoke a reverence for God, while not necessarily intending to endorse the full Qur'anic context of the phrase (such as Surah Al-Kahf 18:24). In a similar way some Hindu Christ-followers say the Sanskrit word *tathastu* (so be it) to conclude their prayers to the triune God. And though they, along with most Hindus, are not usually familiar with the word's specific origins in Hindu traditions, the word nonetheless *feels* more authentic and appropriate in their prayers to God than the foreign loan-word "amen." In each of these cases the person uses the word or phrase to evoke its positive, general associations within their own communication. The words are, in a sense, musical phrases that bring added harmonies to the Christ-follower's faith expressions.

While persons using evocative extraction largely have a positive assessment of and give voice to a text's general context and associations, those using *exploitative extraction* use a text in ways that shut down or contend with its original context.[9] A well-known example of this in religious contexts can be seen in polemic tracts and speeches, where an author/speaker may use a story, idea, or verse from another tradition with little or no regard for its context and interpretive tradition. The communicator in these instances may essentially de-contextualize, de-historicize, and quite radically reinterpret the text, often with the goal of supporting their case against that other religious traditions and in favor of their own. One example from the

---

[8] Steve Moyise, "Does the NT Quote the OT Out of Context?" *Anvil* 11:2 (1994), 139. Quoting Thomas M. Greene, *The Light in Troy: Imitation and Discovery in Renaissance Poetry* (New Haven: Yale University Press, 1982), 39.

[9] It is important to note that exploitative extraction as I describe it stretches Greene's, Hays', and Moyise's category of "exploitative imitation" on which it is based. For them, even when the Renaissance poets (Greene) or the New Testament writers (Hays, Moyise) used exploitative imitation they still had a reverence for the text. See also Swanson's similar point in "Beyond Prooftexting," 317.

Hindu context is the way some Christian apologists have used the passage from the Bhagavad Gita 4:7-8.[10] In the passage's wider context Krishna is explaining humanity's struggle between *dharma* (righteousness) and *adharma* (unrighteousness), and how he as the Supreme One, or God, intervenes to help humanity move more strongly towards *dharma*. Some Christian apologists, however, have focused on verse 8, ignoring its literary context and re-translating it as "I have come to destroy sinners." Extracting the verse in this way then allows them to contrast it with 1 Timothy 1:15 ("Christ Jesus came into the world to save sinners") and support their argument that Hinduism claims to destroy sinners whereas Christianity provides salvation to sinners.[11]

Reproduction

Green's second intertextual strategy is *reproduction*. This strategy in some ways falls on the opposite end of the spectrum to extraction. For whereas in extraction a person fragments and often decontextualizes a text, in reproduction the person acknowledges, and even celebrates, the text's full context. For example, a writer may paraphrase or quote a lengthy amount of text with a minimal amount of embellishment or deviation, and with obvious deference to its context.[12] In religious contexts, persons may use reproduction when they find that the text (speech, story, practice, etc.) and its interpretive tradition highly resonates with and contributes to their own beliefs or practices. As a historical example from the Muslim context, Mark Swanson found that some Christian apologetic works from the 8th century drew on Qur'anic language and prayers in ways that expressed high appreciation for aspects of their Muslim context. One writer, for instance, used substantial sections of the Qur'an to help form his apology's opening prayer. In such instances writers seemed to have found within parts of the Qur'an "a world

---

[10] "Indeed, whenever righteousness decays, O Son of Bharata, and unrighteousness increases, then do I manifest myself. In order to protect the good and to destroy evildoers and to establish righteousness, age after age I come to be." Gavin Flood and Charles Martin (eds), *The Bhagavad Gita: A New Translation, Contexts, Criticism* (New York: W.W. Norton & Company, 2015), 24.

[11] As one 19th-century tract summarizes, "(Since) we are sinful, guilty, and condemned, Krishna will surely destroy us… (but) Jesus Christ came into the world to accomplish a work of mercy, benevolence, love, and salvation." Rev. Baba Padmanji, "A Comparison of Hinduism and Christianity," in J. Murdoch (ed.), *English Translations of Select Tracts Published in India* (Madras: Christian Knowledge Society's Press, 1870), 54. For a contemporary example see the testimony of a Hindu-background Christian in Nepal. Tony Reinke, "Nepal's Most Unlikely Church Planter," *Desiring God*, August 7, 2014, https://www.desiringgod.org/articles/nepals-most-unlikely-church-planter. Accessed April 1, 2019.

[12] Hays, *Echoes of Scripture*, 173.

of prayer and praise which they could happily visit, even if they would not settle there permanently."[13]

As another example from the contemporary context of insiders, Hindu Christ-follower Dayanand Bharati and other insider Christ-followers often sing or pray what some Hindus call the *Pavamana mantra*. This well-known prayer from the Brihadaranyaka Upanishad, when translated says,

> Lead me from untruth to the truth
> Lead me from darkness to light
> Lead me from death to immortality

Though the prayer in its original context may have been part of a sacrificial ritual to the deity Soma, Hindus now utilize it as a prayer of blessing that can be appropriately directed to any one of their preferred deities. For their part, Hindu Christ-followers pray this in their gatherings to reference the biblical God. In this sense their use of it is similar to that of other Hindus who recognize it as a sacred text and prayer that has a universal application (even though they may not know or give attention to the text's specific context in the Vedas). They thus reproduce it as it is used in popular Hindu tradition and bring it into the universe of their faith in Christ.

Heuristic

It may be apparent that these first two strategies, though having quite different approaches to a text's tradition, do not engage deeply with the *discontinuity* and *tension* between the text's and communicator's traditions. Rather, as a general rule, both seek to reduce and minimize tension; extraction by allowing the new context (for example Christian theology, or an interpretation of biblical scripture) to completely reshape a text in its image, and reproduction by allowing the text to speak without much challenge to the original context.

In contrast, and in between these poles, are two intertextual strategies that seek to grapple with tension more substantively. In the *heuristic* approach a communicator values aspects of a text as it has been interpreted by its community. But they also acknowledge that, while some aspects of a text's interpretative tradition may be in continuity with their own tradition, beliefs, and/or framework, other aspects of it are in tension with it, thus creating a cultural, ideological, or theological gulf between the two. To deal with this gulf and the tension it creates, the communicator *partially* reinterprets the text according to their own framework, but with respect for where it comes from and what it conveys in its original context. In this way, as Thomas Greene explains, the communicator's new speech or work "distinguishes itself from the older voice, finds its own public accent, but it does so, can

[13] Swanson, "Beyond Prooftexting," 315.

only do so, after sensitively apprehending that other accent in something like its particular timbre and personal force."[14]

One example of the heuristic approach from Christian theological history is the well-known "fulfillment theology" developed by numerous scholars and missionaries in India in the late 19th and early 20th centuries.[15] One of the early developments of this theology came from Krishna Mohan Banerjea, who developed this heuristic-like approach in his engagement with the Vedas.[16] A Christian convert from Hinduism, Banerjea sought to prove that the Vedic deity Prajapati was a prophecy in the Hindu context about Christ. In the Vedas Prajapati is often depicted as the creator of the world and, in one instance, Prajapati does this by offering himself as a sacrifice.[17] For Banerjea this story, along with the Vedic emphasis on ritual sacrifice, demonstrates the shrouded remnants of an ancient revelation given by God to Moses. And, though obscured by time, for Banerjea this revelation could be understood to depict the importance of dealing with sin through sacrifice, something ultimately satisfied and fulfilled by Jesus Christ.[18] Banerjea acknowledges that the story's interpretive tradition, via later commentaries and tradition, sits in tension with his own interpretation. But he deals with this by claiming that these traditions obscured the real truths of the story. It is only the biblical witness, and particularly its witness of Christ, that can clear the fog brought by centuries of wrong interpretations of these scriptures and illuminate the truth they contain. Christ ultimately resolves the tension and corrects Hindus' deficient knowledge of the text.

In contemporary settings many Christians, including Christ-following insiders, draw on a heuristic approach to deal with tensions between traditions. For example, some Buddhist followers of Christ, particularly in their evangelism, call Christ *Phra Sri Ariya Mettrai*. Many Buddhists throughout Southeast Asia know and venerate *Phra Sri Ariya* as the future Buddha and venerate him through the many various images, statues, and oral and written stories.[19] For their part, many Buddhist Christ-followers see *Phra*

---

[14] Greene, *The Light in Troy*, 42.

[15] For an overview of these see Paul Hedges, *Preparation and Fulfilment: A History and Study of Fulfilment Theology in Modern British Thought in the Indian Context* (New York: Peter Lang, 2001); Ivan M. Satyavrata, *God Has Not Left Himself Without Witness* (Eugene, OR: Wipf and Stock, 2011).

[16] Satyavrata, *God Has Not Left Himself Without Witness*, 92-95.

[17] Rig Veda 10.90.

[18] For a description and analysis of the development of Banerjea's fulfillment theology see Satyavrata, *God Has Not Left Himself Without Witness*, 91-137.

[19] *Mettrai* or *Maitreya* literally means "the future Buddha." In various Buddhist scriptures, such as the Lotus Sutra, he is portrayed as a Bodhisattva, or one who is close to buddha consciousness, and is described as the one who would come in the future and will lead countless beings to the path of the Buddha and Nirvana. Aphilak Kasempholkoon, "Phra Sri An (Maitreya) as a Hero: Structural Analysis of Phra Sri

Sri Ariya as Christ, the being who will one day return to bring blessing and salvation. They acknowledge a tension between interpretations but deal with this by allowing their understanding of Christ to reinterpret the person of *Phra Sri Ariya*. Some also deal with this tension by using *Phra Sri Ariya* as a bridge helping Buddhists to begin reading about Christ and ultimately rely on the biblical scriptures to inform them of his person and truths. In their opinion, Buddhist Christ-followers can eventually stop using the term *Phra Sri Ariya* and adopt the Thai Christian name of *Phra Yesu* (Lord Jesus).[20] These Christ-followers thus use a heuristic approach to, from their standpoint, update and correct the *Phra Sri Ariya*'s personage and narrative via the truths of Christ as a bridge to faith in Christ

Dialectical

The last intertextual strategy, the *dialectical* approach, also acknowledges the tension of traditions but, rather than seeking to resolve it, allows the past text to have *and retain* its voice. In this case the communicator senses that, as Steve Moyise says, "neither (tradition) is able to absorb or master the other."[21] Doing so may allow for tension but can also create the space for mutual critique and provide the communicator with a "dynamic source of artistic power."[22]

Hindu Christ-follower Dayanand Bharati, whom we met at the beginning of the previous chapter, is often dialectic in his posture towards various Hindu scriptures, stories, practices, and teachings. One such example is his reflections on and practice of Hindu *bhakti*,[23] a prominent concept in various Hindu traditions, scriptures, poems, and songs and often translated into

---

An Myths in Thai Society," *Manusya: Journal of Humanities* Special Issue No. 19 (2011), 21.

[20] Personal correspondence, Banpote Wetchgama, July 1, 2019. Banpote relates the story of a Buddhist woman who, prior to following Christ, was reticent to listen to others share about him. However, a member of Banpote's church asked her if she would like to hear the story of *Phra Sri Ariya* (Jesus). She agreed and, after hearing his account of Jesus, "opened her mind" and decided to join him in further Bible study. After 7–8 months she declared she was a follower of Christ.

[21] Moyise, "Does the NT Quote the OT Out of Context?," 140.

[22] Greene, *The Light in Troy*, 46. For Richard Hays, much of the New Testament writers' engagement with the Hebrew scriptures reflects a dialectical approach. For example, Paul lets the Hebrew scriptures speak "in ways that cannot be fully controlled or manipulated." Hays, *Echoes of Scripture*, 168. In Romans Paul "needs the blessing of Scripture, and Scripture's witness to God's election of Israel stands in judgment of all formulations of the gospel. On the other hand, Scripture's witness gains its eschatological coherence only in light of the gospel, and the gospel stands in judgment of Israel's unbelief. The voices contend in counterpoint… Scripture refuses to be assimilated to a one-sidedly Christocentric reading." Hays, *Echoes of Scripture*, 177.

[23] Dayanand Bharati, "Canon," 2020, Unpublished paper.

English as "devotion." For Bharati this term closely relates to the biblical ideas of having faith in, knowing, and having a personal relationship with God, as seen in the many biblical scriptures that speak about God's love towards us and the reciprocal love of people back to God. But though examples of these can be found in various places in the biblical scriptures, Bharati finds no single biblical term or concept that expresses the range of emotion or the depth of relationship that is conveyed by the concept of *bhakti*. In addition, Bharati finds that even those instances of biblical scripture that speak of love and devotion lack the depth and development found in the Hindu tradition of *bhakti*. Instead, he finds that much of the biblical witness, particularly Paul's writings in the New Testament, emphasize a rational faith response to God. And while he agrees with these teachings, Bharati also longs for language and concepts to express the depth of a person's love and devotion to God. He thus finds that *bhakti* provides for him and other Hindu Christ-followers a refreshing lens through which to interpret his faith in Christ. "*Bhakti* as a personal relationship with God," he says, "with or without any understanding of all the doctrinal aspects of it, can help a *bhakta* [Christ-follower] to go even beyond the [biblical] scripture to trust her God. Though nothing can separate us from the love of god (as said by Sevanand [Paul]), [this verse] emphasizes what God has done for us rather than what a *bhakta* can do by *bhakti*."[24] Paul, Bharati is saying, discusses God's love towards us and our rational response to this love, but the language of *bhakti* enriches this further by suggesting language for a deeply emotional, relational commitment that in turn propels a person to do something – in this case, to give total surrender to the devoted (God). Because of this he can say, "Thus *bhakti* as it is in the Hindu religious tradition helps one to understand the *muktivedic* (biblical) revelation about the love 'of' God in a new perspective."

But while the concept of *bhakti* instructs the biblical scripture on its points, Bharati also finds that the biblical scripture speaks back to *bhakti*. He explains, "In the Hindu tradition, *bhakti* begins as a relationship and most of the time remains the same without ever worrying much about learning more about God to grow in faith." Biblical scripture, however, directs and helps the Christ-follower to "know the mind, will, and purpose of God" in a way that Hindu tradition does not emphasize, or claim is possible. In addition, though the Hindu traditions allow for *bhakti* to be expressed to a variety of deities, none express a *bhakti* in Christ, something which is unique to the biblical scripture. In this way the biblical scripture speaks back to Hindu scriptures and traditions of *bhakti*, adding its voice of insight about Christ and the ability to know God.[25]

---

[24] Bharati, "Canon."

[25] We could categorize as dialectical the wide range of Christian theologians who have engaged with non-biblical scriptures to create a theological synthesis between

The Intertextual Charisma of the Spirit

As some of our examples from above indicate, insiders are not the first Christ-followers to believe that, while the biblical canon is authoritative, the charisma of the Spirit can provide revelation through non-biblical scriptures. As well, Christ-followers, including insiders, seek to listen to and honor the voice of those non-biblical scriptures while dealing in various ways with their discontinuity with the biblical scripture. However, whereas most Christ-followers maintain these approaches as Christians outside the Hindu, Muslim, and Buddhist communities, insiders are uniquely doing this from *within* their religious communities. Due to this embeddedness, they more regularly, and in very practical ways, deal with the questions of how they should read their own community's scripture from the vantage point of a Christ-follower.

In summary, what does this indicate about insiders' alternative missiological imaginary as it regards scripture? First, the engagement of scripture is deeply *relational*, and in at least two ways. One, the involvement of the Spirit in the process of revelation indicates that discernment and interpretation are not simply a rational question or exercise. Rather, though interpretation involves the intellect, we also are dependent on God relating to us, and us relating to God, to discern the Spirit's presence in other scriptural traditions. Two, insiders alert us to the importance of scriptural engagement in relationship with community. Though many Christian scholars and missionaries have developed interpretations of various scriptures, insiders are particularly mindful of the way in which their co-religionists will respond to their Christ-oriented interpretations of these. While they know that not everyone will accept or be convinced by their interpretation, they nonetheless assert that the Spirit is at work to provide an interpretation that is faithful to the gospel *and* speaks to their community.

Second, insiders alert us to how the Spirit does not simply lead someone to "use" a non-biblical scripture in a particular way, but how the Spirit is involved in the non-biblical scripture's wider tradition. Recall Bharati's insight regarding *bhakti* and the way it enriches the biblical witness. Though he may not phrase it in this way, his interpretation suggests that something of the Spirit's work is evident in the *bhakti* interpretive tradition itself, as well as in the specific scriptures and the different songs that it produced.

The understanding and interpretation of biblical revelation and scripture is one important, even central, aspect of any missiological imaginary, including those of insider Christ-followers. The various strategies that these persons follow is not homogenous, and not always new within Christian history. But insider Christ-followers are not theorizing such approaches in a

---

those and the Christian tradition. For sake of space I will not discuss such theological works since few, that I am aware of, have been embraced by or created grass-roots groups or movements, the focus of my enquiry here.

disconnected way. For them the dialectic role of the Spirit in biblical scripture *and* their community's textual traditions enrich and help shape a vision of how God wants to transform those communities from within. Similar emphasis is evident in other areas of their faith as well, including their understandings of Christ and salvation.

8: Insider Imaginaries of Salvation

"But do insiders believe that Jesus Christ is God and the only way for salvation?"

This is a question frequently posed by Christians. For many Evangelical-oriented Christians, it is *the* question of importance. Scholars, leaders, and those interested in Christian mission may disagree or debate many things, including how to read the Bible and other scriptures, but most all will agree that the doctrine of salvation through the person and work of Christ is central to the Christ-following faith, and one of the pivotal points differentiating Christ-following faith from other religious traditions. Of particular concern to many, then, is if and how insider Christ-followers regard the person and work of Christ, and the nature of God's salvation.[1]

But while this is certainly a crucial issue, and one we must explore, I suggest that we not simply focus on verifying or scrutinizing insiders' soteriological orthodoxy. Rather, and in keeping with our focus, we want to consider how God's Spirit may be opening new vistas and imaginaries through various insiders and their understanding of Christ and salvation. Recall again the importance of and our focus on *missiological imaginaries*; the fundamental ways Christ-followers constitute their world and what Christ calls them to do and be in it. Such imaginaries are *missiological* because they shape the Christ-followers' witness – their practices, relationships, speech, beliefs – about how God is re-creating them, their communities, and even their religious traditions. Thus, in this chapter I will explore the ways in which insiders are developing new imaginaries – ones that God's Spirit may be guiding and building on the rich biblical repertoire of salvation images.

---

[1] Though the person of Christ (Christology) and the work of Christ (soteriology) have often been discussed quite separately, scholars have in recent decades acknowledged that discussion of the two belong together. Theologians, as Kärkkäinen says, have "a growing realization of the connection between 'functional' (what Christ has done for us) and 'ontological' (who Christ is in his person) Christologies." Veli-Matti Kärkkäinen, *Christology: A Global Introduction*, 2nd ed. (Grand Rapids, MI: Baker Academic, 2016), 4.

Images of Christ and Salvation

As we have begun to see, and will further explore in this chapter, the stories of various insiders highlight the many ways in which insider Christ-followers' salvific concerns and approaches to Christ are shaped by the frameworks of their religious communities. Most of these Christ-followers are not, as we have said previously, familiar with or necessarily concerned with the more Western and academic formulations of Christology and soteriology – or even those developed by Christian scholars in their regions. Rather, through their experiences and negotiations there has often emerged a hybrid religiosity that conceptualizes and interprets the notion of humanity's "problem" and the nature of Christ's "good news" via their own cultural and religious frameworks. These "theologies of the road" or missiological imaginaries, provide us with the chance to see what Glen Stassen called a "thicker Jesus" and, we may add, a thicker salvation.[2]

How might the Spirit be "thickening" our Christological and salvific imaginaries through insider Christ-followers? One way we can understand this is to note the basic mode by which the New Testament itself presents Christ and salvation – through the use of images and examples. As Brenda Colijn notes, scholars have long acknowledged that the New Testament does not develop a clearly laid-out, systematic doctrine of salvation.[3] Rather, we are given a "variety of pictures taken from different perspectives."[4] Taken together, the metaphors and images of Christ and salvation "balance and qualify one another" and provide a rich tapestry of meaning from which Christ-followers through the centuries have gained profound hope and guidance.[5] They have also inspired countless articulations of theology and a broad repertoire of liturgies, music, and other reflections. On the flip side, however, the prevalence of images has also created deep conflict and divides within the Church, particularly for those who would seek to focus on or privilege particular images of Christ and salvation to the neglect of others.[6]

---

[2] Glen Harold Stassen, *A Thicker Jesus: Incarnational Discipleship in a Secular Age* (Louisville, Kentucky: Westminster John Knox Press, 2012).

[3] Brenda B. Colijn, *Images of Salvation in the New Testament* (Downers Grove, IL: IVP Academic, 2010), 13.

[4] Colijn, *Images of Salvation*, 14.

[5] Colijn, *Images of Salvation*, 16.

[6] Colijn notes twelve interrelated images, including a committed relationship with God and God's people, citizenship in a new country where everyone follows Jesus, sharing in the life of God, a fresh start for human beings and creation itself, being rescued from danger in order to be safe and whole, liberation from captivity or bondage, restoration of broken relationships and a broken world, vindication as members of the true people of God, being chosen by God for service and blessing, an intimate spiritual union with Christ and other believers, a special vocation to be God's priestly people, and a pilgrimage or struggle that requires endurance. Colijn, *Images of Salvation*, 23.

In a similar way, the biblical text does not provide a singular title for or characterization of Jesus. Here again, we are presented with a variety of titles, each pointing to a particular way in which Jesus relates to God and creation.[7] After the texts were written church traditions further developed these images and probed more deeply issues such as Christ's deity, the relationship of Christ's deity and humanity, and the relationship of Christ to the Father and Spirit.[8] In more recent years, and particularly with the growth of theologies outside of the West, theologians and church communities have championed biblical images that were often neglected in Euro-centric, masculine theologies, including Jesus as Liberator for the Poor and Marginalized (Latin America and India), Ancestor (Africa), the Cosmic Christ (Asia), the gender-affirming Logos (womanist), the Black Christ (Black American), Immigrant (Hispanic), and many others.[9] There is amongst all of these a common core; namely, as Kärkkäinen says, "that something crucial happened in this One who is confessed as the Lord and Savior by all Christians of all times."[10] This common core, however, is enriched by a diversity of particulars regarding the nature of Jesus' crucial work, along with his related titles and roles.

Why does biblical scripture provide us with a diversity of images of salvation and Christ? One reason, as Colijn notes, is that each image answers a set of questions that would have been particularly important to Jesus' and the biblical authors' varied audiences.[11] In other words, God intended his salvation to be broad enough to address the wide range of distortions that were introduced into God's creation through sin. In one sense, the impact of sin on creation could be likened to the multiple cracks that crisscross a broken mirror. All parts of the mirror experience the cracks and distortions, but each part experiences a different crack that distorts the mirror in a different way. God's good news is that each part of creation can be healed and re-created of the particular "cracks" that have affected them. God's salvation is "good news" for all creation precisely because it addresses the specific questions and points of brokenness experienced by particular communities.

But another important function of images in general, and the images of Christ and salvation presented in the biblical witness in particular, is that

---

[7] Kärkkäinen notes a variety of titles and characterizations in the New Testament gospels and Paul, many of which derived from the religious categories of the authors' Jewish faith. These include Christ/Messiah, Son of God, Son of Man, Lord, Son of David, Logos (John), Suffering Servant (Mark), King of the Jews (Matthew), Friend of All (Luke), Word of Life (John). Particular for Paul was Jesus Christ as the Eschatological Christ, the Wisdom of God, the Reconciler, the Covenant Maker, Our Righteousness, Humble Servant, Embodiment of Fullness, and God's Mystery. Kärkkäinen, *Christology*, chapters 1-2.

[8] Kärkkäinen, *Christology*, chapter 3.

[9] Kärkkäinen, *Christology*, chapters 6-7.

[10] Kärkkäinen, *Christology*, 9.

[11] Colijn, *Images of Salvation*, 16.

these allow for all aspects of creation, including the variety of cultural and religious communities, to find God's good answers and news for their particular questions, in part within the existing language and images of hope, healing, and re-creation of their traditions. Indeed, as Kärkkäinen notes, no one picture of Jesus and his work has ever been dominant throughout church history.[12] Rather, and along with what we noted in chapter 3, God's Spirit has long worked throughout creation, instilling and inspiring in them questions, longings, and images that lead them towards and resonate with the various biblical pictures of Christ and salvation.

In light of this, the question we pose is, what about Christ, and God's salvation through Christ, have various insiders found to be "good"? What pre-existing images and conceptions about what is needed and good has the Spirit provided in their traditions, and how have they found at least some of these to resonate with, or even be fulfilled through, the work and teachings of Jesus? And how are these creating unique missiological imaginaries that shape insiders' witness and being in the world? Because it would be beyond the scope of this chapter to try and answer these questions for all insiders in all contexts, I will instead turn to specific groups and the particular experiences, conceptions, and images that they find important and helpful as they have embraced salvation through Christ.

Christ as Creator: Native American Christ-Followers

In reflecting on the importance of Christ for his Native American people, Casey Church (whom we met in chapter 5) recalls the Native saying, "Our circle has been broken and needs to be mended."[13] He explains, "Native American lifeways and identities are continually under stress. To survive we must regain what we have lost of our world by redefining and reshaping what remains."[14] This need for wholeness – re-creation – is what Casey sees Christ providing for him, his people, and all of creation.[15] Recall how, when Church experienced his pivotal vision of Christ, it was a historic, Jewish Christ who met a Native boy. Each "stared deeply into each other's soul," and the boy, "knowing nothing of Western Christian tradition, responded by taking a piece of rabbit and bowl of water, raising it to the twilight sky, and saying 'As I eat this flesh and drink this water I do this to remember what the man on the

---

[12] Kärkkäinen, *Christology*, 9.

[13] Church, *Holy Smoke*, 8.

[14] Church, *Holy Smoke*, 8.

[15] In a similar way Richard Twiss, the influential Native American Christ-follower, leader, and author, found that through Christ he and other Native Americans could experience "liberty, wholeness and a sense of Creator's affirmation as tribal/indigenous people." Twiss, *Rescuing the Gospel from the Cowboys*, 228-229.

middle pole (cross) was doing for us.'"[16] The Native boy knew that this man was suffering to bring healing to his people, and responded in worship using elements important to and full of meaning for his community.

As the above story and others from chapter 5 start to suggest, the alternative imaginaries of many Native American Christ-followers seek to re-envision Christ and, in a sense, *release* Christ from the captivity of colonial Western theological traditions and categories. They respond to what Randy Woodley characterizes as the "Evangelical (imperial) hermeneutical lens that has often reduced Jesus and his work to *the savior of the world and one's own personal Lord and Savior*."[17] When Christ is reduced in this way, he says, "We limit Jesus – or maybe a better way to say it is we try to control Jesus by limiting our theological image of him, and people who try to live for Jesus end up with a very limited imagination concerning what Creator expects and what is possible in our world."[18] What is needed, Woodley and others suggest, are new images that open up new possibilities, and particularly for Native Americans whose communities and traditions have found little place in the missiological imaginaries of Western Christianity.

In response, Native American Christ-followers draw on various images from their traditions that also resonate with the biblical witness to Christ. For example, Richard Twiss and some of his Lakota people speak of Jesus as *Chanku* – the Road or Waymaker.[19] They draw this image from John 14:6 as well as the popular Lakota metaphor of the Red Road (*Chanku Luta*) which itself, as we discussed in chapter 4, is derived from Black Elk's vision regarding God's good way of life that brings wholeness and healing to a people and their land. Twiss and others also speak of Jesus as "brother" or companion; the one who journeys with and comes alongside persons in their spiritual and life journeys.[20]

But one of the more prominent images used by many Native American Christ-followers is that of Jesus as "Creator." Here again is an image that draws from biblical texts like Colossians 1:16,[21] that resonates with various Native American titles and concepts related to divinity, and that, as Richard Twiss says, addresses the desire for "liberty, wholeness and a sense of Creator's affirmation as tribal/indigenous people."[22]

---

[16] Church, *Holy Smoke*, 13.

[17] Randy Woodley, *Decolonizing Evangelicalism: An 11:59 p.m. Conversation* (Eugene, Oregon: Cascade Books, 2020), 21. Italics his.

[18] Woodley, *Decolonizing Evangelicalism*, 21.

[19] Richard Twiss, *One Church, Many Tribes* (Ventura, Calif.: Regal, 2000), 35.

[20] Twiss, *Rescuing the Gospel from the Cowboys*, 120.

[21] "For in him all things were created: things in heaven and on earth, visible and invisible, whether thrones or powers or rulers or authorities; all things have been created through him and for him."

[22] Twiss, *Rescuing the Gospel from the Cowboys*, 228-229.

But in what ways does identifying Christ as Creator translate as "good news" for Native Americans? First, for many Native Americans, Christ as Creator emphasizes that Christ, his presence, and his work, are completely stable. Though nature changes and has cycles, and people's societies shift, the Creator oversees and remains present in the midst of any and all changes. As Randy Woodley says, "Christ is not just King, but Creator. Kings come and go, but the Creator is eternal."[23] Such an understanding of Christ gains particular potency when seen against the backdrop of the tremendous trauma and losses that Native American communities have felt over the last centuries. Christ was present and grieved by what occurred before and is present and offering healing now.

Second, Christ as Creator highlights the ways in which Christ seeks to reconcile all of creation. For Native Americans this reconnection to creation has several implications. One is that Christ reconnects people with the physical creation, particularly the land. The importance of land and place for anyone, but particularly for Native Americans, cannot be overstated. As Church says,

> We call the land our Mother because it gives us everything we need to live. Without her we would die. She gives us water and food, from her comes our shelter and our garments for warmth. There is a cycle of life we respect; we know we are a part of this cycle. Before modern funeral rituals, our bodies were allowed to return to the land. The land is made up of our ancestors from the beginning of time – this is another reason we respect her.[24]

As Church indicates, land is not only a source for life, it is foundational to a people's identity.[25] However, with the painful history of displacement, "Native people need to identify with a location, but we have lost our location… We have lost land and identity, but wherever we are there is land and a chance to identify once again with her."[26] In this context, Christ as Creator helps to connect Christ and the work of Christ with the land and creation. As Terry LeBlanc expresses it, "The Spirit of Jesus is the universal presence of the Creator within Creation."[27]

---

[23] Randy Woodley, *Shalom and the Community of Creation: An Indigenous Vision* (Grand Rapids, MI: Eerdmans, 2012), 39.
[24] Casey Church, "Place-Displaced: A Native American Perspective," *Fuller Magazine* 17 (2020), 52.
[25] See Willie Jennings' discussion of how European Christianity disrupted indigenous understandings of identity and land. Jennings, *The Christian Imagination.*
[26] Church, "Place-Displaced," 52.
[27] LeBlanc summarizing the perspective of Richard Twiss. Terry LeBlanc, "Richard Leo Twiss Memorial," *Cultural Encounters* 9:2 (2013).

But creation, as Native American traditions are intensely aware, is holistic and includes the land, the animals, the elements, and, of course, peoples. In this regard, Christ as Creator also emphasizes Christ's role in creating *all* peoples, along with people's capacity and creativity to form cultural traditions. And because of Christ's eternal and stable presence, we can be assured that Christ is not a disconnected creator who was only involved in the origins of creation. Rather, Christ *continues* to be involved in creation, inspiring the creation of relationships, communities, and cultural traditions marked by *shalom* or, as Woodley expresses it, the "Harmony Way."[28]

This focus on reconciling all of creation through Christ intersects with another important value for Native Americans – community. Woodley weaves these two themes together when he says that, ultimately, Christ as Creator seeks to create what he calls a "community of creation" that represents God's *shalom* in all its fullness.[29] This includes the cultural identities and traditions of people, the physical creation, and all other aspects of it. In this way "all of creation is participating in the new community, not just humans,"[30] helping to expand the field of Christ's salvation to include, not only the salvation of individuals, but the restoration and re-creation of all creation.

Third, in addition to emphasizing Christ's stability and reconciling work, for many Native Americans the Creator Christ is one that restores dignity to their identity and traditions. Western Christians, as Twiss notes, have often failed to recognize "the *pervasive presence* of Creator – regardless of time and space,"[31] including the way in which Christ was and is present in Native American traditions. Christ as Creator, however, helps to counter colonial narratives regarding Native American culture, religious traditions, and practices. In other words, to assert that Christ is the Creator equally of *all* parts of creation decenters the (explicit or implicit) message that Western culture and Christianity is the only, or best, vessel through which Christ can be encountered and known. This image provides Native Americans language with which to see Christ as evident in their traditions from their origin. Woodley explains, "The problem when the Europeans came is that they believed they had all of Jesus and the natives had nothing of Jesus. But if the church believes that Jesus is the Creator, then they have to affirm that Jesus has been here all along, in the Sun Dance, the Stomp Dance, the Midewiwin Lodge. It's not the task of the church to change those ways but rather to accept them as truth where they are."[32]

---

[28] Woodley, *Shalom and the Community of Creation*, xv.
[29] Woodley, *Shalom and the Community of Creation*, 40.
[30] Woodley, *Shalom and the Community of Creation*, 40.
[31] Twiss, *Rescuing the Gospel from the Cowboys*, 69. Italics his.
[32] Steve Heinrichs, "Living Vulnerability: Indigenous Perspectives on Evangelism," *Anabaptist Witness* 3:1 (2016), 51.

In addition, Christ as Creator, as seen from the counter-colonial viewpoint of Native Americans, reconceptualizes the "problem" that God's good news seeks to address. As Terry LeBlanc argues, "theology must move its place of departure out of Genesis chapter 3, the depravity of humanity and the fall of creation, into Genesis chapter 1 and 2 – the plan and intent of God. This does not mean ignoring the obvious – separation from the Creator post Genesis two – it simply means asking different questions about the nature of the breech [sic], the impact of sin, and the purpose of its expiation."[33] In doing so, God's salvation becomes particularly good news for those who have experienced the trauma of colonization. As Terry and Jennifer LeBlanc summarize, "We have come to describe this Good News to our own people in this way: the Creator of all has, through the person, work, life, teaching, death, and resurrection of Jesus made the way for human beings to be brought back into right relationship with the Creator, right relationship with one another, and right relatedness to the rest of creation."[34]

As suggested at the beginning of this section, Native Americans are aware that these imaginaries not only communicate good news to their own people but can also help to enrich the impoverished imaginaries of Western Christians. As Woodley says, such imaginaries, if embraced by Western Christians, could help move them "from provincialism to a point where they understand that embedded within Jesus' indigenous teachings of the community of creation is a key, not just for saving us, but also for healing our planet."[35] In reflecting on Jesus' inaugural sermon in Luke 4, which draws from Isaiah 61 and 58, Woodley notes that the actions in Isaiah 58:6-8 – bringing freedom, food, shelter, and clothing – are the preludes for light (a symbol of salvation), and healing. Because of this Woodley suggests "we should probably stop using the word 'salvation' and instead use the word that it comes out of, which is 'healing.'"[36] The goodness of God's reconciling work through Christ, Woodley would suggest, extends beyond the individual and, in fact, is most fully experienced when individuals of *all* peoples participate in Christ's "community of creation," thus becoming Christ's healing agents.

Good News with Muslim Followers of Christ

In Muslim contexts there is much discussion regarding the nature of Jesus. Traditional Muslim teaching regards Jesus as a prophet, but still a created being and not God. Salvation, from the Muslim perspective, is experienced

---

[33] Terry LeBlanc and Jennifer LeBlanc, "NAIITS: Contextual Mission, Indigenous Context," *Missiology* 39:1 (2011), 93.
[34] LeBlanc and LeBlanc, "NAIITS," 93-94.
[35] Woodley, *Shalom and the Community of Creation*, 40.
[36] Heinrichs, "Living Vulnerability: Indigenous Perspectives on Evangelism," 54.

when a person dies and goes to heaven after having spent a lifetime, or at least significant effort, in submitting themselves to God and his ways as outlined in the Qur'an. Thus, despite many similarities between the Christian and Muslim traditions, there appears to be a great divide regarding Jesus and if/how people receive salvation. How, then, do many Muslim followers of Christ view Jesus in ways that reflect their tradition *and* are faithful to the biblical witness?

One example comes via Isaac, a person that visited Yussef, whom we met in chapter 5, early one morning in 2002.[37] Isaac was a *murshid* or *pīr* (revered leader), of a Muslim Sufi movement, a branch of Islam which I will describe more fully below. The movement had grown to several thousand followers and was organized into local groups that were led by 250 group leaders, all of whom followed and disseminated Isaac's teachings. The day before his visit to Yussef, Isaac hosted a gathering for his leaders, during which the leaders entered a ritual of *dhikr*, or repetitive prayer focused on Isaac as the *pīr*. This practice, reflecting the Sufi Muslim teaching of the need for an intermediary through whom persons can reach God, was common among groups like Isaac's and helped his disciples focus on God via the *pīr*'s devotion.[38] However, and unbeknownst to the disciples, Isaac had recently started to doubt his own relationship to God, and even his own salvation. And as he observed the disciples express their dependence on him and his ability to help guide them to heaven, his doubts grew stronger. He was keenly aware that he himself was not God, nor even a prophet, and he wondered, "If I have questions about whether or not I will go to heaven, how can I take these people to heaven?" That evening, after the conclusion of the gathering, he expressed his concerns to God and asked that he would be shown the *sirāt mustaqīm*, the true path to salvation.

That night as he slept, he had a dream during which a person, whom he sensed was Jesus, appeared before him in white clothing and gave him instructions to go to a specific village and location. There, Jesus told Isaac, he would then meet and listen to a person (Yussef), who was the grandson of the very *Sufi* master of whom Isaac himself had been a disciple. Excited by

---

[37] This account is drawn from a video (2020), personal correspondence, and Brown, "Brother Jacob and Master Isaac."

[38] Sufi scholar David Cashin explains the *dhikr*, saying "The disciple is generally unable to control his mind. Since God has no definite form, a man cannot all at once fix his mind on him, so he requires something tangible for the proper control of his mind. Unless the mind is fully controlled it is not fit for *dhikr* (chanting of the names of God). Hence the visualized image of the *murshid* (guide) is indispensable as an instrument for the concentration of all thoughts to one point. This gives rise to the very common expression: 'The face of the pīr is the means of salvation.'" David Cashin, "The Influence of the Esoteric Cults Upon the Sufis of Bengal" (unpublished thesis, University of Stockholm, 1988), 58.

this specific and clear dream, and the connection to his own *Sufi* master, Isaac set off that morning.

When Isaac arrived at Yussef's house he told Yussef about his vision, as well as his prayer and desire to learn about the *sirāt mustaqīm*. Could Yussef share with him the path of salvation? Using biblical scripture and the Qur'an, Yussef proceeded to share about God's creation, humanity's disobedience and alienation from God, and God's re-creation through Jesus. He also shared his own testimony about coming to faith in Christ in 1969. After hearing these things, Isaac was convinced he had heard the true message of salvation and wanted to follow Christ and take baptism. Yussef, however, asked him to wait, saying "God has made you a great leader, and he wants all of your followers to know that Jesus the Messiah, and He alone, is the way of salvation. Go home and tell your wives and children first that Jesus is the Lord and Savior, and then tell your closest disciples." Isaac agreed to this and invited Yussef to come and help him share this Good News with his people.

Two weeks later Yussef came to Isaac's home and all 250 of Isaac's leaders gathered, ready to listen to Yussef. Isaac told his disciples about his own prayer and the vision he received, and then asked Yussef to share again the way of salvation. After Yussef had done so, he invited all the leaders to put their faith in Jesus as their Lord and Savior. The leaders agreed but requested that they be allowed to first go back and share this news with their own families. When Yussef returned a few weeks later all the leaders had shared and were ready to be baptized as Muslim Christ-followers. Yussef baptized Isaac and his family, Isaac then baptized his leaders, and finally Yussef instructed the leaders to go home and baptize their own family and community members. To this day Yussef continues to meet with Isaac and the leaders, providing teaching and contextually relevant Bible translations to further strengthen the growing movement.

How did Isaac's experience as a Sufi Muslim, influenced by the religious and cultural context of his region, shape his understanding of Christ and salvation? To understand this let us briefly explore the Sufi Muslim context of his region. Sufism is in general a form of Islam that emphasizes devotion to God through a particular spiritual guide or *pīr* (Muslim saint), with roots in South Asia extending back to at least the 11th or 12th centuries. It has had significant influence in the area as seen not only in the numerous Sufi orders that exist to this day, but also in the ways these have influenced people's practice of Islam in general. In fact, even though perhaps only 5-10% of Muslims are formally part of a Sufi order, some scholars estimate that perhaps two-thirds of Muslims in the region have been influenced by one or more orders, and many Muslims regularly visit the gravesites of *pīrs* and attend Sufi rituals in the hopes of receiving a blessing from the spirits of the *pīrs*.[39]

Because Sufi orders and teachings are often shaped by the practices and emphases of the Sufi leaders themselves, Sufi teachings can be quite diverse. There are, however, several themes that many Sufi groups in this region share, and which shape and reflect wider religious and cultural values. One is the emphasis on *fānā*, or annihilation. According to this teaching an individual's ultimate goal is to lose themselves, and particularly that which separates them from God, in God himself. To help reach this, they can go through numerous small and intermediate "annihilations," facilitated by mediators such as Muhammad or a Sufi master or *pīr*.[40] One way to continually minimize or annihilate the self is to give deep devotion to the *pīr* and his teaching and guidance, including practices such as *dhikr* – repetitive prayer focused on the *pīr*.

The focus on and respect given to a Sufi master and/or a *pir* intersects with strongly held cultural norms characterized by hierarchy. Culturally, a person's hierarchical status in the community reinforced and expressed ascribed characteristics such as age and wealth. In addition, those who are socially "higher" can also be regarded theologically as more pure and closer to God, depending on their reputation.[41] These social and theological hierarchical norms in turn relate closely with a culture of patronage, in which "a person of higher rank is accorded the right to extract labour, service, and respect from persons of lower rank."[42] When persons from different statuses enter into a patronage relationship, they do so based on a set of reciprocal exchanges. For instance, in exchange for a client's honor, obedience, service, and loyalty, a patron may provide resources and protection that the client

[39] In a PhD study of insider groups in Yussef's region, John Stephenson characterizes this interest in *pīrs*, whether living or dead, as part of a wider religious/cultural emphasis he calls *pīrism*. He also makes a distinction between *pīrism* and *Sufism*, saying "Pirism is the broad term for the notion of a figure of spiritual power who may act on an individual's, or group's, behalf as a patron figure. Sufism is the philosophical and religious stream of Islamic devotion that centres around a spiritual guide who has links back to the originator of the movement, and thence to Muhammad. Thus sufi guides are *pīrs*, but not all *pīrs* are sufi guides." John Stephenson, "The Messiah Most Honourable: The Christological Views of Muslim Background Followers of Iśā āl Mosiho in a South Asian Country" (Doctor of Philosophy thesis, Glasgow, private publication, 2016), 53.

[40] Those Sufi masters that can somehow demonstrate real or perceived spiritual lineage going back to Muhammad are deemed to be particularly important and effective mediators in this regard.

[41] These also tend to have the resources to more carefully follow the Muslim instructions for a proper lifestyle, such as the resource to provide a secluded room in which the family's women can observe *purdah*. Stephenson, "The Messiah Most Honourable," 38.

[42] Stephenson, "The Messiah Most Honourable," 39.

needs. In other words, clients hope and expect that their "upward" service will be rewarded by an expression of downward grace or blessing, called *doya*.

But how does one with low power and prestige approach and gain the favor of a potential patron and secure his *doya*? In such cases a client may approach a person who can act as mediator or broker. Such persons have more status than the client and are accessible to both the client and the potential patron. Here too clients enter into a patron/client relationship with the mediator, giving that person their service and loyalty, through which they can eventually and ultimately offer loyalty to and gain the *doya* of the "big man" patron.

The cultural norms of status, patronage, and mediation seen here are not exclusive to South Asian Sufi, or even Muslim, communities. However, as Stephenson shows, these norms often provide images and language for Muslims, Sufi Muslims, and even Muslim followers of Christ to understand their faiths in unique ways.[43] For Christ-followers, we could say that the Spirit, via biblical scripture, is speaking through, affirming, and also reshaping the cultural norms and images to form unique missiological imaginaries – ways of constituting and interacting with the world in light of God's good, re-creating project.

Consider Isaac's story above. First, for many Muslim Christ-followers Christ is the mediator through whom they gain access to God and God's *doya*. As an example, Stephenson explores a Muslim story he finds to be paradigmatic for the way the Muslim Christ-followers he interviewed understand Christ. On the day of judgement, the story says, it is true that Allah will judge each person according to their good and bad deeds. But *before* commencing this process he will first call Muhammad to his side, excluding him from the weighing of deeds. Muhammad in turn will call out his spiritual "brothers" and "cousins," or those who closely followed him, to

---

[43] Stephenson, "The Messiah Most Honourable," 38. In fact, Sufis sometimes use the logic of these norms to help defend themselves against criticism from Muslims regarding the Sufis' orthodoxy. For example, in a tract from the 19th century a Sufi devotee defends the role of *pīrs*, saying, "God says in the *Koran*, 'you must have an intermediary through whom you should approach me. Without such an intermediary no one can expect any [spiritual] satisfaction.'" The tract goes on to say "Without an intermediary, nothing can be achieved… If for any worldly reason anyone files a suit, he has to look for a pleader. One who goes to court without a pleader has to face the anger of the office orderlies… One who does not have a *pīr* will face the same situation [when he comes to God]. On the day of judgement only the Devil will be on his side." As quoted in Rafiuddin Ahmed, *The Bengal Muslims 1871–1906: A Quest for Identity* (New York: Oxford University Press, 1981), 62. See also Arthur F. Buehler, *Sufi Heirs of the Prophet: The Indian Naqshbandiyya and the Rise of the Mediating Sufi Shaykh* (Studies in Comparative Religion: Columbia: University of South Carolina Press, 1998), 134.

come to his side and so also avoid the scrutiny of deeds. Many Muslims implicitly or explicitly sense, hope, or believe that Muhammad will call certain *pīrs*, who in turn will call their devoted followers. As one Muslim Sufi told Stephenson, "My *pīr* will be called too, and because I am *in him* I will be saved."[44] The *doya* or grace comes ultimately from God but is mediated first through Muhammad, the patron and mediator *par excellence*, and then by extension to those closely associated with him.

In their application of this story and these cultural norms, Muslim Christ-followers affirm the idea of the mediation of grace, but view Muhammad quite differently from their wider Muslim community.[45] As they have read biblical scripture, they have decided that Christ was not simply a prophet less than, or even equal in importance to, Muhammad. In a context with a finely tuned hierarchy, two leaders or patrons cannot be on par with each other.[46] Christ-following leaders thus lead their people through a process of Bible study and help their people transvalue Isa (Jesus) above Muhammad. But what does this mean? Through his interviews with Christ-followers Stephenson noted language that reflected patronage imaginaries. Salvation through Christ, some said, was following Jesus very closely, or even "taking Jesus' hand." This is imagery that, Stephenson notes, "draws on their previous belief structure and everyday experience of needing to follow someone who knows the way [and] needing to be joined with someone who is powerful to save and faithful to do so."[47]

Second, the mediator or *pīr* draws a community of people around him who express devotion to the *pīr* and his teaching. There is a fine line being drawn here – the *pīr* is not the object of worship, for that would clearly violate Muslim teaching against idolatry. But the *pīr* represents and provides an accessible pathway to God. Though God cannot and should not be visualized, persons can visualize the *pīr* as the representative of God and (at least some of) God's attributes. For Muslim Christ-followers, this connects to the scriptural understandings of Jesus as "radiance of God's glory and the exact representation of his being" (Hebrews 1:3). To express devotion to Jesus, then, is to by extension express devotion to God himself.

But, many Christians will want to know, do these Christ-followers believe that Jesus is God and embrace the language (controversial in Muslim

---

[44] Stephenson, "The Messiah Most Honourable," 153.

[45] In contrast to many Muslim-background Christians who view Muhammad as a deceiving and dangerous historical figure, many Muslim Christ-followers largely view him in neutral and/or somewhat positive ways, whether as a mere human with some good teaching, or even a type of prophet. However, in interest of space I will not probe the various debates and discussions of how Christ-followers should regard Muhammad.

[46] As Stephenson expresses it, "two leaders is one too many." Stephenson, "The Messiah Most Honourable," 159.

[47] Stephenson, "The Messiah Most Honourable," 165.

contexts) that Jesus is God's Son? As interviews from studies conducted by Stephenson and Jan Hendrik Prenger illustrate, there is certainly a diversity of views among Muslim Christ-followers regarding language of the deity of Jesus.[48] However, both Stephenson and Prenger find that most of the Muslim Christ-followers they interviewed have a "high Christology" and affirm all that the Bible affirms about who Jesus is and the nature of salvation, using their own questions and categories.[49] For example, one of Stephenson's respondents says,

> He is our salvation giver because he is our Lord (*Probhu*). He is our Lord (*Probhu*) and was born as a man without the seed of a man, and he was exactly man like us and in the shape of a man he came to this world. After coming to this world he shed blood for our sins. After his death, again he rose after three days and commanded us… Now he is in fourth heaven and sat at the right hand of Allah now. In this way, many proofs can be seen that he is the only salvation giver (*Uddhārkortā*) and he is our saviour (*Nājātdātā*), he is our only Lord (*Probhu*) and he is the owner (*Mālik*) of all things.[50]

Another respondent shared how in his reading of the Qur'an he came to understand Jesus, saying,

> [In reading] *Sura Maida*, from 109 to 120 I received a hint that *Īśā Kālemātullāh* [Word of Allah] will intercede. But that *Hojrot* [Prophet] Muhammad will intercede, I couldn't find this anywhere in the Qur'an. And in the Bible there is more, that *Īśā Kālemātullāh* is the Saviour (*Uddhārkortā*) of mankind. [But] that *Hojrot* Muhammad will save, this statement is not in the Qur'an.[51]

It is true that many of these Christ-followers prefer to refer to Jesus as "word of God" rather than "son of God." This was *not*, as the interviews show, because they denied Christ's status, nor the salvation that God offers through Christ. Rather, as Prenger summarizes, many find it hard to explain to their Muslim community how Christ could be both God *and* God's son.[52] In addition, Muslims resist this title because of the Qur'anic teaching that God cannot have a son. In this the Muslim Christ-followers emphasize titles and descriptions that avoid the controversy and confusion while still acknowledging that Christ is one with God.

---

[48] Prenger, *Muslim Insider Christ Followers*.
[49] Prenger, *Muslim Insider Christ Followers*, 86; Stephenson, "The Messiah Most Honourable," 147-148.
[50] Stephenson, "The Messiah Most Honourable," 122-123.
[51] Stephenson, "The Messiah Most Honourable," 123-124.
[52] Prenger, "Muslim Insider Christ Followers," 267.

Good News with Buddhist Christ-Followers

In Southeast Asia, Pba, a Buddhist Christ-follower, has read biblical scripture and made sense of Christ and Christ's salvation in terms of categories common to her and her wider Buddhist community. Pba was raised Buddhist and, similar to Vichaka whom we met in chapter 5, integrated popular animistic beliefs in spirits and ancestors into her ritual beliefs and practices.[53] Because of this Pba would visit the pagodas (temples) to pray and ask monks to pray for her, observe popular festivals such as *Awk Phansa* (breaking a season of fasting), and offer incense and prayers at shrines dedicated to certain spirits when she had a particular need. Such practices were meaningful to her and deeply integrated into her and her community's identity.

Though it was not common for persons in her community to formally study the tenets of Buddhism, she and most others learned through stories and informal discussion that good actions (*dana*) such as going to the temple, giving an offering, and honoring an ancestor provided one with merit (*punya*). This, in turn, would combat bad karma and improve this and their next life. They also believed that spirits, both good and bad, could protect and improve their life. For this they could offer incense at shrines and also request local shamans to access the spirit realm and make requests of the spirits on their behalf.

Pba knew of some Christians in her area and their deity named Jesus, but since they seemed to distance themselves from others, she felt that Jesus was a deity that was relevant to and would only listen to Christians. One day, however, a Christ-following friend-of-a-friend talked to Pba about Jesus. Pba was not interested until her friend clarified that, contrary to what Pba had heard and assumed, Jesus was not the deity of a particular religion and did not require persons to convert religions. Rather, Jesus was the God of immense power and care and, if Pba chose to follow Jesus, he would show her just how much this was true. Intrigued, Pba began praying to Jesus, thinking more about him, and learning about him through her friend. As she did so she soon sensed a change in her life and situation. Her business and family life improved, and her problems with anger started to lessen. She became more patient with her family and others, which brought a much calmer and more peaceful atmosphere to the household.

In addition, Pba began to understand the incredible differences between Jesus and what her community knew and taught about other Buddhist deities and powers. The Buddha, she had been taught, was a source of teaching, but not God and not someone that would answer or help people. Jesus on the other hand paid attention to and seemed to really love her and her family.

---

[53] This testimony is based on the interviews in Marie Bauer, "What Happens When Buddhists Follow Jesus? A Peek into the Transformed Lives of Southeast Asian Women," *Resonance: A Theological Journal* 4:1 (2018), 86-93.

Whereas she had normally practiced rituals like candle- and incense-lighting and bowing to the Buddha image to worship and appease the Buddha, Jesus did not require anything of these things. Also, in the midst of the typical Buddhist petition she was taught to promise the Buddha certain gifts, such as a pig's head, alcohol, or eggs if her prayer was answered. But Jesus was not interested in bribes. In contrast with how she experienced spiritual faith previously, the nature of a relationship with Jesus was characterized by freedom; freedom from bribery and manipulation, and freedom from many of the vices and challenges she had experienced in her family and life.

Not unlike some of the cultural norms of South Asia, Buddhists in Southeast Asia often emphasize the importance of depending and relying on others, and particularly those with status and power. As Paul De Neui highlights, a question that many Buddhists of this region ask of themselves and each other is, "Where is your place of dependence?"[54] Persons will often have at least one, and often more, persons or power-figures on whom they depend, including their parents, a monk, or a spirit. In addition, persons commit themselves to a patron, but only for as long as the relationship is mutually beneficial. If and when a person finds a better patron that meets his or her present, and often shifting, needs, they can shift patrons. Spirits, deities, or Buddhist saints can also serve as patrons, leading Buddhists like Pba to come to sacred spaces to offer incense or other offerings depending on their need, and often at critical moments such as exams, needing a job, or needing healing.

What does Pba's experience begin to suggest about the imaginaries Buddhist Christ-followers are shaping as they regard Christ and salvation? Certainly one element, which we also see in the Muslim examples above, is the importance of depending on a patron to provide good things for life's circumstances, and to help protect against the bad. Sometimes such relationships can feel exploitative, particularly when they cost a person more and more of their resources, time, and devotion. But this is where Pba's realization of the contrast between Jesus and other spirits/deities is particularly significant – Jesus is the *benevolent* patron who does not exploit people in their hardships. Yes, devotion is important but, as Pba learned, her relationship with Jesus transformed from one of obligation and devotion into one of relationship. Jesus is still, and will always remain, the powerful patron deity, but one that constructs the patron/client relationship in a radically different way from other patrons.

Another feature is the emphasis on help with and release from suffering of the effects of *karma* – the chains/effects of past bad actions that keep a person from flourishing in life. Pba and other Buddhist Christ-followers intentionally retain and use the word *karma* in addition to the word for "sin," since the prevalent word used by Christians for "sin" usually denotes

---

[54] Paul De Neui, Personal conversation with the author, July 2019.

horrendous actions like killing and continual stealing; actions that common persons do not commit, at least on a regular basis. *Karma*, on the other hand, can refer to a bank account of spiritual power of sorts that accumulates over time (throughout past lives and the present), stemming from small and big actions, good and bad.

Of particular concern to most Buddhists is bad *karma* and the ways this impacts not only the afterlife and future lives, but also the quality of life and relationships in the present. Though the sufferings that people experience are sometimes caused by natural circumstances or their faulty vision of reality, suffering also quite often reflects people's past bad actions. Remember from chapter 5 Vichaka's description of how he felt Jesus released him from hundreds of "chains" – the effects of all his bad decisions – that had accumulated and held him down. For Vichaka these *karma*-induced "chains" were at once practical (finances, work, etc.), but also emotional and relational. And the release he experienced from the chains of bad karma through Jesus opened up a pathway for a new life, including a deeper and deeper knowledge of and relationship with God.

For Christ-following Buddhists like Pba and Vichaka, Jesus is "good news" because Jesus guides them towards the wisdom, decision making, peace, happiness, and family fealty that they desire for various situations of life. For them Christ comes to represent not another religious community, nor a different system of beliefs. Of course, as they grow in their understanding of Jesus, they learn through biblical scriptures of various ways that Jesus challenges various cultural norms, including the norm of changing patrons and loyalties when something does not work out as expected. In other words, though not every need and desire will be met in the way they would like, they grow in their trust that Jesus provides the pathway towards fulfilling lives and relationships. Nonetheless, we again see how the Spirit speaks through, affirms, and also reshapes images and norms of their religious traditions to form in them alternative missiological imaginaries that assess the world, God's work, and their role in this in light of Christ.

Conclusion: Salvific Imaginaries and the Hope of the Gospel

In his letter to the Colossians Paul affirms the church's faith and love, which he credits to the "hope laid up for you in heaven" (1:5). And though the Greek word for hope, *elpis*, is sometimes interpreted as hope for eternal life, it can also refer to an expectation of good. Indeed, lest Paul's readers see the hope of the gospel as something only to be experienced in a distant future, he continues to describe it as "bearing fruit among yourselves from the day you heard it and truly comprehended the grace of God." The good things that the Colossians could expect via the forgiveness and redemption of Christ could be experienced both *presently* and *ultimately*. And because these good things were based on a new reality – Christ – the church could and should put aside, or transvalue, some of the practices and ways of thinking through which they had previously received hope (2:16-19).

In a similar way many insider Christ-followers are finding hope – the expectation of good – through various images of Christ and salvation. In each case the biblical Christ connects with particular images and norms while challenging and expanding these in significant ways. And yet, rarely do Christ-followers understand the fullness of Christ and Christ's salvation instantly. Rather, people normally understand and practice the goodness of God's work in Christ gradually, over time. They, like any Christ-follower, engage in a process of transformation or, as we often call it, "conversion." What does this process look like, and how does it contribute to their missiological imaginary? It is to this that we turn next.

9: The Journey of "Conversion"

Our conversation regarding insider imaginaries of Christ and salvation has thus far highlighted the ways in which the Spirit interacts with existing images and norms, helping persons see how God through Christ wants to bring salvation and healing to their particular brokenness. We see that God does not ignore or replace the religious images of a community. Neither, however, does God leave them unchanged. Rather, people comprehend and embody God's work in them and their context gradually, over time. Much like how God created the world and humanity in Genesis 1-2 over time and progressively continues the work of re-creation then, now, and into the future, so also the salvation and transformation of people's imaginaries do not occur in an instant. Salvation – the process of bringing us and all creation into the fullness of Christ (Eph. 4:13) – is a process of gradually reshaping the ways we assess ourselves, our communities, traditions, and hopes in light of Christ. Thus, to better understand the missiological imaginaries of insiders, it will help us to give attention to this transforming process of salvation.

We can begin with a familiar question: what does it mean for insider Christ-followers to turn to, move towards, or "convert" to Christ? In 1972, when he was 18 years old, Richard Twiss moved to the Rosebud Reservation in South Dakota to join the growing American Indian Movement (AIM) and protest centuries of injustice inflicted against Native American tribes.[1] As a member of the Lakota Native American tribe Twiss' move reconnected him with his family's culture and the community his parents had moved away from in order to find jobs when he was a child. But though he found the work of the movement and his cultural reconnection exciting he began to disagree with the methods and motivations of some of its leaders. He soon grew disillusioned with the movement as a whole and, entering a downward spiral of drug and alcohol abuse, eventually moved with friends to the Hawaiian island of Maui. One afternoon while traveling across the island two young Christians approached and shared with him a simple message about Jesus' plan for his life. Twiss listened but was not at all interested; for him

[1] This and the following stories come from Twiss, *Rescuing the Gospel from the Cowboys.*

Christianity was the "destructive religion of the white man," and he said as much to the two Christians.[2]

But though he tried to forget about the encounter he continued to think about the Christians' words for the rest of the day. Late that night, after he and some friends had binged on hallucinogenic mushrooms, he found himself engulfed with anxiety and paranoia over the fear of dying. At the height of the experience, he thought of the Christians' words and cried out, asking Jesus to come into his heart and forgive him for all the wrong he had done. He later recounts that at that moment "the effect of the drugs left, the fear disappeared, and a most awesome sense of peace literally flooded my being from the top of my head to the bottom of my feet. I felt clean, forgiven, and filled with joy."[3] He sensed that this came from the Creator himself, in the person of Jesus Christ, and he committed himself to be a follower of Jesus.

Excited about his experience and his new faith Twiss soon moved to Alaska to join an Evangelical discipleship program. He learned much from their teachings and practices, but a question continued to vex him: how did everything he was learning about Christ connect with the Lakota heritage that he had come to value so deeply? One day he posed the question to one of the pastoral leaders of the program. In response, and quoting Galatians 3:28,[4] the leader told Twiss that cultural identities did not really matter to God, since God would ultimately blend all cultures into one. "So Richard," the leader concluded, "don't worry about being Indian anymore – *just be like us*."[5]

The implied "us," as Twiss heard it, was White Christian culture. He knew that Christ could bring freedom from a life of drugs and other forms of bondage, but the price of this freedom was the giving up of Twiss' Native American identity. Twiss was torn but accepted the exchange, spending the next 12 years learning and leading others in a form of Christianity divorced from his Native American identity and culture.

But though Twiss did not integrate his faith with his heritage at this point, he continued to maintain relationships and some cultural connections through regular visits to the Lakota Rosebud Reservation. Through these visits, together with his growing acquaintance and friendships with Christians who were learning about "contextualization," he began to revive his questions about integration. Gradually Twiss realized that, contrary to what he had been taught, God had high regard for his Native American identity and culture. As a result, Twiss started experimenting and adapting various ceremonies and symbols important to his people and, as he did so, grew more and more convinced that the person and work of Christ were not meant to bring the

---

[2] Twiss, *Rescuing the Gospel from the Cowboys*, 103.

[3] Twiss, *Rescuing the Gospel from the Cowboys*, 103. Italics his.

[4] "There is neither Jew nor Greek, slave nor free, male nor female, for you are all one in Christ Jesus."

[5] Twiss, *Rescuing the Gospel from the Cowboys*, 104. Italics his.

pain he felt when he disconnected his cultural identity and heritage from his faith in Christ. Rather, and through the reincorporation of and reconnection with these important parts of his tradition and identity, he discovered that Christ's salvation could and should bring to his people a deepening sense of freedom and wholeness. In Christ it was possible to be the "whole person" that the Creator had designed him and them to be.

In a similar way Native American leader Randy Woodley tells the story of a man in his community in Nevada who identified strongly with and regularly practiced the rituals of his Native American heritage and community.[6] At first he was, not unlike Richard Twiss, very resistant to talk about Jesus or church because of the historical trauma caused by Christian boarding schools. Woodley was sensitive to this trauma and had, as part of his own personal journey and ministry, found ways – including building a sweat lodge – through which he reconnected his faith in Jesus with his tradition. Woodley's friend spent time with him in his sweat lodge and, after seeing and experiencing the ways in which Woodley followed Christ as a Native American, eventually began to follow Christ himself.

One day soon after this Woodley met with some local pastors and, over the course of their conversation, shared about his friend's decision to follow Jesus. Coincidentally, right after this Woodley's friend walked into the place where they were meeting. The pastors quickly realized this was the same person Woodley had just told them about and one excitedly greeted the man saying, "I'm so glad to hear that you're now a Christian!" Woodley's friend, however, did not take this comment well and exclaimed, "I ain't no Christian!" After the initial confusion, one pastor sought to clarify, "But Randy told us you had recently begun following Jesus." "Oh, I see what you mean now. Yeah, I'm following Jesus Christ – he's Grandfather's Son – but I ain't no Christian. Don't call me that."[7]

Of course, many Native American Christ-followers do not have the visceral reaction to the word "Christian" that Woodley's friend had. And yet these types of reactions and experiences illustrate for Woodley that, for many in his community, the word and identity of "Christian" is "not the good news we intend it to mean. Rather, it is the bad news of colonialism, oppression and even genocide."[8] For Native American communities and many other groups around the globe Christianity has sought to not only convert them to a new religion, but to overthrow and colonize their story, and even to erase large parts of it forever. Twiss, Woodley, and others, however, are developing imaginaries of how Jesus does indeed transform a community and its story, but does not overthrow or colonize it.

---

[6] Randy Woodley, *Living in Color: Embracing God's Passion for Ethnic Diversity* (Downers Grove, IL: InterVarsity Press, 2001), 52.
[7] Woodley, *Living in Color*, 52.
[8] Woodley, *Living in Color*, 53.

To provide one more introductory example of what it means for insider Christ-followers to turn to or "convert" to Christ, in the last chapter we met Pba, a Buddhist Christ-follower from Southeast Asia. As we saw, Pba was aware of a small socially and culturally isolated Christian community that followed a deity named Jesus. Pba and her community gave little consideration to the Jesus deity since the Christians felt that this was *their* deity, responsive only to those who had converted, taken baptism, and become Christians. Because of this, when a Christ-follower approached Pba one day and invited her to meditate and pray to Jesus, Pba initially declined. This particular person, however, was a part of a Buddhist Christ-following group and clarified that, contrary to what Pba had heard and assumed, Jesus was not the deity of a particular religion, nor did Jesus require persons to convert religions. With her new friend's guidance Pba began to pray to Jesus and experience changes in her family, business, and personal life.

As Pba grew in her understanding and practices of following Jesus, she found that Jesus provided her with wisdom for her and other people's lives. For example, as a member of the village leadership council she started leading a community health committee and people came to her for advice regarding health issues and other related matters. She also began a group she called "The Savior Club" to help with community and temple events and have discussion meetings about God. Pba chose not to use the name "Jesus" in the club's meetings so as not to imply that the group was "Christian." However, as more people became involved with the group, she engaged them individually in book studies and invited them to start praying to Jesus, just as she had done at the beginning of her journey. In so doing many people have become interested in learning more about Jesus. For Pba's people faith in Jesus is a process, just as it was for Pba herself. Jesus had been patient with her, bringing her blessing and gradually prompting changes in her life. But these were incremental and did not require her to give up her Buddhist and community identity wholesale.

ReImagining Conversion

In our last chapter we considered the ways in which God uses and works through a community's existing religiosity to answer questions about goodness and salvation, and what Christ means for these. But we have also begun to hint at and notice the ways these salvific imaginaries raise the related question of what it means to "convert" to Christ. Of course, and as we have already discussed, the idea that Jesus requires people to change as they enter into God's kingdom is an inescapable and crucial theme of the NT. And yet, as students of mission history know, missionaries have intensely debated and disagreed about the nature of that change in any given context. What practices, knowledge, or commitments are crucial for conversion? Does conversion occur at a particular moment, or through a process? What does one "convert" from, and to? Is "conversion" even the right word to use?

Such questions are obviously complex. To begin with, then, it will be helpful to sketch a framework for understanding the issue of "conversion." From there I will then examine how the hybrid religiosities of various insiders, such as those of Twiss, Woodley, and Pba, contribute to their understanding and practice of "conversion."

The Journey to and with Christ

Christians of many traditions, and particularly of Protestant and Evangelical denominations, are familiar with a genre we could call the "personal testimony" narrative. Though it can take various forms, a common feature of such narratives is an event or situation that precipitates a crisis, out of which the person learns about Christ and decides to "convert" or become a Christian and follow Jesus. Another feature often included in such testimonies is a clear differentiation of what life was like "before Christ" and what life was like after turning to Christ.[9] As such, this way of shaping and narrating conversion often presents a strong dichotomy between the old and the new lives of believers. And in the testimonies of Christian converts from other religions, the "old" invariably includes their and their community's religiosity and religious traditions. Though these may have at one time been personally meaningful the person was compelled to leave them in favor of the "new" life of following Christ.

But does the biblical witness require that "conversion" to Christ follow such narratives? Does it entail such differentiation between a before- and after-Christ state? Though there are many theological and religion-specific studies on this point, for our purposes a recent examination of the topic of conversion from Luke-Acts by Joel Green provides a helpful framework with which to put various insider experiences in conversation.[10]

---

[9] This general outline in many ways extends back to the Apostle Paul and Augustine, whose stories of "dark to light" conversions provided the Christian tradition with classic prototypes for conversion narratives.

[10] Biblical scholars widely acknowledge that "among the NT writings, none is more concerned with conversion than Luke-Acts," though there is less agreement about what conversion entails for Luke-Acts. For missiological studies on conversion see Alan Tippett, "Conversion as a Dynamic Process in Christian Mission," *Missiology* 5:2 (1977), 203-221; Richard Hibbert, "Negotiating Identity: Extending and Applying Alan Tippett's Model of Conversion to Believers from Muslim and Hindu Backgrounds," *Missiology* 43:1 (2014), 59-72; Joshua Iyadurai, "Christian Conversion in India: Political Exploitation or Personal Transformation?" in Rebecca Samuel Shah and Joel Carpenter (eds), *Christianity in India: Conversion, Community Development, and Religious Freedom* (Minneapolis: Fortress Press,

An initial question regards the biblical terminology of "conversion." What words do the biblical writers use to describe what it is that persons are to *do* in relation to Christ and the gospel? In Luke-Acts the two words that perhaps relate closest to the English-language word and concept of conversion are *epistrepho* ("to turn") and *metanoia* ("repent").[11] Though these words are often interpreted in primarily cognitive terms – for example, what someone does when they decide to *believe* in Christ – the biblical texts show that "turning" or "repenting" involve a wider set of factors and have very practical implications for the people involved. *Epistrepho* involves the "transformation of day-to-day patterns of thinking, feeling, believing, and behaving" and, relatedly, *metanoia* regards a change of thinking that reshapes a person's values, behavior, and purpose.[12] In other words, the change involved in following Jesus requires and involves all aspects of a person's being.

But though the biblical terms point to a holistic transformation, the specific details of how this transformation and change comes about differ from narrative to narrative. There is, much to many evangelists' frustration, no one singular biblical pattern of conversion. Despite this there are several themes that most narratives share. One particularly prominent theme can be described through the metaphor of *journey*. That is, though persons may be presented with the need to make an important decision or decisions, the transformation/change of conversion is an *ongoing* process with *many* points of decision, engaging many aspects of a person's context. In other words, Luke-Acts (together with the First Testament scriptures it draws on) signals that it is not simply one point of a path that is important, but rather multiple aspects of the path.

The stories and reflections of contemporary insider Christ-followers often reflect the sense that conversion is a journey. For example, from the Native American perspective, Richard Twiss says, "True conversion – becoming transformed, and over a lifetime *conformed* to the person of Jesus – is a gradual and erratic process… It is an organic process of spiritual transformation as we engage the sacred ways of our Creator, bound by the

---

2018); Peter Thien Nyunt, *Missions Amidst Pagodas: Contextual Communication of the Gospel in the Burmese Buddhist Context* (Carlisle, UK: Langham, 2014).

[11] Though some argue that these terms have distinct meanings – for example, that *metanoia* is used more often of Gentiles – Green shows that Luke-Acts does not make such a clear distinction and instead tends to use the two terms interchangeably. Neither is it helpful, nor biblically accurate, to try translate the words as "repentance" for Jews and "conversion" for Gentiles, though the shaping that occurs because of a person's repentance/conversion may certainly look different depending on a person's cultural context. Joel B. Green, *Conversion in Luke-Acts: Divine Action, Human Cognition, and the People of God* (Grand Rapids, MI: Baker Academic, 2015).

[12] Green, *Conversion in Luke-Acts*.

limitations of our existence as finite human beings."[13] Recall as well how Black Elk, described in chapter 4, appreciated and appropriated the Jesuit "red road" map as a tool and metaphor for the Christ-journey. Though Twiss, Black Elk, and others certainly point to and talk about particular points of the road that may traditionally be described as a "point of conversion" (like Twiss' magic mushroom experience) they come to understand such moments not so much as the point of conversion, but rather as key experiences that joined with other experiences along a long journey of transformation.

Journeys can indeed be long and ongoing, and can helpfully draw our attention to a more expansive work of God's Spirit in the transformation process. From a biblical perspective we can consider three "directions" of gaze and attention: the present path itself, its origin, and its destination. We will look at each of these in turn along with the ways they resonate with the missiological imaginaries of insider Christ-followers.

Attention to the Present Path

One implication of understanding conversion as a journey is that the turning/repenting of the Christ-follower engages and reshapes a person's *existing* pathway. That is, while persons are certainly called to shift their overall direction (towards Christ, towards a future kingdom and heaven, etc.), they are also engaging a process of remaining on and reconstructing their existing pathway. In this sense the biblical writers do not always, or even usually, conceive of dichotomous and *different* paths, but instead that persons reshape and redirect the path they are following.[14] This is certainly the case in the transformation story of Saul/Paul in Acts 9. Saul receives the ability to physically see again after his blinding experience and he also receives the ability to perceive more deeply the work of God for him and all people. But notice that Saul is *not* called away from his tradition. Instead, he is called to re-understand what had previously been shrouded to him – God was indeed present and working in and through the Jewish people, but through Christ the history and trajectory of this work now took on new meaning and expression.

It is true, of course, that God revealed himself to and interacted with the Jewish community in a unique way. And yet it is not only Jews who are encouraged to follow Jesus via the pathway of their heritage. In speaking to Gentiles in Acts 14 and 17, for example, Paul draws on starting points common to his and their traditions – God as creator of "the world and everything in it" (17:24), including all persons and nations (14:15-16). In addition, in Athens Paul references a local shrine to "the unknown god" and quotes the wisdom of poets familiar to his audience. Paul is decidedly *not* telling them that he is bringing a new story, and neither does he use similes

---

[13] Twiss, *Rescuing the Gospel from the Cowboys*, 34.

[14] Green, *Conversion in Luke-Acts*.

such as "some of your beliefs are like our own."[15] God's path is not one that simply parallels theirs. Rather, as Mary E. Hinkle says regarding Acts 14, "Paul and Barnabas argue that their (Jewish) story is the Lycaonians' story too, even if it sounds at first like new information to them."[16] In other words, to have faith in and follow Jesus does not require people to follow a new path or tradition, but to see that God is and has already been *on their path*, albeit in ways they had not yet seen.

This path, of course, does not only involve individual persons themselves. Rather, the transformation of conversion engages persons' contexts, including their relationships and the practices, morals, and rituals that they share with others in their community. It is not, as is sometimes pictured, primarily an "individual-oriented, feeling-based, interior religion,"[17] or what Arthur Darby Nock called a "reorientation of the soul of an individual."[18] Instead, as Green shows using the hermeneutical lens of cognitive science, Luke-Acts has in view an ongoing transformation of the self that involves dispositions and behaviors. And, most importantly, this transformation is not just facilitated through an individual's personal prayer to God (as important as that may be), but is also facilitated "through relational interaction and engagement in the practices of one's group of reference."[19] Green explains this through the idea of a person's *habitus*, or their embodied and often unconscious or pre-conscious practices.[20] A person's *epistrepho* ("turning") and *metanoia* ("repentance/change of mind") towards Christ and Christ's kingdom always involve the shaping and reshaping of the person's mind, opinions, allegiance, embodied practices and behaviors, all which are interpreted via the person's relational context, their existing pathway.

As we have seen, the focus on the present path in its totality is certainly a perspective taken by many of the insider Christ-followers we have

---

[15] Mary E. Hinkle, "Preaching for Mission: Ancient Speeches and Postmodern Sermons," in Robert L. Gallagher and Paul Hertig (eds), *Mission in Acts: Ancient Narratives in Contemporary Context* (American Society of Missiology Series: Maryknoll, NY: Orbis Books, 2004), 99.

[16] Hinkle, "Preaching for Mission," 96.

[17] Green, *Conversion in Luke-Acts*, 8.

[18] Arthur Darby Nock, *Conversion: The Old and the New in Religion from Alexander the Great to Augustine of Hippo* (London: Oxford University Press, 1933), 7-8.

[19] Green, *Conversion in Luke-Acts*.

[20] As Green states, *habitus* is "embodied history, internalized, and… operative at a preconscious level." Because of this, "Behavior is not an add-on to conversion… not even an important one. Rather, conversionary practices are constitutive of conversion. This is because conversion refers to transformed patterns of human life, that is, to transformed patterns of thinking, feeling, believing, and behaving. Practices serve not only as the window through which one's deepest commitments are on display, therefore, but also as the per se embodiment of those commitments." Green, *Conversion in Luke-Acts*, 68.

encountered. These tend to resist the assumption that conversion must involve giving up a religious identity, community, tradition, and many of the practices that go with these. Rather, Christ meets persons in the middle of their whole context, including their community, religiosity, and tradition, and helps them reimagine these from within. As they do so they re-envision their pathway, allowing God's Spirit to guide them via biblical scripture and insight about how their present dispositions, actions, practices, rituals, etc. can and should be reshaped in light of God's presence. For example, in the Buddhist context David Lim (who helped develop the "Four Noble Truths of Christ" that was helpful for Vichika, whom we met in chapter 5) works with persons like Vichika and Pba, whom he calls "New Buddhists." He finds that it is important for them to know that "their decision to follow Christ simply entails the willingness to redefine the meanings of Buddhist forms into Christ-centeredness" without changing their Buddhist identity and community.[21]

In a similar way, Peter Thein Nyunt, who has helped form groups of Buddhist Christ-followers in Myanmar, speaks about the importance of what he calls "cultural conversion" among Buddhists. Christ, he says, calls Buddhists to reorient themselves, their views, behaviors, and allegiances, but they should be "allowed and encouraged to express [their] new faith within [their] own culture," including their Buddhist religiosity and traditions. We can recall how for Pba, Vichika, and others in the Buddhist context it was truly good news to learn that Jesus was not the god of foreigners or the Christian community. Rather, they found Jesus responsive to them, their questions, and their needs, and willing to extend grace and blessing to them as Buddhists.

But notice too how, for these Buddhist Christ-followers, trusting in Jesus is a process where he gradually transvalues Buddha, the ancestors, and various religious practices in their estimation. Often Jesus is at first an intriguing candidate among various powers to learn about, perhaps on par with and not completely replacing these others. However, as they turn to Jesus more and more and learn about his life, teaching, and what this means for this life and the coming Nirvana-kingdom, Jesus begins to supersede Buddha and ancestors in importance. Eventually their understanding of the Buddha and the ancestors is transformed – the Buddha is someone who perhaps had some wise things to share, and the ancestors are beings whose memory and ongoing existence they continue to honor, but these do not have an influence on their own lives in the present.[22]

[21] Lim, "Contextualization of Merit-Making," 86.

[22] For example, a Buddhist Christ-follower, Simaan, at first continued to seek the help of her ancestors by offering to them incense and prayers, even while praying to Jesus. In recent months, however, she gradually stopped burning incense to her ancestors, though she felt the freedom to do so.

Interestingly, for these Christ-followers the process of Christ transvaluing Buddha and ancestors relates closely to a new understanding of if/how to depend on self. For them and their Buddhist experience, the merit they seek from Buddha and ancestors when doing a good action or bringing an offering ultimately represents a dependence not on those beings, but on themselves and their own ability to manipulate the beings or spiritual system via their rituals.[23] One Buddhist Christ-follower named Nary, for example, reflects,

> If you go to the temple and ask for blessings from the spirits that means you are depending on yourself. But if you go to the temple and ask for blessings from Jesus that isn't depending on yourself, that is depending on Jesus. We light incense like before but we ask for blessing from God; we ask for God to lead us on the good path and we ask him to look after our ancestors so that we are not under the power of evil spirits… If you pray but only focus on the problem, it means you are not really depending on God at all. And if you just continue to worry about a problem after you finish praying, that is a sure sign that you're depending on yourself.[24]

Notice how Nary performs the same action – asking for blessing using the attending rituals. However, for her there is a profound contrast in the *significance* of that ritual when directed towards God versus the spirits. As Nary and Buddhist Christ-followers like her learn how God through Christ is the one who provides forgiveness and merit, independent of incense, offerings, and other rituals, they start to feel a new freedom. The significance of these rituals is no longer tied to their own financial, temporal, and clever ability to present the right combination of elements to powerful beings. Rather, the significance of rituals shifts; the Christ-followers still conduct some of these rituals, but the rituals now direct their attention to God and remind them that they do not need to depend on themselves any longer.

Attention to the Pathway's Origin

A second focal point when considering a journey and pathway is to recognize and give attention to where one is journeying from, or the *origins* of a particular pathway. This is deeply important, particularly when considering if and how transformation engages the received religiosity, heritage, and traditions of the past. How do the biblical narratives help us understand the way conversion relates to our past? Here we can examine the relationship of conversion to the phrase and idea of the forgiveness of sins. As N.T. Wright shows, the biblical expression "forgiveness of sins" is connected to the idea

---

[23] For an analysis of the reciprocal exchange and appropriation of blessings through various Buddhist rituals in this region see Donald K. Swearer, *The Buddhist World of Southeast Asia*, 2nd ed. (New York: State University of New York Press, 2010), 20-22.

[24] As translated by Surya (pseudonym) March 13, 2021.

of restoration as most clearly seen in Israel's Exodus and later exile. Repentance is "what Israel must do if her exile is to come to an end."[25] As Israel repents and (re)turns to loving God with all their heart, God forgives and delivers them from slavery and exile. Thus, in the New Testament when John the Baptist and other biblical actors and writers talk about God's "forgiveness of sins," they are using language that calls their audience to remember how God was a part of their history, bringing correction and restoration.[26]

In addition, the biblical writers use a variety of metaphors to further describe God's actions, such as God's desire to move people from darkness to light, from crooked to straight ways, and from outside to inside. Each of these reminds the audience of the ways God has invited prior generations to redirect their pathway away from a particular way of seeing the world, a moral space, or a set of formative practices, and towards those that are more desirable and relationally whole.[27] This looking back thus has a double focus; it calls people to remember, rediscover, or perhaps realize for the first time the ways in which God was present with the community and themselves before their present moment, and it also calls them to recognize and repent of the ways their present actions and pathways have moved them away from, and not towards, the wholeness that God desires.

The importance of the origin of a religious tradition are quite evident in the reflections of many insiders. From their perspective Christ meets them and is a part of their present path, and even a part of their received religious traditions and practices. But they also begin to reinterpret their traditions, stories, and significant leaders/prophets/seers, with the lens of Christ. With this they consider the ways those paths were in some ways "crooked" and in need of God's redirection, but also how God's Spirit was perhaps moving in and seeking to bring direction to the tradition and community all along. In chapter 6, for example, we explored the ways insiders interpret the records of past revelation – scripture, myths, and various practices – of their traditions in light of their faith in Christ. Through various intertextual methods these believers reinterpret aspects of revelation their traditions considered sacred.

Insiders, in a sense, begin to *re-story* their community's past and tradition via their experiences and insights regarding Jesus. This is not unlike the ways in which the Apostle Paul re-stories the traditions of the Lystrans and Athenians in Acts 14 and 17. As we saw above, in both of these locations Paul is speaking to non-Jews whose heritage and story are very different from the Jewish communities to whom he often preaches. He cannot make reference to many of the Jewish stories and persons that he normally

---

[25] N.T. Wright, *Jesus and the Victory of God Vol 2: Christian Origins and the Question of God* (Minneapolis: Fortress Press, 1996), 187.

[26] Green, *Conversion in Luke-Acts*, 65.

[27] Green, *Conversion in Luke-Acts*, 87-91.

references when recounting the history of God's work. He could educate these audiences on that history, but doing so is not only unnecessary, it could convey the wrong message. Though Paul knows that God had indeed been at work in a special way through the Jewish people, Paul highlights the shared starting point of creation and re-stories God's work in all humanity, including the Lystrans' and Athenians' histories.

But here we need to be careful. Westerners may assume that this process of reinterpretation is like a sifting of traditions, with biblical scripture being the "sieve" that sifts out truth from non-truth. But this would be a decidedly Western way of looking at story, tradition, and history, where the concern is to ascertain and communicate *facts* as carefully as possible. The more factual an account is, the more truthful it is. From this perspective Western Christians may then expect that believers would reinterpret their tradition, clarifying in what ways its stories, practices, etc. do or do not line up with biblical truths.

But this would *not* be the way many religious communities understand the role of story. Rather, when recounting traditional stories, and even biblical scripture, many would perhaps agree with what Randy Woodley says of Native Americans. "Our first thought is not 'what's true' and 'what's not true,'" he says. "That doesn't really matter. What matters is the truth of the story, not whether the story is true."[28] Indeed, when recounting his community's origin stories Woodley finds no need to debate if or how these match the biblical story of creation in Genesis 1 and 2. It is clear that the Genesis story provides for him a core framework, but not in terms of facts. Rather it clarifies for him a sense of the relationality of God as Creator of people and place, truths that speaks to his community and which are expressed in his own community's traditions. For example, when reflecting on the Genesis story of creation, he says,

> It is common for indigenous peoples to understand the primary emphasis of God's love in terms of place, and as a result, according to relationship in a particular place. The context of relationality, as it relates to place, already exists in indigenous people's own stories. What has not been presented clearly to Native Americans is the following Christian storyline: Jesus, as the Creator-Son, brought the good news of the relational aspects of the Trinitarian God to earth by creating a place. Eden was where human beings were placed in order to enjoy the fullest possible sense of place on earth. God's original intention was to allow humans to relate in the parameters of a shalom garden. One could say that the garden culture was the original human culture from which one could come to know God, a God who relates in and through community. This divine community is a model for all human societies, including Native

[28] Joel Mayward and Randy Woodley, "What's the Truth in the Story? An interview with Randy Woodley," *The Other Journal: An Intersection of Theology and Culture* 33 (August 23, 2021), https://theotherjournal.com/2021/08/23/truth-story-interview-with-randy-woodley/, accessed July 12, 2022.

> Americans. It is this story to which Native Americans can relate, because it is the same story we already know in our own context and in our own place. Each Native American place of covenant is our "Eden."[29]

Notice how for Woodley the biblical story of creation provides not a history that conflicts with Native American accounts of creation. Rather the biblical story, when viewed from the Native American perspective, enters into the stories of Native Americans, adding to and affirming aspects of those stories. This re-storying is not a violent, colonial take-over and displacement of a people's tradition and stories, but an entering into those stories, showing how God has always journeyed with the people.

Attention to the Pathway's Destination

A final theme (for our purposes) that arises from conversion-as-journey is that conversion is oriented towards God's eschatological purpose. Christ-followers are called to not only reshape their existing pathways and to re-story the narratives and traditions of the past, but to also move in a new direction, towards a new destination. Here again, the biblical witness does not always spell out a clear focal point or destination. Instead, it uses images of God's kingdom present and coming, and provides through the life of Jesus glimpses of how that kingdom can be embodied and enacted by his followers. We could say that, though conversion involves a directionality, it focuses not so much on an address than on a state of being, both personal and relational. This new state, partially realized now and fully realized at some point, is what compels Christ-followers to embark on the journey and do the often hard work of re-envisioning the past and reshaping the present.

Many insiders, in their reflections, evidence a shift of eschatological focus. Sometimes, perhaps often, it is a gradual shift, since the turn to Jesus often is more focused on the transformation that occurs in the present versus a concern for what will happen in the future and after death. And, as would be expected, different religious communities weigh the importance of future and afterlife differently than others.

For some Sikh followers of Christ, for example, the New Testament teaching of heaven provides definition and focus for what some feel is an underdeveloped or ambiguous teaching in their Sikh tradition. One of the concepts that Sikhs sometimes use to refer to an afterlife is *sachkhand* – the abode of truth. But this concept is used and can be interpreted in various ways. In some cases, it can refer to a physical location or room, denoting that the Guru's truth and presence are especially located in these places. In other instances, it can refer to a mystical state of union with God, often understood as after death (or after many deaths and rebirths). And still in other cases

---

29 Woodley, *Shalom and the Community of Creation*, 115-116.

sachkhand can refer to a transformed state of mind – a union with truth – that can occur in the present life.

For Sikhs, of course, all of these uses are meaningful and poetic expressions pointing to a transcendent connection with God. However, some Sikh Christ-followers, after reading the New Testament and encountering the various explicit and implicit understandings of heavenly relationship and presence with God, find *sachkhand* leaves them with a comparative lack of clarity. The relatively clearer biblical vision of an identifiable space that is meant for relationship between people and God is a vision of hope that generates excitement. One Sikh Christ-follower, for example, shares how in her Sikh community *sachkhand* is seen as simply experiencing good things in this life, including wealth. As she expresses it,

> Everyone says that *sachkhand*… is only on earth. If we are enjoying money and everything, that is heaven. If we do not have money and honors, we are in hell. So, they mostly believe there is no heaven and no hell [afterlife]. Heaven and hell is on earth… [If I ask] where is heaven and hell, they say, "If you have spent a good life here then it's heaven here."

In contrast, however, she finds hope and comfort in the vision of heaven as a place that brings perfect connection with God and relief from the worries of her life. She does agree that aspects of the salvation and goodness that Jesus provides (such as healing) can be and are experienced now. But the biblical vision of union with God helps her redirect her understanding of God's direction for her and her Sikh community.

Whereas teaching on the afterlife sometimes receives less emphasis and definition in traditions like Sikhism, other traditions forefront it more strongly. The Qur'an, for example, as well as other Muslim writings and teachings, describes and discusses the Day of Judgement and who will be able to enter Allah's *junnah*, or paradise/garden. Though Muslim scholars may debate the particulars, most would agree that it is those who have maintained certain practices, including for example the confession of the *shahadah* (there is no deity but Allah and Muhammad is his prophet).

For their part, Muslim Christ-followers largely retain the Muslim vision of an afterlife *junnah* created by God for those who follow him and his ways. However, they learn to regard Christ as the pathway, the means and criteria, by which God will allow them into *junnah.* Some Muslim Christ-followers in South Asia, for example, see Jesus as the one that "takes his own" to heaven. In this they affirm the Muslim vision of an afterlife governed by Allah and, in line with some Sufi teachings, and as we saw in chapter 8, the role of an exalted mediator (like Muhammad and Sufi masters) to act as a mediator. From their readings of biblical scripture, however, it is Jesus who will intercede and secure a place for his followers on the day of judgement. As one Christ-follower says,

> He [Jesus] will be given supremacy over Heaven and He will take each of His followers to Heaven… He is able to take us to Heaven and he is able to give us peace. He is preparing a building for us in Heaven where we will live.[30]

This re-visioning of the future and the elevation of Jesus' role in it in turn impacts the way these believers evaluate Jesus in the present. As another Christ-followers shares,

> Because He [Jesus] says, "The one who gives me a place, the one who believes on me, the one who accepts me, I will take him to Heaven, I will take them to my place"…We looked at those things and [believed] them… We have the belief that He will take us to Heaven.[31]

John Stephenson, in his study on Sufi Muslim Christ-followers in South Asia, notes that in these and many other responses Christ-followers were continuing to reflect cultural and Sufi Muslim understandings of heaven and atonement. When thinking about why they had access to heaven via Jesus, these believers were not seeing Jesus as paying off some price created by sin. It is not, as Christian theologians have often framed it, a forensic atonement. Rather Jesus' atonement is relational. They often express this through the word *supāriś* (recommendation), or "the process of presenting one's client to a provider."[32] One Christ-follower elaborates on Jesus' mediating, recommending role in this way,

> There is only one mediator [*supāriśkārī*], who can always access Allah on behalf of people. He is *Īśā Māsi*, who is Allah and man in one and the same person. Being a man he comes to *supāriś* for people and being Allah he comes. He returns back to Allah to recommend for people. As a man He had to suffer a cruel death for the sin of man. He had to earn total holiness and by earning this holiness He was able to gain access to Allah. Only He has the authority to *supāriś* to Allah those who come through Him for any help. He is the real *supāriśkārī*.[33]

For these Christ-followers Jesus has transvalued Muhammad and other mediators through his life, death, and resurrection. He has become, in their estimation, the true mediator that can help them as mere people gain access to the "big man," Allah himself, and the *junnah* he has prepared. It is apparent they see some resonance between the Muslim and biblical eschatological visions, but the pathway is redirected and changed with the new and heightened estimation of Jesus.

---

[30] Stephenson, "The Messiah Most Honourable," 168.
[31] Stephenson, "The Messiah Most Honourable," 168.
[32] Stephenson, "The Messiah Most Honourable," 165.
[33] Stephenson, "The Messiah Most Honourable," 166.

Conversion of Religion?

As we conclude our discussion of insider Christ-followers' imaginaries regarding conversion, we should address one last and common question: are there occasions where conversion does indeed necessitate leaving one's religious community and no longer identifying with that tradition? Depending on the specific circumstances, some Christ-followers hold more tightly to and value their birth religious tradition more than others. For example, Joshua Massey discusses how Muslims in some regions are "disillusioned" with Islam, or at least the version of it they have experienced, because of the oppression they have experienced by Muslim government and religious leaders. Many Iranian Muslim-Background Christians, for example, converted to Christianity partly in reaction to the oppressive religious/political policies they experienced under the government of the Ayatollah Khomeini.[34] Such persons felt little affinity for Khomeini's version of Islam and its vision for their present and future. Jesus, however, offered a welcome alternative vision. For these, conversion to Christianity and separation from Islam made sense.

However, for other Christ-followers, and particularly for the insiders we have listened to, religious identity is very important. Often this is because of the relationships they have and enjoy within that community – relationships that could be severed if they "converted" to Christianity. It is also often out of a sense of appreciation for aspects of the tradition itself – the affective feelings of joy and contentment that it has brought them at times, and the ways it has helped order their lives. In such cases they find that Christ offers a way that is not so much opposed to their tradition and identity, but one that is superior and that emerges from within. They often react against what they feel are colonial and misdirected Christian teachings requiring them to convert out of what they value and into a foreign tradition. Some of these hold their identities tightly despite Christian pressures to release them.

But there are also insiders who, while valuing their religious identity, hold it openly. Yussef, the Muslim Christ-follower who converted to Christianity and then returned to his Muslim community and tradition as a Christ-follower, continues to counsel others to retain their Muslim identity as Christ-followers. However, he is also open to the leading of Christ in people's lives, and to the possibility that Christ-followers in future generations may prefer to change their religious identities. As he says in one interview,

> I follow *Isa al Masih*. He's my Savior. That's all. We want to put less light on religion because we don't want to say, he is a Christian and he is a Muslim. That name should not become a big part of our life. Our life is about following the teachings and instructions of Allah. If I follow *Isa al Masih*, I am not

[34] Joshua Massey, "God's Amazing Diversity in Drawing Muslims to Christ," *International Journal of Frontier Missions* 17:1 (2000), 13.

becoming a Christian, and I'm not becoming a Muslim. What I am is what I am.[35]

He goes on to say,

> I will not be upset if the second-generation defines theology and doctrine and decides that we don't need to call ourselves Muslims. We can be called something else. I will not be upset because I am depending totally on God. He will lead them.[36]

For Yussef, and many other insider Christ-followers, Christ does not require a change of religion, but neither does Christ oppose it. And yet they develop a new imaginary that re-visions what the turn to Christ can look like and mean for them and their communities. Jesus has met them where they are, helped them to re-story their and their tradition's past and re-vision the future, in ways that include those traditions but are not limited to them.

As noted above, this pathway – the ongoing work of God's salvific transformation – is not simply one's own. Rather, individuals share the pathways of life, culture, and religious tradition with their communities. And, of all those community connections and relationships, it is often those of a person's family that are particularly important. Familial relationships, as we know, often shape persons' religious paths in powerful and profound ways, and persons in turn often have strong influence on the religious paths of those in their family. But, in terms of following Christ, a person's family can also be a potential hindrance or barrier. How does the ongoing re-creating work of God reshape family? It is time to explore this question in more depth.

---

[35] Prenger, "Muslim Insider Christ Followers," 101.
[36] Prenger, "Muslim Insider Christ Followers," 360.

10: Insider Missiologies of Family

In many cultural and religious traditions people's religiosity – their subjective appropriation and interpretation of religious traditions – is experienced and expressed in community. That is, while religiosity is individual, it is not seen as individualistic. The same is often true among Christ-followers in non-Western contexts, for whom God's work through Christ is "good news" because of the way it impacts, heals, and reshapes not only themselves personally, but also their communities and families. For insiders too, the components of their missiological imaginaries we have thus far explored – learning of God through canon and charisma, intertextually reading religious and biblical texts, making sense of Christ's salvation through religious imaginaries, and gradually seeing this salvation transform their existing religious pathway – are often experienced and shaped in the context of relationship with community and family. Unfortunately, however, the legacy of Western Christianity and mission has often presented salvation and transformation/conversion in very individualistic ways, causing great tension and division between Christ-followers and their families.

For example, when the prominent Indian theologian Yisu Das Tiwari (1920–1987) decided to follow Christ and take baptism at the age of 22 his Hindu father at first sent him to a mental asylum. Tiwari was eventually released but persisted in his desire to become Christian and take baptism, at which point his father banished him from his family and household. This devastated Tiwari. He later recalled, "When I decided to be baptized, I did not think that I was 'leaving' Hindu society. I thought I was adding something new; something glorious to my Hindu heritage… Soon, I discovered this was not possible… [M]y own family shut the door, literally, on my face. I was driven out."[1] Over the course of many years Das became a respected theologian, professor, and leader in the Indian Christian church. One of his deep desires was to find connections between the Christian faith and Hindu traditions. Because of this he wrote and taught in compelling ways how Christianity could be understood via the categories of Hindu philosophy and religious traditions. But despite such creative work, the pain of family rejection never seemed to have left him. Prior to his death 64 years after his

[1] Ravi Tiwari, *Yesu Das: Witness of a Convert* (Delhi: ISPCK, 2000), 5-6.

conversion his son asked him whether, if he was able to go back, he would "take the same course" of joining the church and provoking his family's rejection. In response Tiwari replied, "Christ… has never left me, I will never leave him, but I would have not joined the Christian community; I would have lived with my people and my community and been a witness to them."[2]

As we have seen, many Christ-followers have experienced similar pain and regret. Some, like Yussef and Vijay, have even returned to their family and religious community. In so doing they and others like them have echoed Tiwari's words, "I would have not joined the Christian community." In saying such things insiders are often not, as I have argued in previous works, rejecting church.[3] Rather, they reject the claims that the "church" and Christian community are synonymous and that they have to leave their family to be a part of the church.

In addition, for many persons "family" does not only include those who are living. Rather, and even for Christ-followers in some contexts, family include those who have died but are still believed to in some way be present: their ancestors. Many cultures and religious traditions honor ancestors, and particularly parents and other close family who have recently died. Such ancestors, in these religious frameworks, are understood to still be very much present, at least for a time and in a different form. Because of this living family members are expected to honor these ancestors in various ways. Many Buddhists in Southeast Asia, for example, regularly offer rice, money, and other offerings to their ancestors at local temples, believing that the ancestors enjoy and can use such offerings in their spiritual setting. The family also believes that the offerings will please the ancestors and keep them and their ancestors in good relationship. When some Buddhists begin to follow Christ, they continue to present ancestor offerings at the temple, though they gradually change their understanding of what this means. Nonetheless, for these Christ-followers, recently departed family are still family who deserve to be remembered, honored, and related to in some way. And though Christ changes the nature of the relationship, the Christ-followers reject the idea that they can no longer acknowledge and be in relationship with departed family.

In this chapter I want to address a crucial question: for insiders, how does the gospel of salvation – God's ongoing, re-creative work – relate to and impact the family? How is God uniquely, alternatively, shaping their missiological imaginaries in regards to family? And, consequently, how do insiders deal with the difficulties of remaining faithful to and not compromising their faith in Christ while trying to remain in good relationship with their families? No doubt many readers of this book will have already wondered about, for example, how these Christ-followers regard Jesus'

---

[2] Tiwari, *Yesu Das*, 24.

[3] Duerksen, *Ecclesial Identities in a Multi-Faith Context*; Duerksen and Dyrness, *Seeking Church.*

teaching about leaving father, mother, family, for the sake of God's kingdom. Some may even wonder, are insiders truly "counting the cost" of following Jesus if they are not willing to leave family and community for his sake? Or, if they do not understand their actions in these ways, how *do* they understand the relationship of the gospel to family?

These are important questions, not only because of the ways insiders are interpreting certain biblical texts, but because of the implications of the place of family – including the question of deceased family – in God's missiological work. I will begin by examining the sayings and approach of Jesus on family along with a theological framework for understanding family. From there I will consider how these may help us understand the approaches and testimonies of insiders themselves. Lastly, I will briefly consider the question of ancestors from the standpoint of an insider missiology of family.

Jesus and Family

Christians have long been perplexed by some of Jesus' teachings on, and his seemingly negative assessment of, family. The 19th-century biblical scholar Ernest Renan, for example, claimed that Jesus "completely trampled under foot family, worldly pleasure, and all temporal care."[4] In fact, in Renan's view Jesus was so focused on his mission that he "revolted" against parental authority as a child and as an adult had little regard for "the ties of blood."[5]

Not everyone in Renan's time or now would be comfortable characterizing Jesus as so completely calloused to and unconcerned about family. And yet the biblical witness records instances where Jesus does indeed use strong, even culturally offensive, language regarding ties to family relationships. He tells his disciples that he came to put people against their fathers (Matt. 10:35), that they should be ready to leave family and home (Mark 10:28-30) and not love family more than him (Matt. 10:34-39), and that they should hate and renounce their family to follow him (Luke 14:26-27, 33), not go to their funerals (Luke 9:57-62), or even *call* someone "father" (Matt. 23:9).

However, at other times Jesus seems to affirm family roles and relationships. He criticizes Pharisees and legal experts who prioritize a religious tradition over God's instruction to honor and care for their father and mother (Matt. 15:3-9). He also affirms marriage (Matt. 19:4-6), gives special attention to children (Matt. 19:13-14), and feels compassion for parents (Mark 5:21-43, 7:25-30, Luke 7:11-14). In addition, Jesus uses the

---

[4] Ernest Renan, *The Life of Jesus* (Boston: Roberts Brothers, 1896), 420.

[5] Renan, *The Life of Jesus*, 108.

analogy of an earthly father's virtues in order to illustrate God's goodness as a heavenly father (Luke 11:11-13).[6]

First, as we know, it is important to consider the audiences and churches that the gospel writers had in mind as they narrated Jesus' words. Though the gospels were written to churches in diverse historical and cultural contexts, in general many were already experiencing a growing divide and tension between themselves and dominant Jewish groups. This tense parting of ways was one that, as Barton says, "began at the most mundane level, that of domestic relations and household ties."[7] In other words, the gospels were written to Christ-followers who knew the pain of being divided and estranged from families because of their commitment to Christ. The gospel writers knew that Jesus' words about the possibility – even the inevitability – that divisions would occur between followers of Jesus and their families would help normalize the experience of these churches. The writers thus sought to assure the early churches that, while Jesus affirmed the institution and relationships of family, he also affirmed that it should be subservient to the values, identity, and mission of being part of God's kingdom.

Second, and relatedly, Jesus' "anti-family" teachings are best understood as part of his wider teachings regarding the coming kingdom of God. One of the characteristics of this new kingdom was that God would reconstitute a new Israel as a new community or type of family. This family would not be marked by lineage or blood-ties, but rather by their commitment to Jesus and his teachings. Many persons in this community, particularly in the early decades, were of course still Jewish with Jewish family ties. However, as followers of Jesus and his teaching they were now set apart from their wider Jewish community. In fact, one of the ongoing questions for Jesus' disciples and the early Jewish church community regarded who among Jews is a part of, or inside, God's people, and who is no longer a part of God's people.

Jesus' twist to all of this, of course, was to flip around what group is "inside" what. From a sociological perspective the disciples and early church originated as a movement within the Jewish community. But Jesus reframes the relationship of his disciples with their community/family; while sociologically many of the "new Israel" may be "inside" and a part of the wider Jewish community, the kingdom of God that that this new Israel represents relativizes the Jewish, and any other, community and family. Ultimately the Jewish identity, along with its cultural norms and expectations, is made subservient to and is "inside" the kingdom of God. If and when cultural norms, including commitment to one's family, comes into conflict with God's kingdom the latter takes precedence. Discipleship to

[6] For further discussion on these points see Ieuan Ellis, "Jesus and the Subversive Family," *Scottish Journal of Theology* 38:2 (1985), 178-179.

[7] Stephen C. Barton, *Discipleship and Family Ties in Mark and Matthew* (New York: Cambridge University Press, 1994), 222.

Jesus, as Barton summarizes, "relativizes all other ties of allegiance and makes possible access to a new solidarity, the eschatological family of 'brothers, sisters and mothers' who do the will of God."[8]

This relativizing of family in relation to God's kingdom is certainly what passages such as Mark 3:31-32 seek to depict. In this narrative Jesus' mother and brothers come to and literally stay outside of the house where Jesus is, sending word to him through others. Their action of staying outside of the house and away from Jesus seems to indicate some tension, and hints at the type of relationship they had to God's work through Jesus. Their intention is to "take charge of" or violently seize Jesus because they think that he is "out of his mind" (3:21). Mark indicates that the family's action and intent is related to others who in Mark's gospel stand outside of God's work. For instance, as Paul Middleton shows, the word used for seizing or taking charge (*krateo*) in 3:21 is the same word used of the chief priests, scribes, and elders when they later seek to arrest Jesus in the temple (12:12). In addition, the family's accusation of madness comes after and is linked to the scribe's accusation that Jesus is possessed by Beelzebul (3:22). In other words, Jesus' family has the same overall opinion of and relationship to Jesus as the hostile leaders, marking them as outsiders not only of Jesus' sub-community of disciples but of the kingdom of God.[9]

It is not hard to understand why Jesus would relativize one's commitment and relationship to family when they are clearly hostile to and against God's work. But what about times when families are perhaps more benign in their opinion of Jesus and God's kingdom? According to Mark, even here Jesus' disciples may need to be ready to leave family. For example, his disciples abandon family businesses including, for James and John, their father (Mark 1:20). When Peter states that they have abandoned everything to follow him (10:28), Jesus doesn't comfort and tell them that they will regain it all. Rather, he affirms that following after him requires breaking familial ties – that they will need to "abandon" house, brothers, sisters, mother, father, children, and fields, and that this will be experienced with persecutions. In these instances, Mark implies, people are not persecuted simply for following Jesus. Rather, they are persecuted when following Jesus compels them to leave family and other things.

But, and third, here too such instructions need to be read in the wider context of Jesus' teaching and example. When done so we see that family is only one of many things that Jesus calls his disciples to re-evaluate. For

---

[8] Barton, *Discipleship and Family Ties*, 225.

[9] Paul Middleton, "Suffering and the Creation of Christian Identity in the Gospel of Mark," in J. Brian Tucker and Coleman A. Baker (eds), *T&T Clark Handbook to Social Identity in the New Testament* (New York: Bloomsbury, 2014), 136.

example, in Luke 14:18-20 Jesus tells a parable about a man who invites persons to his banquet. In response to the invitation people give various excuses for why they cannot come, including needing to see a field, needing to try out five yoke of oxen, and having "just got married." Though marriage is something Jesus affirms at other times, it can also be one of various possible things, including material possessions, that distract persons from joining the banquet of the kingdom.

The key insight here is that Jesus is not necessarily calling into question particular items (fields, oxen) or persons (spouse, father, mother, brother, sister, etc.). Rather Jesus is concerned that his disciples re-evaluate their *relationship* to these. In other words, it is not a family (or any other person or item) that hinders someone in following Christ per se, but the person's relationships to these things. Likewise, Jesus does not critique the institution of family, but rather the way in which those relationships could cause someone to compromise their commitment to God's purposes.

But if and when the relationship is found to be threatening to the disciple's path, is rejection of family, wealth, status, etc. Jesus' main or only solution? Though, as we have seen, there are certainly times when disciples should sever compromising relationships, there are also times when family, wealth and other relationships can and should be subject to God's process of transformation. Jesus' own incarnation itself models this. As Barton explains, "We may say that the revelation of the divine glory in the incarnation and the passion is not a denial of the body and bodily relatedness in the form of human institutions like marriage and family ties: it is their transfiguration in the light of the greater reality of the triune life of God."[10] In other words, God's kingdom does not (always) stand opposed to family, social status, material possessions, etc. Instead, there are times when Jesus reshapes these according to the kingdom's own values. One of the marks of discipleship is to discern God's transformative purposes for someone or something, and one's own role in that transformation.

Fourth and finally, family in Jesus' context, and that of Paul's teaching, was often understood in light of the Greco-Roman *oikos* (household). Biblical scholars have long noted that the *oikos* was the central and basic economic and social structure for society. As Roger Gehring notes, "Scarcely anything determined daily life more than the *oikos* with its network of relationships… By belonging to an *oikos*, each individual gained a sense of identity within society as a whole; it provided them an 'inside' and an 'outside,' not only a dwelling place but also a home."[11] Jesus, his disciples, and Paul regularly utilized the *oikos* in their ministries. Paul in particular

---

[10] Stephen C. Barton, "Living as Families in the Light of the New Testament," *Interpretation* 52:2 (1998), 137.

[11] Roger W. Gehring, *House Church and Mission: The Importance of Household Structures in Early Christianity* (Peabody, Mass: Hendrickson Publishers, 2004), 17.

often based new church communities in households, utilizing their houses as places of worship and their kinship and relational networks as natural avenues for witness and church growth. The *oikos* household thus was not only a potential barrier but could also be a basis and catalyst for God's work.

A Wider View of Family

That God seeks to transform families and make them integral to his kingdom comes into clearer focus when we take a step back and consider a wider view of Scripture's vision regarding family. Ray Anderson does this by beginning with the Genesis creation narrative itself. The origins of family, according to Anderson, along with God's purposes for it, are found in Genesis 1 and 2. Here the narrative says that God created people in his image, and that man and woman then became "one flesh." This indicates God's purpose for family – people come together and relate as (not simply form or create) family to help reflect God's image and likeness.[12] Family is thus created by and finds its purpose in something outside of itself: God's own creative Word. What is the purpose of God's creative Word, and the reason God created anything at all? Intrinsic to God's Word, creation, being, and indeed all relationships, is love. God envisioned all social relationships to be formed and, when needed, re-formed by love.

This is significant because, as human social relationships, including family, are created by God to reflect his image and the love intrinsic to it, such relationships are only effective to the extent that they uphold that core reality.[13] Various biblical writers pick up and elaborate on this. The writer of Ephesians, for example, begins a section in chapter 5 with the practical instruction "walk in love, as Christ loved us." He then describes what this love looks like in a variety of family and social relationships. For the writer all relations are to be subsumed by and subordinate to the core reality of love.

Though Jesus, in his statements, may seem to in some ways contrast this vision of family, Anderson argues that Jesus did not actually reject or dissolve family. Rather, and similar to what we have discussed above, Jesus brings family into the service of God's "new order" which is, in fact, "the original order" of God's creation.[14] "The same God," Anderson says, "who has established family as the basic unit of human social existence is the Lord to whom each family and each family member owes worship and obedience."[15] Jesus brings the gospel message about the kingdom of God, but he also brings "a gospel of the family," shown through Jesus' own

[12] Ray S. Anderson and Dennis B. Guernsey, *On Being Family: A Social Theology of the Family* (Grand Rapids, MI: Eedrmans, 1985), 20.
[13] Anderson and Guernsey, *On Being Family*, 21.
[14] Anderson and Guernsey, *On Being Family*, 140.
[15] Anderson and Guernsey, *On Being Family*, 142.

participation in and upholding of the family relationships in his own life. There is, Anderson concludes, "a gospel of the family as well as a gospel of the kingdom."[16]

But rather than seeing the good news of kingdom and family as different from or in conflict with each other, God designs family and kingdom, and the two gospel emphases, to have a "symbiotic relationship."[17] How can this be? For Anderson, drawing on Bonhoeffer, the connection between them is found in the person and role of Jesus as a mediator. Bonhoeffer pictures Jesus as the ultimate Mediator, not only between people and God, but also between people themselves. When Jesus calls us to discipleship, says Bonhoeffer,

> We learn that in the most intimate relationships of life, in our kinship with father and mother, brothers and sisters, in married love, and in our duty to the community, direct relationships are impossible. Since the coming of Christ, his followers have no more immediate realities of their own, not in their family relationships nor in the ties with their nation nor in the relationships formed in the course of living. Between father and son, husband and wife, the individual and the nation, stands Christ the Mediator, whether they are able to recognize him or not. We cannot establish direct contact outside ourselves except through him, through his word, and through our following of him. To think otherwise is to deceive ourselves.[18]

Bonhoeffer goes on to point out that, though it is true that Jesus as Mediator can separate people, he can also unite. He explains the implication: "Thus although the direct way to our neighbor [including family member] is barred, we now find the new and only real way to him, the way which passes through the Mediator."[19]

Jesus as Mediator, then, becomes the good news, the restorer of family relationships, returning them back to God's original purposes. And, in light of this, Christ-followers have a range of possible responses and postures towards family. If/when the family relationships are hostile towards or a hindrance to a person's commitment to Christ, Christ the Mediator relativizes those relationships in favor of God's kingdom purposes. Again, family relationships are only one of many that the Christ-follower needs to subsume under and re-evaluate in light of Christ. But family and its relationships are also unique in that they reflect part of God's created order. Family ideally reflects aspects of God's purpose and image, and particularly the core reality of love. But family, like the rest of creation, is also marred by sin. In light of this Jesus stands as Mediator between God and people, and in the midst of

[16] Anderson and Guernsey, *On Being Family*, 142-143.
[17] Anderson and Guernsey, *On Being Family*, 142.
[18] Dietrich Bonhoeffer, *The Cost of Discipleship* (London: SCM Press, 1959), 86.
[19] Bonhoeffer, *The Cost of Discipleship*, 90.

people's social relationships. Through Jesus such relationships can be restored, returned and re-centered on God's loving purpose.

An Insider View of Family

The above discussion of Jesus' teachings on and God's wider purpose for family helps us to see that biblical scripture does not present only one response to the question of familial and communal conflict. Rather, Christ-followers can have various responses, particularly when they are seeking for familial transformation in ways that do not hinder or become hostile to their faith in Christ. The key is seeing Christ as Lord, or Mediator, over those relationships.

But how does this help us grasp the various ways insiders understand family? To begin with, it is important to understand that insiders coming from non-Western cultures often include a wider number of people in "family" and "household," and often rely on those relationships for more purposes than do persons from Western contexts.

In parts of South Asia, for example, families often live in *bāṛis*, or households and house structures that normally include numerous extended families. Traditionally the structure of the *bāṛi* is enclosed and faces inward, creating a natural compound with only a few windows and a single doorway facing the outside. The bounded structure of the *bāṛi* reflects the way people think of the family and its relation to the wider concentric circles of social relationships. As John Stephenson shows, South Asian Muslim family members make a strong distinction between those on the inside and those outside of their *bāṛi* and feel an obligation to family that they do not feel to others. For instance, it may be acceptable to overcharge a neighbor for something, but not a family neighbor in the *bāṛi*.[20] Of particular importance is the role of the father, the top patron, of the family. Everyone is beholden to the father and seeks to honor him and be good "clients" in the hierarchical understanding of the culture.[21] The *bāṛi*, then, is the unit that in many ways gives and sustains life, both materially and relationally. Materially, extended family members often share finances and resources with each other. Relationally, the family's collective cohesion, and the design of the unit, allow them to watch out for each other and ensure each other's safety. The *bāṛi* becomes for Muslims the core system of guidance, instruction, and support.

For the Muslim Christ-followers that Stephenson interviews, and many others that we have met, the household functions in ways very similar to the Greco-Roman *oikos*. These are social structures that provide people's identities, economic well-being, and sense of "place" within society. And

---

[20] Stephenson, "The Messiah Most Honourable," 36.

[21] Stephenson, "The Messiah Most Honourable," 40.

much of this, to recall Anderson's argument, reflects aspects of God's created design for people's nurture, protection, and development.

And yet, biblical teaching also demonstrates that the *oikos* (or South Asian *bāṛi*) are not without their challenges. In fact, as Destro and Pesce discuss, Jesus did not view the *oikos* as simply a neutral social structure. It was true that they could be important and helpful bases for ministry and identity, but they were also in need of transformation. Jesus often challenged householders to be sure to offer hospitality and to do so without expecting any reciprocal benefit or advantage. In so doing he challenged the ways that the patron/client hierarchies of the *oikos* culture operated.[22]

Yussef, whom we met in previous chapters, is familiar with the *oikos* of biblical culture and the *bāṛi* of his own and regularly teaches on the importance of the family identity as well as its relative importance in relation to God's will. He understands his Muslim identity, and the family into which he was born, as part of God's providence. He says, "We are born in a Muslim family. This is a God-given identity. He could have allowed me to be born in a Christian family, and then I would've had a Christian identity. This is God's decision, and I should remain there."[23] And yet, as we have seen, Yussef also holds this Muslim identity, and the relationships of the Muslim family, as contingent on Christ for their meaning and purpose. If being a "Muslim" in identity, or staying in the family or *bāṛi* (or *oikos)* structure, becomes a barrier to being a disciple of Jesus, it is not incumbent to maintain these.

This has certainly been the case for many Christ-followers who have faced and continue to face opposition and even persecution from their families. One Muslim Christ-follower and leader shares how his relationships are impacted, often negatively, because of his decision to follow Jesus. He says,

> Jesus says in Matthew when he is sending his disciples, I am not here to make peace but to give you difficulties in your life. When you are accepting me you will get many difficulties. Your family members can be against you. You will be beaten and threatened. People will take you out of your house. We are not free.[24]

Christ-followers and their family relationships, he asserts, are not "free" to operate as normal. They may have personal freedom from sin, but following Jesus also brings challenge.

In a similar way another Muslim Christ-following leader reflects on the accusation Christians sometimes make that he and many Muslim Christ-

[22] Adriana Destro and Mauro Pesce, "The Interstitial Movement of Jesus and the Oikos," in Adriana Destro and Mauro Pesce (eds), *From Jesus to His First Followers: Continuity and Discontinuity: Anthropological and Historical Perspectives* (Leiden: Brill, 2017).
[23] Prenger, "Muslim Insider Christ Followers," 208.
[24] Prenger, "Muslim Insider Christ Followers," 345.

followers in his region remain Muslim in order to avoid persecution. In response he says,

> They [insiders] go to deep levels talking about what the Bible says, pray for each other, applying it. They are far braver, far more ready to suffer than those in a Christianized context. That is my experience. How many people have to be killed for us to be seen as brave enough? Let me introduce you to some of the people who are grieving and suffering, and let's see if you are asking that question again. I think if anything, it is the traditional model that is more fearful. They don't even really engage with anyone, and certainly not with Muslims.[25]

Though insiders sometimes find it difficult to remain within their *oikos*, they prefer to do so if at all possible. Doing so is certainly important to them for their own sense of well-being. But they also often have a sense of God's mission and calling for them to remain in their *oikos* to help bring God's good news and transformation to those they love and value. We can thus at this stage ask, for those insiders who successfully maintain relationship with their family structure, what does a "gospel of the family" look like? David Anthony presents us with a case study via a movement started by Ismail, a Muslim Christ-follower. Soon after beginning to follow Jesus, Ismail's thoughts and concern turned towards his family. How could he share about the miracles that Jesus had done for him and the new life he was beginning to live? One day he pondered on this question, telling Anthony,

> If I change my religious name to Christian, my family will not allow me to visit them again. Even if they allow me to come to visit, they will forbid me to speak of Christianity. I know of a few Muslims from my tribe who changed their names from a Muslim name to a Christian name and have declared themselves as Christians. I tell you the truth, David; they are like a fruit seed placed on top of a big rock. They cannot do what Jesus tells us to do, to go and help others believe, because they cannot grow roots into their own culture. What do you think? Can I have Jesus and stay a Muslim?[26]

In analyzing this notice that, in one sense, Ismail was beginning to sense a conflict between two missiological imaginaries, both of which were informed by biblical scripture and culture. One was the imaginary he was familiar with: Christ-followers were part of a different "religion" that was separate and incompatible with his own. Christ-followers should thus declare themselves "Christian" and take various steps to symbolize this (such as name change). This teaching was perhaps in some ways based on, or

[25] Prenger, "Muslim Insider Christ Followers," 219.

[26] David Anthony, "The Oikos and the Wineskins," *International Journal of Frontier Missiology* 34:1-4 (2017), 16-17.

reinforced by, scriptures such as the "anti-family" teachings of Jesus we have discussed.

The other possibility was an imaginary that valued and loved family relationships, and found identity, meaning, and security in these. Ismail's desire to care for, love, and honor family connected with his scriptural understanding that Christ would want his family and community to accept Christ as well, and that Ismail should share about and seek to persuasively show others what Christ had done for him. In other words, he could continue to participate in the household structure and enjoy its benefits, but now for the purpose of introducing his family member to Christ.

Which imaginary or response was right? Christ was now in the midst of his life and family and, as Bonhoeffer would say, acting as the Mediator of those relationships. This new reality, and new place of Christ in his life and relationships, called for a response. Anthony explains that Ismail took time to pray and deliberate. As he did so he read Matthew 5:15 ("Neither do people light a lamp and put it under a bowl. Instead they put it on its stand, and it gives light to everyone in the house (*oikos*)"). As he read this he sensed that God was calling him to be God's "lampstand" for his family, and that the most effective way to do this was to, if at all possible, remain in their midst and in good relationship so that they too could hear about Christ. Anthony summarizes Ismail's decision, saying, "Rejection from one's *oikos* may be a result of striving to fulfill the Great Commission, but it is not the objective. The objective is to 'Go and make disciples of all nations' (Matt. 28:19-20)."[27] For Ismail, this meant first being a "light" to his household by remaining with them while also doing what he could to stay true to his faith in Jesus.

Ismail decided to retain his Muslim identity and remain in his community. He shared his faith with family members, not as a convert to Christianity, but as a Muslim who followed Christ the Messiah. On hearing Ismail's testimony his family's first response was "Have you become Christian?" Ismail assured them he had not changed his religion, but now considered Jesus his Master and Messiah. It was a question that others also continued to ask, particularly as more and more of his family members started to follow Christ. Ismail patiently answered their questions, using passages from the Qur'an to show that, as he understood it, his faith was consistent with his Muslim identity. Response was divided. More and more decided to follow Christ, while others remained uncertain of Ismail's teaching. However, even those that were uncertain accepted that the Christ-followers were Muslim, even if strange Muslims.[28]

As the movement grew family relationships began to be transformed. Wives remarked on the new level of respect and care their husbands gave to

---

[27] Anthony, "The Oikos and the Wineskins," 9.

[28] Anthony, "The Oikos and the Wineskins," 17.

them and their children. Other men became more peaceful and less inclined to gamble, allowing their households to be better fed and provided for.

After a few years the movement multiplied, with groups of families in several villages regularly meeting together for prayer and worship. They also continued to study the biblical scriptures and to deliberate on their family relationships. One day as a group discussed the parable of the old and new wineskins in Matthew 9:17, one leader, Mohamed Beni, shared the way this related to him and his family. When he had originally decided to follow Christ he followed the advice of Christian friends and told his family that he had "become Christian." Doing this, his friends told him, would ensure that he was not denying Christ. When Mohamed told his family they threw him out of the household.

Some time later, however, Mohamed met and began studying the Bible with a group of Muslim Christ-followers. Together they considered other biblical responses to family, leading Mohamed to decide he had made a mistake. He returned to his family, telling them he was not a Christian, but rather a Muslim devoted to following God. He shared about his faith in Jesus, along with Jesus' death and resurrection. His family were "delighted" with his desire to return and accepted him back immediately. As he continued to live and share with them, they gradually became "open to a new perspective about the Messiah." For Mohamed Matthew 9:17 related directly to his experience. He says,

> This parable of the wineskins is about my life. I am the new wine who tried to place myself into the old wineskins. The old wineskins are Christianity. When I did this I tore my family apart and like this parable, my opportunity to tell my family and village about Jesus was spilled out and lost, I thought, forever. Brothers, we in this meeting, who are Muslims, must understand that we are the new wine and if we are to reach our people we must create new wineskins. The old wineskins of Christianity have never held the gospel for my people. Our own families and our own villages are the new wineskins. We who are the new wine must place ourselves in these new wineskins.[29]

Ismail's and Mohamed's missiological imaginary regarding family could have been shaped by many factors. Indeed, in Mohamed's case he originally adopted the imaginary of his Christian friends which, as we have discussed, certainly reflects one aspect of the biblical message. But they also found that Christ does not mediate relationships in just one way. Some may indeed need to leave, or be ready to be thrown out from, their families for the sake of maintaining their commitment to Christ and his gospel. But this is far from the only option, and Ismail and Mohamed, led also by biblical scripture, and perhaps the Spirit, developed ways to remain with family for the sake of

[29] Anthony, "The Oikos and the Wineskins," 19.

being agents of transformation. The gospel of the kingdom meets the gospel of the family in a creative way.

Christ-Followers and the Ancestors

As briefly discussed at the beginning of this chapter, many cultures and religious traditions consider "family" to include not only living relatives, but also those who have died – their ancestors. Though the dead family member is no longer physically alive, he or she is still present in spirit, at least for a period of time, and the living and dead continue to be in relationship with each other. In some Theravada Buddhist communities in Southeast Asia, for example, a person may become a *phi ta yai* (ancestor spirit), a good and benevolent spirit that resides in heavenly realms or sacred spaces. While they wait for their consciousness (*vinyana*) to be reborn into another life, they continue to protect and provide assistance to the living, particularly their family members, and to punish bad persons.[30] Alternatively, if persons have committed some sin in their life they may at their death temporarily become a *preta*, or hungry ghost.[31] During this time they exist in a liminal in-between state, unable to "eat," move into a more preferable existence, or properly bless their living family members with good health, crops, or other services.

In such contexts what does it look like for families to honor and remain in relationship with their dead relatives? One common way is through various forms of prayer, often by the living and/or a monk or intermediary to the dead relative. Such prayers may simply be expressions of thankfulness, but may also ask for some blessing from the dead. Another common form of honor, which I will return to below, is through giving alms or gifts to the dead relative for his or her benefit. After the living offer prayer and/or alms the dead "communicates" or reciprocates back to the living by possibly answering the prayer and giving a blessing, such as a good crop or other outcome. A third way that relationship can be expressed is through more immediate "two-way" conversation between living and dead. In some situations, for example, spiritual specialists may mediate a conversation where the living and dead ask after each other's well-being and if/how they can help the other.

---

[30] Alexander Horstmann, "Reconfiguring Manora Rongkru: Ancestor Worship and Spirit Possession in Southern Thailand," in Kirsten W. Endres and Andrea Lauser (eds), *Engaging the Spirit World: Popular Beliefs and Practices in Modern Southeast Asia* (New York: Berghahn Books, 2011), 186; Charles Keyes, "From Death to Birth: Ritual Process and Buddhist Meanings in Northern Thailand," *Folk* 29 (1987), 188.

[31] Erik W. Davis, *Deathpower: Buddhism's Ritual Imagination in Cambodia* (New York: Columbia University Press, 2015), 163.

How do some Christ-followers relate to ancestors in light of such practices? As an example we can consider the experience of Awn, a Buddhist Christ-follower in South Asia. Awn and her husband Somsak lived with and shared about Christ with her father and family for many years, such that her father became a Christ-follower. Following his death and funeral Awn's family visited a Buddhist lay-person who specialized in communicating with the dead. During the ceremony, and after asking some initial, personal questions to ascertain that they were indeed conversing with the father, the family began to ask after his well-being. One of Awn's sisters asked where he was residing and if he needed anything. The father (via the specialist) responded, "You do not need to make merit for me, I have all the merit I need. You do not need to build me a house (spirit house). My father in heaven has built me a house in heaven. Follow Somsak and Awn. They taught me how to enter this place of peace and joy. Follow them."[32]

This example contains several important expressions of relationship. First, we can note the norm and practice of gift-giving or alms. What John Clifford Holt observes regarding Sri Lankan Buddhists could also applies here when he says, "Almsgivings are by far the most common form of familial rites observed in Buddhist Sri Lanka, the occasions par excellence wherein solidarity among family members (dead or alive) is reaffirmed and celebrated."[33] Alms can take various forms, including food, money, or other items. In some cases family members may even offer their dead relative the gift of a small house (of around 1 ½ meters in height), containing an array of household items, including mattresses, kitchen items, mats, etc. Family member normally give gifts such as these to the monks at a temple, who in turn perform a chant of dedication. This chant signifies that the items presented to the monk have been transformed and transferred to the relative for their use.[34]

Buddhists have varied understandings of why alms are helpful and important to their relatives. Some believe that the essence of the items is quite literally transformed and conveyed to their relative for their benefit, alleviating hunger or providing them with other means by which to exist. However, and perhaps more prevalently, many believe that alms provide

---

[32] Somsak (pseudonym), email to the author, January 16, 2019.

[33] John Clifford Holt, "Gone But Not Departed: The Dead Among the Living in Contemporary Buddhist Sri Lanka," in Bryan J. Cuevas and Jacqueline I. Stone (eds), *The Buddhist Dead: Practices, Discourses, Representations* (Honolulu: University of Hawaii Press, 2007), 330.

[34] The monks then take the actual physical items and store them for later use by them or others. Keyes, "From Death to Birth," 193; Patrice Ladwig, "Can Things Reach the Dead? The Ontological Status of Objects and the Study of Lao Buddhist Rituals for the Spirits of the Deceased," in Kirsten W. Endres and Andrea Lauser, *Engaging the Spirit World: Popular Beliefs and Practices in Modern Southeast Asia* (New York: Berghahn Books, 2011), 26.

them and their dead relative with merit through which both can be eventually transformed and guided to a new, higher state.[35] In either case, though, the family views almsgiving as more than a transaction. Rather, the act helps to sustain the bonds of the familial pact; the living express concern for the well-being of the dead, and the dead continue to be good patrons to the living younger dependents of their family.[36]

In light of this, notice the features of Awn's interaction with her Buddhist Christ-following father above. The father does not deny that he needs things in his new state. However, he professes that these things (house, merit) are already being provided for him. The family does not, indeed cannot, provide anything to him that he does not already have. Relatedly, the interaction between the father and family reflects the cultural value of patronage, though in a transformed way. As discussed above, patronage towards spirits and dead family members is expressed much as it would be towards a living person. That is, a person of lower status or need submits to and puts themselves under the benevolence and at the service of someone with greater wealth, status, or power. In exchange the person of higher status protects and helps the person of lower status in their times of need. Buddhists often regard spirits and dead family members as those of higher status, deserving honor and service, and as those who can bless the living with health, prosperity, and other goods.[37] Similarly, Awn's family continues to honor and approach their father as an elder and patron of the family. Indeed, he continues to function in this role and instruct his family to follow the (Christ-following) teachings of Somsak and Awn so as to also enter the same place of "peace and joy." However, the patron–client relationship has also been transformed. The father has, at it were, a new and higher patron (his "father" Jesus, though he does not name him), who is providing for and blessing him. The power of blessing no longer comes from the ancestor patron but now instead comes from Jesus.

This transformed understanding of ancestor relations is similar to the experiences of other Buddhist Christ-followers we have met, such as Nary in the last chapter. Recall her transformed understanding of almsgiving when she said, "We light incense (to our ancestors) like before but we ask for

---

[35] Keyes, "From Death to Birth," 192.

[36] As David Lim notes, "Many… believe that their ancestors actually need to be provided for by their descendants; and others do not believe that the ancestors are even aware of what their descendants do for them, but that their expression of filial piety is what is most important. Whether or not the ancestor receives what is offered is not really the issue. Rather, the act is a way to respect, honor and look after ancestors in their afterlives, as well as to insure their continuous good relations with living descendants." David S. Lim, "Contextualizing Ancestor Veneration: An Historical Review," *International Journal of Frontier Missiology* 32:3 (2015), 110. See also Holt, "Gone But Not Departed," 343.

[37] Bernard Formoso, "Thai Buddhism as the Promoter of Spirit Cults," *South East Asia Research* 24:1 (2016), 132.

blessing from God; we ask for God to lead us on the good path and we ask him to look after our ancestors so that we are not under the power of evil spirits."[38] In other words, many still feel that giving a gift of incense is somehow honoring their ancestors, but now direct their prayers to Jesus.[39]

Such a way of relating to ancestors has, of course, often been rejected by Christians, believing it to be a form of idolatry.[40] Similarly, communication with ancestors, such as between Awn's family and her father, sounds to Christians dangerously close to necromancy or sorcery, practices that biblical scripture sometimes prohibits (as in Deut. 18:10-13). Because of this most Christians have what David Lim calls the "rejectionist view" with regard to ancestor veneration, and normally disciple new believers to no longer go to ancestor shrines or participate in related practices.

There are other ways of assessing such practices, however. For example, regarding the communication with the dead, it is helpful to see that the prohibitions made in Scripture are most usually warning against the efforts of the living to gain some sort of knowledge about the future. And while this can certainly be one motivation for contemporary ancestor veneration and communication, many if not most practices do not focus on gaining additional knowledge about the future, but rather on seeking for the well-being of family members.

Similarly, David Lim contends that the practices of ancestor veneration are *not* expressions of worship since most make a distinction between ancestors and deities. Rather, the practices are acts of filial piety, similar to what they would offer to living family members. It is a continuation of the honor, care, and good conduct that one would direct towards household members, as well as a recognition that God continues to care for the dead, just as he does the living.[41] As Lim says,

> They perceive the dead to be separated from human society merely by a curtain of invisibility. In these communalistic cultures the concepts of being surrounded by a "great cloud of witnesses" (Heb. 12:1) and "the communion of saints" (essential to the Apostles' Creed) make perfect sense. The Christian

---

[38] As translated by Surya (pseudonym) March 13, 2021.

[39] And, as mentioned previously, not all Buddhist Christ-followers sense the need to continue the practice at all. Recall Simaan, who gradually stopped burning incense to her ancestors.

[40] For a historical summary of this view see Lim, "Contextualizing Ancestor Veneration: An Historical Review." Though this has been the prevailing view among Christians since the 18th century, earlier missionaries to China, such as the 6th-century Nestorians and the 17th-century Jesuits, were more accommodating and accepting of ancestor veneration.

[41] David S. Lim, "Contextualizing Ancestor Veneration: A Theological Survey and Practical Steps for Implementation," *International Journal of Frontier Missiology* 32:4 (2015), 186.

> faith is continuous with the faith of ancestral heroes, and God is as much *the* god of our ancestors as He was the "God of Abraham, Isaac and Jacob."[42]

Similarly, theologian Simon Chan argues that Asian Christians can draw on the Christian teaching of the "intermediate state," a space and time where persons reside between death and final judgement. For some theologians in church history, such as Augustine, this space was envisioned as a temporary state in which persons resided while awaiting the resurrection of the dead. Some have also envisioned this state as allowing some amount of communication between the living and dead. Indeed, for Chan, the intermediate state means that the "communion of the saints" can be enjoyed not only among living saints, but also between those living and dead.[43] After all, if persons share concerns with and ask persons living to pray for them, why not also the dead who stay in an intermediate state?[44]

Notice that Asian Christ-followers like Lim and Chan are *not* challenging the basic ontology regarding ancestors. Similar to what many Christians have historically believed, the dead continue to "live" in a different state, and one that is not entirely removed or walled-off from the living. The relationship between dead and living still exists. But to return to Bonhoeffer's point above, their relationship now has Jesus standing as a Mediator. Jesus reaffirms the family relationship as part of God's created order, but also reorients the relationship under and according to the kingdom of God. Gradually the Christ-followers come to see and trust that the relative is under Christ's care now, making alms unnecessary. In addition, whatever "merit" they or their relatives receive are now gifts not from them, but from Christ.

As discussed in chapter 1, Western Evangelical missionaries have often emphasized the importance of "people groups" and "people movements," including family networks, for mission strategy. The gospel, it is asserted, spreads quickest and most effectively along kinship and ethnic lines. Many insider Christ-followers would probably agree and argue that this is one reason why they elect to not become "Christian." However, our discussion in this chapter suggests that insiders have not simply adopted a Western mission strategy. Rather they have developed a missiological imaginary that emphasizes the importance of relationships and the cultural logics of their particular contexts. For some the importance of relationship and community

---

[42] Lim, "Contextualizing Ancestor Veneration: A Theological Survey," 186.

[43] Simon Chan, *Grassroots Asian Theology: Thinking About Theology from the Ground Up* (Downers Grove, IL: IVP Academic, 2014), 190.

[44] Chan also suggests that, because salvation involves "the need to grow into a fuller and more explicit knowledge of God through Jesus Christ," it may be possible for ancestors to gain this in the intermediate state. Death may not "seal the soul in its final condition until final judgement," but rather "Through the church on earth, deceased ancestors who did not hear the gospel in life are given the opportunity to hear it" and grow in it further. Chan, *Grassroots Asian Theology*, 195-196.

extends even to ancestors, challenging Western Protestant conceptions of who constitutes family. All of this reflects God's project of re-creating in us and our relationships the *imago Dei*. Insiders' emphasis on staying in relationship with their religious community, which is connected to wider kin community, is certainly helpful for the purpose of witness and sharing Christ with those people. However, more than a witness strategy, it also prompts us to see how salvation includes the restoration and re-signifying of relationships, including and particularly kin relationships.

11: Conclusion

The story is told among the Parsis of India that when their ancestors fled Persia by boat they eventually ended up on the coast of modern-day Mumbai in western India. Upon arrival one of their senior priests approached the king of the territory to ask for asylum. In response to the priest's request the king sent out a jug that was filled to the brim with milk. His territory, he was saying, was already full to the brim and would not be able to accommodate the new arrivals. In response the Parsi priest slipped a coin into the milk to indicate that they, the Parsis, would be able to enrich society and integrate into it without displacing anyone in the kingdom. He then also put a pinch of sugar into the milk and said, "Your highness, as the sugar sweetens the milk so shall we endeavor to sweeten your lives with our industry."[1] With this answer the king accepted the asylum seekers into his kingdom provided they agreed to adopt the local language and dress, explain their religion fully, give up their weapons, and not seek to religiously influence the subjects of his kingdom.[2]

Christ-followers have our own variation of the Parsi's sugar-in-milk imagery, though with a slightly different focus. In one of his teachings Jesus likens the kingdom of God to leaven or yeast in bread (Matt. 13:31; Luke 13:19). The presence and work of God through his people, Jesus indicates, is something that spreads throughout a new context and enriches it. The kingdom of God comes not to displace, overtake, or control a context, but to infuse and transform it from within.

In chapter 1 I suggested that it would be inadequate for us to conceptualize insider missiology as simply a new way to "reach" people in resistant religious contexts, or that insiders maintain their religious identity to avoid conflict. The missiological imaginaries of the insiders we have met, and many others like them, are not simply strategies for evangelism or peacekeeping. Rather, their expressions and practices of faith – their hybrid religiosities – point to new ways of following Christ in non-Christian contexts and enriching those contexts from within.

---

[1] As popularly retold in the novel by Boman Desai, *The Memory of Elephants* (Chicago: University of Chicago Press, 2001), 22-23.

[2] Desai, *The Memory of Elephants*, 23.

As we conclude our study of insider missiology I want to again consider the question: how do insiders challenge Western missiology? In addition to the various aspects of understanding revelation, Christ, salvation, conversion, and community, I now want to suggest some final, interrelated themes that we as Christians can and should consider.

A Mending Missiology

In their decision to remain a part of their religious communities insider Christ-followers are, as we have seen, motivated by multiple goals and hopes. Certainly many insiders, if not most, express a desire to be witnesses to their families and community and sense that extracting themselves from those relationships is not an effective way to do this. In this they also seek to avoid the pain and possible repercussions of being separated from those they love and respect. But, as already mentioned, it would be a mistake to assume that this is the only, or even primary, goal for all. Rather, the stories and imaginaries that we have surveyed would suggest that, ideally, many envision a missiology that maintains, and even mends, relationship and religious traditions.

I draw the language of a mending missiology from the work of Letty M. Russell. In her article "Cultural Hermeneutics: A Postcolonial Look at Mission" Russell considers how a specifically feminist hermeneutic might shape missiology.[3] One theme she highlights is the importance of God's liberating work. Drawing on African women theologians such as Mercy Amba Oduyoye she notes how these and others have critiqued male-oriented theological perspectives, including liberation theology, and offer the voice and experience of women as an important theological corrective. In their estimation God's liberation is tied to relationships, most fundamentally seen in the "circle" of relationships of the trinity that in turn provides a model for "a vision of cooperation, mutuality and care."[4] Letty summarizes the contribution this makes to missiology by saying,

> In this mission God shows no partiality and rejects all attempts to use domination to rule over others in God's name (Acts 10:34; Gen. 11:1-9). From a Christian feminist perspective, *a sending God is a mending God* who invites us to be part of the work of restoring the creation that God intends to make new (Isa. 43:18-21; Rev. 21:5).[5]

---

[3] Letty M. Russell, "Cultural Hermeneutics: A Postcolonial Look at Mission," *Journal of Feminist Studies in Religion* 20:1 (2004), 23-40.

[4] Mercy Amba Oduyoye, "The Story of a Circle," *Ecumenical Review* 53:1 (2001), 97-100; Russell, "Cultural Hermeneutics," 33.

[5] Russell, "Cultural Hermeneutics," 34.

The missiology we need, she contends, is one that "is life-giving for all as we participate in God's action of mending creation."[6]

The concerns and imaginaries we have encountered among insider Christ-followers argue for a similar type of relational, mending missiology. In contexts where religious traditions have contended and competed for adherents and "converts," and where such competition has resulted in violence (whether physical or psychological) on persons and relationships, insiders present an alternative framework. It is one that presents Christ, but seeks to do so in ways that preserves relationships, and brings healing where these have been broken.

Such was certainly the case for persons who returned to their families as non-Christian Christ-followers, such as Vijay and Yussef. As their stories show, many persons become or are familiar with followers of Christ in existing churches – Christians. These churches and their mission agencies often wield a certain amount of power, certainly in finances and other resources, but also in the force of their theological teachings and opinions. The power they exert can be experienced as either helpful or hurtful, depending on how a new follower of Christ chooses to respond. In his study of Muslim Christ-followers in Mindanao, Philippines, Emelito Acoba describes how Christians have often employed what he calls a "hermeneutics of victimization." This, he explains, is a framework that interprets Scripture and people's religiosities via the lens of colonial power. Drawing on the work of James K.A. Smith and Habermas, he suggests that many Christians have unexamined presuppositions in their models of interpretation that cause them to claim a monopoly on the interpretive process. This serves to "deprivilege" and inflict a type of violence on others' interpretive ideas, ultimately "denying the plurality that is vitally constitutive of God's creation."[7] Any persons who "dare to interpret outside the normative power of tradition" are in turn victimized.[8] Acoba sees this most often in contexts where "one is interpreting a Scripture text and fails to arrive at the same epistemological product that is commonly shared by a more powerful… hermeneutical community, such as those belonging in conservative evangelicalism."[9]

The Philippines, and the Mindanao Muslims, have endured various forms of colonialism in their history. In such a context conservative evangelicals' approach to evangelism and discipleship, and their victimization of insiders who pursue a different path, are in Acoba's estimation yet another example of a neo-colonial imposition of power. The ways in which Christians criticize

[6] Russell, "Cultural Hermeneutics," 34.
[7] Emelito Acoba Yango, "Towards a Hermeneutic of Affirmation for Local Theologizing in Closed Access Communities" (Doctor of Missiology thesis, Asia Graduate School of Theology, Philippines, 2009), 92.
[8] Yango, "Towards a Hermeneutic of Affirmation," 92.
[9] Yango, "Towards a Hermeneutic of Affirmation," 92.

and victimize insider Christ-followers are "procedural checks and balances by mission and church institutions to appease the conventions of their funding donors" that reflect "the oppressive dynamics of colonization and victimization."[10]

The corrective to the evangelical hermeneutic of victimization, and one which Acoba observes occurring among the Muslim Christ-followers he works with, is a "hermeneutic of affirmation." Such a framework does not separate Christ-followers from their context but instead seeks to safeguard "the integrity and dignity of the individual in relation to his/her Muslimhood." This is not, for insider Christ-followers, "merely a strategy of manipulation or a cover for non-transparency of identity." Muslim Christ-followers live out their hybrid religiosities on a daily basis and use them to create new theologies appropriate to their context.[11] The Mindanao Muslim Christ-followers affirm their own identity and also challenge and mend the colonial mentality that Christians have implicitly and explicitly forced on the consciousness of their society.[12] I will return momentarily to the ways in which an insider missiology challenges the use of colonial-type power in mission, but here note that, for Acoba, the missiology of Muslim insiders of Mindanao is one that seeks to bring healing and mending to fragmented identities and communities.

A Patient Missiology

In his book *The Patient Ferment of the Church*, Alan Kreider analyzes an under-appreciated teaching of patristic leaders of the early church: their focus on patience.[13] Though many Christians were involved in various forms of evangelism, they also exhibited slow, patient, and clear changes in their habits and behavior. These practices, such as peacefully resisting persecution, caring for each other and the poor, and speaking truthfully marked them as distinct from their wider society. And though their behaviors and practices attracted mockery and derision from some, their steady emulation of the life and values of Jesus also attracted a stream of people to join the church.

But while it was important for the Christ-followers to, in a sense, set themselves apart from the wider society, they did not do so relationally or socially. Rather, in order to be effective witnesses, it was important for them

---

[10] Yango, "Towards a Hermeneutic of Affirmation," 198.

[11] Acoba explains that this also "puts it in opposition to traditional evangelical Christians who seem to think that the domain of theology is under their ownership." Yango, "Towards a Hermeneutic of Affirmation," 215.

[12] Yango, "Towards a Hermeneutic of Affirmation," 216.

[13] Alan Kreider, *The Patient Ferment of the Early Church: The Improbable Rise of Christianity in the Roman Empire* (Grand Rapids, MI: Baker Academic, 2016).

to live out their values among society. They thus lived out their "not of the world" practices in and among the worlds of their communities and families, at least as much as they were allowed to do so. In fact, when his people were accused of being "worthless in [and for] business," Tertullian vigorously defended the solidarity Christians had with their wider society. Though they remained distinct in their morals and in their refusal to take part in idolatrous worship, they participated in all other aspects of life. He explained,

> We are not Brahmans, naked sages of India, forest-dwellers, exiles from life... We sail ships, we as well as you, and along with you; we serve in the army, go to the country, to market with you. Our arts and yours work together; our labour is openly at your service.[14]

As Tertullian argued, Christians were involved a continual interplay between affirming and critiquing their cultural contexts. Kreider summarizes and explains that they experienced both "Gratitude for the beauties in their local cultures" and also "discomfort with the distortions in their cultures to which the gospel had sensitized them." Because of this and their love for their communities, "the Christians attempted to embody alternatives that pointed the way forward for the healing of their cultures. Both as individual believers and also as believing communities, they lived lives that contained a yes and a no. With both they aimed to make a positive contribution to the common good."[15]

In recounting this period of the early church, historians often highlight the "no" of the early church – the ways early Christians were able to persevere and resist pressures that threatened their commitment to Jesus Christ. But, as seen above, the "no" is only one part of a missiology of patience. Along with this must also be the "yes" that allows the radical and transformed nature of the believer's life to be seen among, and hopefully help bring transformation to, the social context itself.

Early churches and Christ-followers in fact held a plurality of opinions about which posture – the "yes" or the "no" of the Christian relationship to culture – they should emphasize. Such can be seen even in the book of Revelation. As Leonard L. Thompson shows, John uses the apocalyptic genre and imagery to strongly denounce and critique Rome, along with any cooperation with its power and systems.[16] That John would have such antipathy towards Rome would make sense, given the strong possibility that he was in Palestine when Roman forces destroyed Jerusalem and its temple

---

[14] Tertullian, *Apology* (trans. T.R. Glover; Cambridge, MA: Harvard University Press, 1931), 191.

[15] Kreider, *The Patient Ferment of the Early Church*, 98.

[16] Leonard L. Thompson, "Ordinary Lives: John and His First Readers," in David L. Barr (ed.), *Reading the Book of Revelation* (Atlanta, GA: Society of Biblical Literature, 2003).

in 70 CE. Though many Christians, especially Jewish Christians, interpreted 70 CE as something of God's judgement on Jerusalem, it also fueled anger towards Rome, as it likely did for John. This, together with other factors, would easily have predisposed John to stand against and voice a strong "no" against any involvement with Roman civic society. This would also shape his counsel to churches; in light of Jesus' imminent return it would be best for churches to stay far apart from the Roman civic culture and for them to critique and discipline any who might have such involvements.[17]

We can see a glimpse of this critique in the Revelation letters to Pergamum and Thyatira. There John denounces a group called the Nicolaitans and prophets such as "Balaam" and "Jezebel" for allowing sexual immorality and eating food offered to idols. The former, as Thompson shows, likely does not refer to sexual activity itself but rather references idolatry. The latter – eating food offered to idols – would be a regular occurrence for persons living and socializing in a civic context where meat was normally offered to idols before serving it to guests. But John's focus was not only on those two practices. Rather, avoiding such practices would help churches remain distinct and separate from civic and imperial society. This wider concern becomes evident throughout the rest of the book, with its vision of a Christ who will soon return and overturn the current order. All throughout, John paints a vision of a Christ who is firmly *against* culture. As Thompson says, "John's emphasis on the imminent return of Jesus is linked to his condemnation of those who participated in the economy and society of the Roman empire."[18]

John, and other Christians like him, advocated for a strong and exclusivist "no" to the surrounding culture. But others – perhaps the majority of ordinary Christians – were more nuanced in the ways they navigated the yes and no. Most lived out their lives in ways that were both distinct from but integrated with their cultural contexts. And, in the end, it was this nuanced approach that helped Christianity spread throughout the Roman Empire, and the world. Thompson's claim bears consideration:

> If the end had come soon after John wrote Revelation, then his isolationism and opposition to the Roman Empire would have been vindicated. But it did not. History in its abundance continued and continues on. And eventually Christianity conquered Rome. The ordinary Christian effected that conquest. As Ernest Colwell observed some time ago, that triumph by the ordinary Christian "was made possible by their *failure* to live as separately and aloof as [many of] their leaders desired."[19] In other words, were it not for the Jezebels and Balaamites and Nicolaitans who accommodated to the Roman world,

---

[17] Thompson, "Ordinary Lives," 42-43.

[18] Thompson, "Ordinary Lives," 44-45.

[19] Ernest Cadman Colwell, "Popular Reactions Against Christianity in the Roman Empire," in John Thomas McNeill et al. (eds), *Environmental Factors in Christian History* (Chicago: University of Chicago Press, 1939), 70. Colwell's emphasis.

> shared life with non-Christians, and risked the wrath of their neighbors, Christianity might have disappeared from the Roman world.[20]

Though there are of course many differences between the communities and contexts of early, "ordinary" Christians and contemporary insiders, both were/are resisting more isolationist visions of what it means to follow Christ. We do not yet have the advantage of much hindsight, but it is possible that the patient missiological imaginaries of some insider Christ-followers will result in long-lasting, growing expressions of God's kingdom among their communities.

A Marginal Missiology

In recent years Christian scholars and leaders have sought to decolonize understandings of Christian mission. What, these scholars ask, does mission look like in an age when "non-Western" churches have surpassed Western churches in number and rate of growth, but the latter still sometimes retain financial and leadership control over mission structures and relationships? Scholars have highlighted numerous themes, including new understandings of and responses to global suffering,[21] reshaped models for mission partnership,[22] non-Christendom bases for understanding God's Spirit and mission,[23] and the missiological insights provided by Majority World women theologians.[24] As Oscar García-Johnson summarizes, the work of decolonizing mission, and any other epistemological framework, involves the "rereading of history and a revision of its epistemological codes. [Decolonization] is a point of departure that seeks to disengage or delink Christian knowledge from the epistemic captivity of Western modernity and coloniality."[25]

But since mission has a long history in Western coloniality, "delinking" the two, at least in practice, is not a straightforward task. Thus, as decolonial scholars (and many from Majority World churches) have pointed out in

---

[20] Thompson, "Ordinary Lives," 46.

[21] Israel Oluwole Olofinjana, "Decolonizing Mission: Learning from the Majority World Template of Suffering and Sacrifice," *Lausanne Global Analysis* 9:5 (2020), lausanne.org/content/lga/2020-09/decolonizing-mission, accessed June 1, 2022.

[22] Taylor Walters Denyer, *Decolonizing Mission Partnerships: Evolving Collaboration Between United Methodists in North Katanga and the United States of America* (Eugene, OR: Pickwick Publications, 2020).

[23] Oscar García-Johnson, *Spirit Outside the Gate: Decolonial Pneumatologies of the American Global South* (Downers Grove, IL: IVP Academic, 2019).

[24] Russell, "Cultural Hermeneutics."

[25] Oscar García-Johnson, "Transoccidentalism and the Making of Global Theology," in William A. Dyrness and Oscar García-Johnson (eds), *Theology Without Borders: An Introduction to Global Conversations* (Grand Rapids, MI: Baker Academic, 2015), 21.

various ways, one of the major issues and challenges in decolonizing mission regards the use and impact of power in all its forms, particularly with mission initiatives that derive from the West. Even Evangelicals, who have sometimes focused less on issues of colonial power, have been mindful of and discussed issues of paternalism since the mid-20th century and have become increasingly aware of this and other forms of power in recent years.[26]

Notice though that García-Johnson highlights the importance of epistemic knowledge – the knowledge we build up about our faith, and the ways we arrive at and organize that knowledge. There is no issue that more quickly raises the specter of power than questions of orthodoxy, however it may be defined. In other words, it is not uncommon that, when churches and organizations feel that their core values, doctrines, beliefs, and practices are under threat, they are tempted to use power to protect them or bring needed correction. In the colonial era such power was occasionally exerted through political and legal policies and enforced through various forms of enforcement. However, more commonly then and now has been the use of soft or other forms of power – financial support, questions of church/denominational membership, and shame and rebukes from prominent leaders.

The specific uses of power and persuasion in mission contexts take a variety of forms. Western organizations focusing on theological education fund a Western-originated curriculum, or a curriculum that clearly derives from and adheres to its theological values, and they employ missionaries and indigenous teachers who will faithfully teach that curriculum. Bible translation organizations will fund the salaries of translators and publications insofar as these follow translation principles that clearly uphold particular theological values. A church-planting organization will support missionaries and indigenous pastors that establish churches according to a particular ecclesial model and that maintain certain theological values. Western mission agencies defund missionaries who they deem have gone too far in supporting insider missiology.

On one level, and in many cases, some level of influence and/or coercive power is to be expected. Organizations and churches always have particular foci and distinctives that they seek to maintain. And as they grow and adapt, particularly across cultures, they often have to grapple with the question of how much innovation can be allowed before their very identity and values are changed. Questions and concerns become particularly heightened when the innovation begins to cross a line historically labeled as theological "heresy." To avoid heresy, or even simply the loss of particular theological

[26] Roland Allen's now-classic *Missionary Methods: St Paul's or Ours?* was an early sketch of themes that would become more widespread decades later. Roland Allen, *Missionary Methods: St Paul's or Ours?* (Grand Rapids, MI: Eerdmans, 1962 [1912]).

emphases, churches and organizations have often had to exert their power and influence in various ways. The threat of these, and sometimes other measures as well, have been the last line of defense against what they feel will otherwise lead to theology and churches that are beyond the pale. And because Western-oriented/originated mission work has often controlled these, and continues to do so, they have often assumed the role of controlling the boundaries of orthodoxy.

But though churches of the Global South have often challenged Western churches on their uses of power and privilege, it is not just "Western" churches that utilize power in these ways. Rather, Christian communities of the Global South, emulating the example of colonial and neo-colonial mission work, often use the power of finances, membership, shame, and others in similar ways. Thus, Western or non-Western Christians alike exert power to scrutinize, reward, or punish those they have influence over. In light of this it is no wonder that many insider movements prefer to remain apart from Christian churches, from whom they often experience ostracism.

It is because of these historic, and ongoing, expressions of colonial missiology that many missiologists have begun to explore the decolonizing themes discussed above. One theme that many scholars and leaders have developed is the place of the "margins" in mission. In their 2013 statement on mission and evangelism entitled *Together Towards Life* the 10th General Assembly of the World Council of Churches highlighted the shift of "mission *to* the margins" to "mission *from* the margins."[27] The margins of global societies – those who more often experience poverty, suffering, and other vulnerabilities – were no longer the focal points for mission, but rather the generative energy for mission. As has often been affirmed in various ways, the Majority World churches who are "outside the gate" of dominant power structures still can and often do shape mission in new and important ways.[28]

In her study of non-Western contributions to decolonial missiology, Eleonora Dorothea Hof argues that marginality, combined with vulnerability, can and should form the new "vocation" of decolonized mission.[29] Colonial models of mission often took advantage of people's vulnerabilities, creating legacies of either dependency or hardened independence. And Christian mission still often focuses on the vulnerabilities, whether of economy, health, knowledge, or other areas, of those with whom they work. Western missions combine the supposed (and sometimes actual) vulnerabilities of the

---

[27] "Together Towards Life: Mission and Evangelism in Changing Landscapes," *International Review of Mission* 101:2 (2012), 250.

[28] Orlando E. Costas, *Christ Outside the Gate: Mission Beyond Christendom* (Maryknoll, NY: Orbis Books, 1982).

[29] Eleonora Dorothea Hof, "Reimagining Mission in the Postcolonial Condition: A Theology of Vulnerability and Vocation at the Margins" (Doctor of Theology thesis, Protestant Theological University, Amsterdam, 2016).

missionized with their own senses of invulnerability, perpetuating colonial patterns of mission. To combat and decolonialize this pattern Hof suggests that Western-based mission reflect on the illusions of their own invulnerability, embrace the *kenosis* or emptying example of Jesus Christ (Phil. 2:5), and "actively undo ourselves of coercive power."[30] Doing so not only begins to address, and hopefully reshape, the distortions of global mission relationships created by colonial patterns, but also cultivates in Western Christians virtues of humility, and even silence, so as to be able to properly hear and learn from those who we have often devalued and marginalized.

Insider missiological imaginaries challenge those in power to honor what Jung Young Lee calls the "creative core" of mission that emerges from the margins of dominant Christian power and orthodoxies.[31] We do this through acknowledging our own vulnerabilities – our historic and colonial tendencies to control and protect God's mission and church from "error," and to coerce persons and systems in ways that exert that control. In so doing we recognize that Western, and Western-influenced missions (including those in non-Western countries), are not the caretakers of mission. Rather, and as the various stories of insiders have suggested, God's Spirit has and continues to inspire and fuel new mission movement and imaginaries. Perhaps those of us seeing this should be humble, and even silent, as we hear and see what God continues to do on the margins of our waning dominance.

Conclusion

Though many of us from the West who are involved in missions and missiology have in recent years and decades grappled more and more with the "rise" of non-Western Christianity and the ongoing legacies of colonialism on mission methods, structures, and missiology, there is still much for us to learn. At the very least we can and should continue to hear the ways in which imaginaries such as those of insiders call us to embrace a mending, patient, and marginal missiology. As we do so we can continue to learn from insiders, and other Christ-followers outside the Western halls of power, about important aspects of our shared faith, such as the nature of God's revelation, Christ's salvation, conversion, and community/family. Such learnings will be more and more possible, and crucial, as we continue to interact in increasingly multifaith contexts.

As we conclude, I want to end where I began. When my friend Jaspreet allowed himself to be vulnerable with me, a White Western missionary, regarding his deep questions on religious identity, it was for me a sign of

[30] Hof, "Reimagining Mission," 302.

[31] Jung Young Lee, *Marginality: The Key to Multicultural Theology* (Minneapolis: Fortress Press, 1995), 96-98.

hope. It was not so much that he seemed interested in that moment in reclaiming his Sikh identity and returning to his Sikh family as a Christ-follower. He did not, and he remains a good friend with a wonderful Christian ministry. Rather, I caught a glimpse of what vulnerable, open conversation about alternative pathways for following Christ could look like. Since that conversation I have wondered: how many more Christian converts have, like Jaspreet, in the silent moments of the night wondered whether they made the right decision, not in following Christ, but in "converting" and becoming a Christian? How many would feel the freedom to share and explore those misgivings and ideas, particularly with a Western missionary? I'm not sure of the answer, but my guess is that there have been and are many who have pondered these questions. What would it look like if Christians, solid in their commitment to Christ and the work of the Holy Spirit, felt free to explore what the Spirit may be stirring through such questions?

One of the gifts that insider imaginaries, such as those we have been privileged to listen to here, present to the global church is the invitation to consider the new works of the Spirit among non-Christian religious communities. Insiders do *not*, as I stated in at the beginning, present us with a perfect, or even preferred, way of following Christ amongst religious communities. The world, and God's kingdom, is much too rich and diverse for such blueprints. Rather, insiders and their imaginaries help us see a glimpse of God's mending and patient mission among those who have been "marginal" to the dominant forms of Christianity. And they invite us, should we choose, to quietly listen, learn, and join with that mission as God leads.

May we do so.

Bibliography

Ahmed, Rafiuddin. *The Bengal Muslims 1871–1906: A Quest for Identity*. New York: Oxford University Press, 1981.

Allen, Graham. *Intertextuality*. The New Critical Idiom. 2nd ed. Abingdon, Oxon; New York: Routledge, 2011.

Allen, Roland. *Missionary Methods: St. Paul's or Ours?* Grand Rapids, MI: Eerdmans, 1962 [1912].

Alma, Hans, and Guido Vanheeswijck. "Introduction." In *Social Imaginaries in a Globalizing World*. Eds. Hans Alma and Guido Vanheeswijck. Boston: De Gruyter, 2018, 1-20.

Anderson, Ray S., and Dennis B. Guernsey. *On Being Family: A Social Theology of the Family*. Grand Rapids, MI: Eedrmans, 1985.

Anthony, David. "The Oikos and the Wineskins." *International Journal of Frontier Missiology* 34:1-4 (2017), 7-23.

Arbuckle, Gerald A. *Culture, Inculturation, and Theologians: A Post-Modern Critique*. Collegeville, MN: Liturgical Press, 2010.

Asad, Talal. *Genealogies of Religion: Discipline and Reasons of Power in Christianity and Islam*. Baltimore: Johns Hopkins University Press, 1993.

Asma, Stephen T. *Why We Need Religion*. New York, NY: Oxford University Press, 2018.

Baago, Kaj. "The Post-Colonial Crisis of Missions." *International Review of Missions* 55 (1966), 322-332.

Barton, Stephen C. *Discipleship and Family Ties in Mark and Matthew*. New York: Cambridge University Press, 1994.

———. "Living as Families in the Light of the New Testament." *Interpretation* 52:2 (1998), 130-144.

Bauer, Marie. "What Happens When Buddhists Follow Jesus? A Peek into the Transformed Lives of Southeast Asian Women." *Resonance: A Theological Journal* 4:1 (2018), 86-93.

Bear, Cheryl. "The Smudge Ceremony: Inspiring Faith in Indigenous North Americans." In *Traditional Ritual as Christian Worship: Dangerous Syncretism or Necessary Hybrid?* Ed. R. Daniel Shaw and William R. Burrows. Maryknoll, NY: Orbis Books, 2018, 190-204.

Bear-Barnetson, Cheryl. *Introduction to First Nations Ministry*. Cleveland, TN: Cherohala Press, 2013.

The Bhagavad Gita: A New Translation, Contexts, Criticism. Eds. Gavin Flood and Charles Martin. New York: W.W. Norton & Company, 2015.
Bharati, Dayanand. "Canon." Unpublished paper, 2020.
Blanchard, Jessica Walker. "'They Came One at a Time': Native-Led Church Planting and Growing the Body of Christ from the Margins of Culture." PhD thesis, University of Oklahoma Graduate College, 2010.
Bonhoeffer, Dietrich. *The Cost of Discipleship*. London: SCM Press, 1959.
Brown, Joseph Epes. *The Sacred Pipe: Black Elk's Account of the Seven Rites of the Oglala Sioux*. Norman, OK: University of Oklahoma Press, 1953.
Brown, Rick. "Brother Jacob and Master Isaac: How One Insider Movement Began." *International Journal of Frontier Missiology* 24:1 (2007), 41-42.
Brueggemann, Walter. *Theology of the Old Testament: Testimony, Dispute, Advocacy*. Minneapolis: Augsburg Fortress, 1997.
Buehler, Arthur F. *Sufi Heirs of the Prophet: The Indian Naqshbandiyya and the Rise of the Mediating Sufi Shaykh*. Studies in Comparative Religion. Columbia: University of South Carolina Press, 1998.
Burrows, William R. "Theological Ideals, Cross-Cultural Realities: Syncretism and Hybridity in Christian Culture Crossing." In *Traditional Ritual as Christian Worship: Dangerous Syncretism or Necessary Hybridity?* Eds. R. Daniel Shaw and William R. Burrows. Maryknoll: Orbis Books, 2018, xxiv.
Cashin, David. "The Influence of the Esoteric Cults Upon the Sufis of Bengal." Unpublished thesis, University of Stockholm, 1988.
Census of India. "Religious Census 2011", https://www.census2011.co.in/religion.php. Accessed July 12, 2022.
Center for the Study of Global Christianity. *Christianity in its Global Context, 1970–2020*. Gordon-Conwell Theological Seminary, South Hamilton, MA, 2013. www.globalchristianity.org/globalcontext. Accessed March 1, 2019.
Chakkarai, V. "Why I am a Christian." *The Harvest Field* 35:3 (1915), 97-102.
Chan, Simon. *Grassroots Asian Theology: Thinking About Theology From the Ground Up*. Downers Grove, IL: IVP Academic, 2014.
Chandler, Paul-Gordon. *Pilgrims of Christ on the Muslim Road: Exploring a New Path Between Two Faiths*. New York: Rowman & Littlefield Publishers, 2007.
Chantlie, Audrey. *The Assamese: Religion, Caste, and Sect in an Indian Village*. London: Curzon Press, 1984.
Charles, Mark, and Soong-Chan Rah. *Unsettling Truths: The Ongoing, Dehumanizing Legacy of the Doctrine of Discovery*. Downers Grove, IL: IVP, 2019.
Chetti, O. Kandaswamy. "Idolatry: A Retrogression." *Madras Christian College Magazine* 14 (June 1897), 705-711.

———. "The Light that Lighteth Every Man." *Madras Christian College Magazine* 18 (July 1900), 181-187.

———. "The Need for Social Reconstruction in India." *Madras Christian College Magazine* (July 1914), 7-18.

———. "Why I am Not a Christian: A Personal Statement." *Madras Christian College Magazine* 32 (January 1915), 352-359.

———. "Announcement Regarding the Fellowship of the Followers of Jesus." *Guardian* April 13 (1933), 179.

Church, Casey. *Holy Smoke: The Contextual Use of Native American Ritual and Ceremony*. Centre for Pentecostal Theology Native North American Contextual Movement Series. Cleveland, TN: Cherohala Press, 2017.

———. "Place-Displaced: A Native American Perspective." *Fuller Magazine* 17 (2020), 52.

Church, Leonard. "Rites of Passage: Implications of the Change Process at Overcomers Alcohol Treatment Program and its Relation to the Change and Transition with the Wiconi Organization." Doctor of Intercultural Studies thesis, Fuller Theological Seminary, 2015.

Colijn, Brenda B. *Images of Salvation in the New Testament*. Downers Grove, IL: IVP Academic, 2010.

Collins, Randall. *Interaction Ritual Chains*. Princeton, NJ: Princeton University Press, 2004.

Colwell, Ernest Cadman. "Popular Reactions against Christianity in the Roman Empire." In *Environmental Factors in Christian History*. Eds. John Thomas McNeill et al. Chicago: University of Chicago Press, 1939.

Corwin, Gary. "A Humble Appeal to C5/Insider Movement Muslim Ministry Advocates to Consider Ten Questions." *International Journal for Frontier Missiology* 24:1 (2007), 5-21.

Costas, Orlando E. *Christ Outside the Gate: Mission Beyond Christendom*. Maryknoll, NY: Orbis Books, 1982.

Costello, Damien. *Black Elk: Colonialism and Lakota Catholicism*. Maryknoll, NY: Orbis, 2005.

Coxe, A. Cleveland. *Ante-Nicene Fathers: The Writings of the Fathers Down to A.D. 325. Volume 1: The Apostolic Fathers, Justin Martyr, Irenaeus*. Eds. Alexander Roberts and James Donaldson. New York: Christian Literature Publishing, 1885.

Cueva, Samuel. *Mission Partnership in Creative Tension: An Analysis of Relationships within the Evangelical Missions Movement with Special Reference to Peru and Britain from 1987–2006*. Carlisle, UK: Langham Monographs, 2015.

Daniels, Gene, and L.D. Waterman. "Bridging the 'Socio-Religious' Divide: A Conversation Between Two Missiologists." *International Journal for Frontier Missiology* 30:2 (Summer 2013), 59-66.

Davis, Erik W. *Deathpower: Buddhism's Ritual Imagination in Cambodia*. New York: Columbia University Press, 2015.

De Neui, Paul H. "Appropriate Typologies for Thai Folk Buddhists." In *Becoming the People of God: Creating Christ-Centered Communities in*

Buddhist Asia. Ed. Paul H. De Neui. Pasadena, California: William Carey Library, 2015. Kindle edition.

Deeg, Max. "The 'Brilliant Teaching': The Rise and Fall of 'Nestorianism' (Jingjiao) in Tang China." *Japanese Religions* 31:2 (2006), 91-110.

DeMallie, Raymond J., Ed. *The Sixth Grandfather: Black Elk's Teachings Given to John G. Neihardt*. Lincoln: University of Nebraska Press, 1984.

Denyer, Taylor Walters. *Decolonizing Mission Partnerships: Evolving Collaboration Between United Methodists in North Katanga and the United States of America*. Eugene, OR: Pickwick Publications, 2020.

Desai, Boman. *The Memory of Elephants*. Chicago: University of Chicago Press, 2001.

Destro, Adriana, and Mauro Pesce. "The Interstitial Movement of Jesus and the Oikos." In *From Jesus to His First Followers: Continuity and Discontinuity: Anthropological and Historical Perspectives*. Eds. Adriana Destro and Mauro Pesce. Leiden: Brill, 2017.

Duerksen, Darren. *Ecclesial Identities in a Multi-Faith Context: Jesus Truth-Gatherings (Yeshu Satsangs) Among Hindus and Sikhs in Northwest India*. Eugene, OR: Pickwick Publications, 2015.

Duerksen, Darren T, and William A. Dyrness. *Seeking Church: Emerging Witnesses to the Kingdom*. Downers Grove, IL: IVP Academic, 2019.

Dulles, Avery. "Revelation and Discovery." In *Theology and Discovery: Essays in Honor of Karl Rahner, S.J.* Ed. William Kelly. Wilwaukee, WI: Marquette University Press, 1980, 1-29.

Dupuis, Jacques. "The Cosmic Economy of the Spirit and the Sacred Scriptures of Religious Traditions." In *Jesus Christ and His Spirit: Theological Approaches*. Ed. Jacques Dupuis. Bangalore: Theological Publications in India, 1977, 211-228.

———. "The Cosmic Influence of the Holy Spirit and the Gospel Message." In *Jesus Christ and His Spirit: Theological Approaches*. Ed. Jacques Dupuis. Bangalore: Theological Publications in India, 1977, 181-210.

———. *Toward a Christian Theology of Religious Pluralism*. Maryknoll, NY: Orbis Books, 1997.

Dyrness, William A. *The Facts on the Ground: A Wisdom Theology of Culture*. Eugene, OR: Cascade, 2022.

———. *Insider Jesus: Theological Reflections on New Christian Movements*. Downers Grove, IL: IVP Academic, 2016.

Elgin, Catherine Z. "Emotion and Understanding." In *Epistemology and Emotions*. Eds. Georg Brun, Ulvi Doguoglu, and Dominique Kuenzle. New York: Routledge, 2016.

Ellis, Ieuan. "Jesus and the Subversive Family." *Scottish Journal of Theology* 38:2 (1985), 173-188.

Escobar, Samuel. "Doing Theology on Christ's Road." In *Global Theology in Evangelical Perspective: Exploring the Contextual Nature of Theology and Mission*. Eds. Jeffrey P. Greenman and Gene L. Green. Downers Grove, IL: IVP Academic, 2012, 67-85.

Fakirbhai, Dhanjibhai. *Immortal Life: The Mukti Marg of Sri Jesus*. New Delhi: BR Publishing Corporation, 2020.

Farrokh, Fred. "Will the Umma Veto SITO? Assessing the Impact of Theological Deviation on Social Acceptability in Muslim Communities." *International Journal for Frontier Missiology* 32:2 (Summer 2015), 69-80.

Formoso, Bernard. "Thai Buddhism as the Promoter of Spirit Cults." *South East Asia Research* 24:1 (2016), 119-133.

Gadamer, Hans-Georg. *Truth and Method.* 2nd ed. New York: Continuum, 2002.

Galang Lufityanto, Chris Donkin, and Joel Pearson. "Measuring Intuition: Nonconscious Emotional Information Boosts Decision Accuracy and Confidence." *Psychological Science* 27:5 (2016), 622-634.

García-Johnson, Oscar. "Transoccidentalism and the Making of Global Theology." In *Theology Without Borders: An Introduction to Global Conversations*. Eds. William A. Dyrness and Oscar García-Johnson. Grand Rapids, MI: Baker Academic, 2015.

———. *Spirit Outside the Gate: Decolonial Pneumatologies of the American Global South*. Downers Grove, IL: IVP Academic, 2019.

Garrison, David. *A Wind in the House of Islam: How God is Drawing Muslims around the World to Faith in Jesus Christ*. Monument, CO: WIGTake Resources, 2014.

Gehring, Roger W. *House Church and Mission: The Importance of Household Structures in Early Christianity*. Peabody, Mass.: Hendrickson Publishers, 2004.

Gibbs, Eddie. "How Appropriate is the Church Growth Paradigm?". In *Appropriate Christianity*. Ed. C.H. Kraft. Pasadena, CA: William Carey Library, 2005, 293-308.

Goh, Robbie B.H. *Christianity in Southeast Asia*. Southeast Asia Background Series. Singapore: Institute of Southeast Asian Studies, 2005.

Green, Joel B. *Conversion in Luke-Acts: Divine Action, Human Cognition, and the People of God*. Grand Rapids, MI: Baker Academic, 2015.

Greene, Thomas M. *The Light in Troy: Imitation and Discovery in Renaissance Poetry*. New Haven: Yale University Press, 1982.

Gregory, Peter N. *Tsung-Mi and the Sinification of Buddhism*. Honolulu: University of HawaiI Press, 2002.

Grenz, Stanley J. "How Do We Know What to Believe? Revelation and Authority." In *Essentials of Christian Theology*. Ed. William C. Placher. Louisville, KY: Westminster John Knox Press, 20-33.

———. *Theology For the Community of God*. Grand Rapids, MI: Eerdmans, 2000.

Gustafson, Hans Stefan. "Descandalizing Multiple Religious Identity with Help from Nicholas Black Elk and His Spirituality: An Exercise in Interreligious Learning." *Journal of Ecumenical Studies* 51:1 (2016), 80-113.

Harrison, Nate. "Native Expresssion." *Fuller Magazine* (2020), 12-19.
Hays, Richard B. *Echoes of Scripture in the Letters of Paul*. New Haven: Yale University Press, 1989.
Hedges, Paul. *Preparation and Fulfilment: A History and Study of Fulfilment Theology in Modern British Thought in the Indian Context*. New York: Peter Lang, 2001.
Heinrichs, Steve. "Living Vulnerability: Indigenous Perspectives on Evangelism." *Anabaptist Witness* 3:1 (2016), 45-55.
Hibbert, Richard. "Negotiating Identity: Extending and Applying Alan Tippett's Model of Conversion to Believers from Muslim and Hindu Backgrounds." *Missiology* 43:1 (2014), 59-72.
Hiebert, Paul G. "Critical Contextualization." *International Bulletin of Missionary Research* 11:3 (1987), 104-112.
———. "Critical Contextualization." *Missiology* 12 (1984), 287-296.
———. *Cultural Anthropology*. 2nd ed. Grand Rapids, MI: Baker, 1983.
———. *The Gospel in Human Contexts: Anthropological Explorations for Contemporary Missions*. Grand Rapids, MI: Baker Academic, 2009.
Hinkle, Mary E. "Preaching for Mission: Ancient Speeches and Postmodern Sermons." In *Mission in Acts: Ancient Narratives in Contemporary Context*. Eds Robert L. Gallagher and Paul Hertig. American Society of Missiology Series. Maryknoll, NY: Orbis Books, 2004, 87-102.
Hoefer, Herbert. *Churchless Christianity*. Pasadena, CA: William Carey Library, 2001.
Hof, Eleonora Dorothea. "Reimagining Mission in the Postcolonial Condition: A Theology of Vulnerability and Vocation at the Margins." Doctor of Theology thesis, Protestant Theological University, Amsterdam, 2016.
Holler, Clyde. *Black Elk's Religion: The Sun Dance and Lakota Catholicism*. Syracuse, NY: Syracuse University Press, 1995.
Holt, John Clifford. "Gone but Not Departed: The Dead Among the Living in Contemporary Buddhist Sri Lanka." In *The Buddhist Dead: Practices, Discourses, Representations*. Eds. Bryan J. Cuevas and Jacqueline I. Stone. Honolulu: University of Hawaii Press, 2007.
Horstmann, Alexander. "Reconfiguring Manora Rongkru: Ancestor Worship and Spirit Possession in Southern Thailand." In *Engaging the Spirit World: Popular Beliefs and Practices in Modern Southeast Asia*. Eds. Kirsten W. Endres and Andrea Lauser. New York: Berghahn Books, 2011, 184-199.
Hunsberger, George. "Conversion and Community: Revisiting the Lesslie Newbigin–M.M. Thomas Debate." *The International Bulletin of Missionary Research* 22:3 (1998), 112-117.
Ibrahim, Ayman S., and Ant Greenham, Eds. *Muslim Conversions to Christ: A Critique of Insider Movements in Islamic Contexts*. New York: Peter Lang, 2018.
Indigenous Pathways. https://indigenouspathways.com/aboutus/. Accessed July 12, 2022.

Irschick, Eugene F. *Politics and Social Conflict in South India: The Non-Brahman Movement and Tamil Separatism, 1916–1929*. Bombay: Oxford University Press, 1969.

Iyadurai, Joshua. "Christian Conversion in India: Political Exploitation or Personal Transformation?" In *Christianity in India: Conversion, Community Development, and Religious Freedom*. Eds. Rebecca Samuel Shah and Joel Carpenter. Minneapolis: Fortress Press, 2018.

Jaz, Abu. "The Cultural Insider, Theological Outsider (CITO): A Conversation with Abu Jaz." *International Journal for Frontier Missiology* 32:2 (Summer 2015), 61-67.

———. "Our Believing Community is a Cultural Insider but Theological Outsider (CITO)." In *Muslim Conversions to Christ: A Critique of Insider Movements in Islamic Contexts*. Eds. Ayman S. Ibrahim and Ant Greenham. New York: Peter Lang, 2018, 423-429.

Jennings, Willie James. *The Christian Imagination: Theology and the Origins of Race*. New Haven, Conn.: Yale University Press, 2010.

Johnson, Keith E. "Does the Doctrine of the Trinity Hold the Key to a Christian Theology of Religions? An Evaluation of Three Recent Proposals." *Southern Baptist Journal of Theology* 10:1 (2006), 24-47.

———. *Rethinking the Trinity and Religious Pluralism: An Augustinian Assessment*. Downers Grove, IL: IVP Academic, 2011.

Johnson, Todd M., and Brian J. Grimm, Eds. *World Religion Database*. Leiden/Boston: Brill, 2020.

Johnson, Todd M., and Gina A. Zurlo, Eds. *World Christian Database*. Leiden/Boston: Brill, 2018.

Johnston, Robert K. *God's Wider Presence: Reconsidering General Revelation*. Grand Rapids, MI: Baker Academic, 2014.

Judson, Jay. "Longing for the Golden City." *Mission Frontiers* (Nov/Dec 2014), 10-12.

Kan, Sergei. *Memory Eternal: Tlingit Culture and Russian Orthodox Christianity Through Two Centuries*. Seattle: University of Washington Press, 1999.

Kärkkäinen, Veli-Matti. *Trinity and Revelation: A Constructive Christian Theology for the Pluralistic World Vol. 2*. Grand Rapids, MI: Eerdmans, 2014.

———. *Christology: A Global Introduction*. 2nd ed. Grand Rapids, MI: Baker Academic, 2016.

Kasempholkoon, Aphilak. "Phra Sri An (Maitreya) as a Hero: Structural Analysis of Phra Sri An Myths in Thai Society." *Manusya: Journal of Humanities* Special Issue No. 19 (2011), 21-32.

Keyes, Charles. "From Death to Birth: Ritual Process and Buddhist Meanings in Northern Thailand." *Folk* 29 (1987), 181-206.

Khodr, George. "Christianity in a Pluralist World: The Economy of the Holy Spirit." In *Living Faiths and the Ecumenical Movement*. Ed. Stanley J. Samartha. Geneva: World Council of Churches, 1971, 131-142.

Kim, Kirsteen. *The Holy Spirit in the World: A Global Conversation.* Maryknoll, NY: Orbis, 2007.

———. *Mission in the Spirit: The Holy Spirit in Indian Christian Theologies*. Delhi: ISPCK, 2003.

Kreider, Alan. *The Patient Ferment of the Early Church: The Improbable Rise of Christianity in the Roman Empire*. Grand Rapids, MI: Baker Academic, 2016.

Kuortti, Joel, and Jopi Nyman. "Introduction: Hybridity Today." In *Reconstructing Hybridity: Post-Colonial Studies in Transition*. Eds. Joel Kuortti and Jopi Nyman. New York: Rodopi, 2007.

Ladwig, Patrice. "Can Things Reach the Dead? The Ontological Status of Objects and the Study of Lao Buddhist Rituals for the Spirits of the Deceased." In *Engaging the Spirit World: Popular Beliefs and Practices in Modern Southeast Asia*. Eds. Kirsten W. Endres and Andrea Lauser. New York: Berghahn Books, 2011.

Larsen, L.P. "Conversion and the Church." *Madras Christian College Magazine* 32 (January 1915), 360-371.

LeBlanc, Terry. "Richard Leo Twiss Memorial." *Cultural Encounters* 9:2 (2013), 21-25.

LeBlanc, Terry, and Jennifer LeBlanc. "NAIITS: Contextual Mission, Indigenous Context." *Missiology* 39:1 (2011), 87-100.

Lee, Jung Young. *Marginality: The Key to Multicultural Theology*. Minneapolis: Fortress Press, 1995.

Lewis, C.S. *Mere Christianity*. New York: HarperOne, 2001.

Lim, David S. "Contextualization of Merit-Making and Grace for Christward Movements in the Karmic World." In *Gift and Duty: Where Grace and Merit Meet*. Ed. Paul H. De Neuii. Eugene, OR: Wipf & Stock, 2017, 67-92.

———. "Contextualizing Ancestor Veneration: A Theological Survey and Practical Steps for Implementation." *International Journal of Frontier Missiology* 32:4 (2015). 183-194.

———. "Contextualizing Ancestor Veneration: An Historical Review." *International Journal of Frontier Missiology* 32:3 (2015), 109-115.

Luzbetak, Louis J. "Two Centuries of Cultural Adaptation in American Church Action: Censure or Challenge?" *Missiology* 5:1 (1977), 51-72.

Mackay, John Alexander. *A Preface to Christian Theology*. The James Sprunt Lectures, 1940. New York: Macmillan, 1941.

Mallouhi, Mazhar. "Comments on the Insider Movement." In *Understanding Insider Movements: Disciples of Jesus Within Diverse Religious Communities*. Eds. Harley Talman and John Jay Travis. Pasadena, CA: William Carey Library, 2015, 109-115.

———. Ed. *The True Meaning of the Gospel of Christ*. 2nd ed. Beirut: Dar al-Farabi, 2016.

Massey, Joshua. "God's Amazing Diversity in Drawing Muslims to Christ." *International Journal of Frontier Missions* 17:1 (2000), 5-14.

Mayward, Joel, and Randy Woodley. "What's the Truth in the Story? An Interview with Randy Woodley." *The Other Journal: An Intersection of Theology and Culture* 33 (August 23, 2021). https://theotherjournal.com/2021/08/23/truth-story-interview-with-randy-woodley/, accessed July 12, 2022.

McDermott, Gerald R., and Harold A. Netland. *A Trinitarian Theology of Religions: An Evangelical Proposal*. Oxford: Oxford University Press, 2014.

McFarland, George Bradley. *Historical Sketch of Protestant Missions in Siam, 1828–1928*. Bangkok: Bangkok Times Press, 1928.

McGavran, Donald Anderson. *The Bridges of God: A Study in the Strategy of Missions*. New York: World Dominion Press, 1955.

———. *Ethnic Realities and the Church: Lessons from India*. Pasadena, CA: William Carey Library, 1979.

———. *Understanding Church Growth*. 3rd ed. Grand Rapids, MI: Eerdmans, 1990.

Merrick, James R.A. "The Spirit of Truth as Agent in False Religions? A Critique of Amos Yong's Pneumatological Theology of Religions with Reference to Current Trends." *Trinity Journal* 29:1 (2008), 107-125.

Middleton, Paul. "Suffering and the Creation of Christian Identity in the Gospel of Mark." In *T&T Clark Handbook to Social Identity in the New Testament*. Eds. J. Brian Tucker and Coleman A. Baker. New York: Bloomsbury, 2014.

Miles, Todd. *A God of Many Understandings? The Gospel and Theology of Religions*. Nashville: B&H Academic, 2010.

Moltmann, Jürgen. *The Spirit of Life: A Universal Affirmation*. Philadelphia: Fortress Press, 1992.

Moreau, A. Scott. *Contextualizing the Faith: A Holistic Approach*. Grand Rapids, MI: Baker Academic, 2018.

Moreau, Scott. "Contextualization that is Comprehensive." *Missiology* 34:3 (2006), 325-335.

Moyise, Steve. "Does the NT Quote the OT Out of Context?". *Anvil* 11:2 (1994), 133-143.

———. "Intertextuality and Historical Approaches to the Use of Scripture in the New Testament." In *Reading the Bible Intertextually*. Eds. Richard B. Hays, Stefan Alkier and Leroy A. Huizenga. Waco, TX: Baylor University Press, 2009.

Munson, Tara Villalba. "Christian Communities in Southeast Asia." In *The Oxford Handbook of Global Religions*. Ed. Mark Juergensmeyer. Oxford; New York: Oxford University Press, 2006, 379-387.

Neihardt, John G. *Black Elk Speaks: Being the Life Story of a Holy Man of the Oglala Sioux*. Lincoln, NE: University of Nebraska Press, 1988 [1932].

———. *When the Tree Flowered: An Authentic Tale of the Sioux Indians*. New York: Macmillan, 1951.

Niles, D.T. *The Preacher's Task and the Stone of Stumbling: The Lyman Beecher Lectures, Yale University*. New York: Harper and Row, 1958.

Nock, Arthur Darby. *Conversion; the Old and the New in Religion from Alexander the Great to Augustine of Hippo*. Oxford: Oxford University Press, 1933.

Nongbri, Brent. *Before Religion: A History of a Modern Concept*. New Haven: Yale University Press, 2013.

Nyunt, Peter Thein. "Emerging Indigenous Leaders for Jesus Movements in the Myanmar Buddhist Context." In *Developing Indigenous Leaders: Lessons in Mission from Buddhist Asia*. Ed. Paul H. De Neui, chapter 10 (ebook). Pasadena, CA: William Carey Library, 2013. Kindle edition

Nyunt, Peter Thien. *Missions Amidst Pagodas: Contextual Communication of the Gospel in the Burmese Buddhist Context*. Carlisle, UK: Langham, 2014.

Oduyoye, Mercy Amba. "The Story of a Circle." *Ecumenical Review* 53:1 (2001), 97-100.

Olofinjana, Israel Oluwole. "Decolonizing Mission: Learning from the Majority World Template of Suffering and Sacrifice." *Lausanne Global Analysis* 9:5 (2020). lausanne.org/content/lga/2020-09/decolonizing-mission, accessed July 12, 2022.

Padmanji, Rev. Baba. "A Comparison of Hinduism and Christianity." In *English Translations of Select Tracts Published in India*. Ed. J. Murdoch. Madras: Christian Knowledge Society's Press, 1870, 46-106.

Pandian, M.S.S. "Nation as Nostalgia: Ambiguous Spiritual Journeys of Vengal Chakkarai." *Economic and Political Weekly* 38:51/52 (2003), 5357-5365.

Parshall, Phil. *Muslim Evangelism: Contemporary Approaches to Contextualization*. Downers Grove, IL: InterVarsity Press, 2003.

Pinnock, Clark H. *Flame of love: A Theology of the Holy Spirit*. Downers Grove: InterVarsity Press, 1996.

Prenger, Jan Hendriik. "Muslim Insider Christ-followers: A Grounded Theory." Doctor of Missiology thesis, Biola University, 2014.

Prenger, Jan Hendrik. *Muslim Insider Christ-followers: The Theological and Missional Frames*. Pasadena, CA: William Carey Library, 2017.

Rajashekar, J. Paul. "The Question of Unbaptized Believers in the History of Mission in India." In *Debate on Mission*. Ed. Herbert Hoefer. Chennai, India: Gurukul Lutheran Theological College and Research Institute, 1979, 323-341.

Reinke, Tony, "Nepal's Most Unlikely Church Planter," *Desiring God*, August 7, 2014, https://www.desiringgod.org/articles/nepals-most-unlikely-church-planter, accessed April 1, 2019.

Reisacher, Evelyne A. *Joyful Witness in the Muslim World: Sharing the Gospel in Everyday Encounters*. Grand Rapids, MI: Baker Academic, 2016.

Renan, Ernest. *The Life of Jesus*. Boston: Roberts Brothers, 1896.

Rheenen, Gailyn Van. "Syncretism and Contextualization: The Church on a Journey Defining Itself." In *Contextualization and Syncretism: Navigating Cultural Currents*. Ed. Gailyn Van Rheenen. Pasadena, CA: William Carey Library, 2006, 1-25.

Rice, Julian. *Black Elk's Story: Distinguishing Its Lakota Purpose*. Albuquerque: University of New Mexico Press, 1991.

Richard, H.L. "Community Dynamics in India and the Praxis of 'Church'." *International Journal of Frontier Missiology* 24:4 (2007), 185-194.

Richard, H.L. "Religious Syncretism as a Syncretistic Concept: The Inadequacy of the 'World Religions' Paradigm in Cross-Cultural Encounter." *International Journal for Frontier Missiology* 31:4 (Winter 2014), 209-215.

Richie, Tony. "The Spirit of Truth as Guide into All Truth: A Response to R.A. James Merrick, 'The Spirit of Truth as Agent in False Religions? A Critique of Amos Yong's Pneumatological Theology of Religions with Reference to Current Trends'." *Cyberjournal for Pentecostal-Charismatic Research* 1 (January 2010), http://www.pctii.org/cyberj/cyberj19/richie.html, Accessed May 29, 2019.

Riesebrodt, Martin. *The Promise of Salvation: A Theory of Religions*. Trans. Steven Rendall. Chicago: University of Chicago Press, 2010.

Russell, Letty M. "Cultural Hermeneutics: A Postcolonial Look at Mission." *Journal of Feminist Studies in Religion* 20:1 (2004), 23-40.

Samartha, S.J. "The Holy Spirit and People of Various Faiths, Cultures, and Ideologies." In *The Holy Spirit*. Ed. Dow Kirkpatrick. Nashville: Tidings, 1974.

Satyavrata, Ivan M. *God Has Not Let Himself Without Witness*. Eugene, OR: Wipf and Stock, 2011.

Schneiders, Sandra M. *The Revelatory Text: Interpreting the New Testament as Sacred Scripture*. 2nd ed. Collegeville, MN: The Liturgical Press, 1999.

Shaw, R. Daniel. "The Dynamics of Ritual and Ceremony: Transforming Traditional Rites to their Intended Purpose." In *Traditional Ritual as Christian Worship: Dangerous Syncretism or Necessary Hybridity?* Eds. R. Daniel Shaw and William R. Burrows. Maryknoll: Orbis Books, 2018, 1-19.

Smith, Christian. *Religion: What it is, How it Works, and Why it Matters*. Princeton, NJ: Princeton University Press, 2017.

Smith, James K.A. *Desiring the Kingdom: Worship, Worldview, and Cultural Formation*. Grand Rapids, MI: Baker Academic, 2009.

Smith, Wilfred Cantwell. *The Meaning and End of Religion: A New Approach to the Religious Traditions of Mankind*. New York: Macmillan, 1963.

Somaratna, G.P.V. "From Becoming the People of God: Creating Christ-Centered Communities in Buddhist Asia." In *Becoming the People of God: Creating Christ-Centered Communities in Buddhist Asia*. Ed. Paul

H. De Neui, chapter 1 (ebook). Pasadena, California: William Carey Library, 2015.

Stang, Charles M. "The 'Nestorian' (jingjiao) Monument and its Theology of the Cross." In *Syriac in its Multi-Cultural Context*. Eds. E. Keser-Kayaalp, H. Teule, K. Akalın, N. Doru, M.S. Toprak. Louvain: Peeters, 2017, 107-118.

Stassen, Glen Harold. *A Thicker Jesus: Incarnational Discipleship in a Secular Age*. Louisville, Kentucky: Westminster John Knox Press, 2012.

Steltenkamp, Michael F. *Black Elk: Holy Man of the Oglala*. Norman: University of Oklahoma Press, 1993.

———. *Nicholas Black Elk: Medicine Man, Missionary, Mystic*. Norman: University of Oklahoma Press, 2009.

Stephenson, John. "The Messiah Most Honourable: The Christological Views of Muslim Background Followers of Iśā āl Mosiho in a South Asian Country." Doctor of Philosophy thesis, Glasgow, private publication, 2016.

Stietencron, Heinrich von. "Charisma and Canon: The Dynamics of Legitimization and Innovation in Indian Religions." In *Charisma and Canon: Essays on the Religious History of the Indian Subcontinent*. Eds. Vasudha Dalmia, Angelika Malinar and Martin Christof. New Delhi: Oxford University Press, 2001, 14-38.

Studebaker, Steven M. *From Pentecost to the Triune God: A Pentecostal Trinitarian Theology*. Grand Rapids, MI: Eerdmans, 2012.

Swanson, Mark N. "Beyond Prooftexting: Approaches to the Qur'an in Some Early Arabic Christian Apologies." *The Muslim World* 88:3-4 (1998), 297-319.

Swearer, Donald K. "Buddhism in Southeast Asia." In *The Religious Traditions of Asia: Religion, History, and Culture*. Edited by Joseph Kitagawa. Oxford: Routledge, 2002, 119-142.

———. *The Buddhist World of Southeast Asia*. 2nd ed. New York: State University of New York Press, 2010.

Talman, Harley, and John Jay Travis, Eds. *Understanding Insider Movements: Disciples of Jesus Within Diverse Religious Communities*. Pasadena, CA: William Carey Library, 2015.

Taylor, Charles. *Modern Social Imaginaries*. Durham: Duke University Press, 2004.

———. *A Secular Age*. Cambridge, MA: Harvard University Press, 2007.

Taylor, John V. *The Go-Between God: The Holy Spirit and the Christian Mission*. Philadelphia: Fortress Press, 1972.

Tennent, Timothy. "The Challenge of Churchless Christianity: An Evangelical Assessment." *International Bulletin of Missionary Research* 29:4 (2005), 171-177.

Tertullian. *Apology*. Trans. T.R. Glover. Cambridge, MA: Harvard University Press, 1931.

Thomas, Joshua. "Native Hermeneutics: Reverse Typology and Remythologization, or: The Theological Genius of Black Elk's Dual

Participation." *Transactions of the Charles S. Peirce Society* 53:3 (2017), 447-465.

Thompson, Leonard L. "Ordinary Lives: John and His First Readers." In *Reading the Book of Revelation*. Ed. David L. Barr. Atlanta GA: Society of Biblical Literature, 2003.

Tillich, Paul. *The Future of Religions*. New York: Harper & Row, 1966.

Tinker, George E. *Missionary Conquest: The Gospel and Native American Cultural Genocide*. Minneapolis: Fortress Press, 1993.

Tippett, Alan. "Conversion as a Dynamic Process in Christian Mission." *Missiology* 5:2 (1977), 203-221.

Tiwari, Ravi. *Yesu Das: Witness of a Convert*. Delhi: ISPCK, 2000.

Travis, John. "The C1 to C6 Spectrum: A Practical Tool for Defining Six Types of 'Christ-Centered Communities' ('C') Found in the Muslim Context." *Evangelical Missions Quarterly* 34:4 (1998), 407-408.

Twiss, Richard. *One Church, Many Tribes*. Ventura, CA: Regal, 2000.

———. *Rescuing the Gospel from the Cowboys: A Native American Expression of the Jesus Way*. Downers Grove, IL: InterVarsity Press, 2015.

Wilder, John. "Some Reflections on Possibilities for People Movements among Muslims." *Missiology* 5:3 (1977), 301-320.

Willard, Dallas. *Renovation of the Heart: Putting on the Character of Christ*. Colorado Springs: NavPress, 2002.

Wimber, John, and Kevin Springer. *Power Evangelism*. San Francisco: Harper & Row, 1986.

Woodley, Randy. *Decolonizing Evangelicalism: An 11:59 p.m. Conversation*. Eugene, Oregon: Cascade Books, 2020.

———. *Living in Color: Embracing God's Passion for Ethnic Diversity*. Downers Grove, IL: InterVarsity Press, 2001.

———. *Shalom and the Community of Creation: An Indigenous Vision*. Grand Rapids, MI: Eerdmans, 2012.

World Council of Churches. "Together towards Life: Mission and Evangelism in Changing Landscapes." *International Review of Mission* 101:2 (2012), 250-280.

Wright, N.T. *Jesus and the Victory of God Vol 2: Christian Origins and the Question of God*. Minneapolis: Fortress Press, 1996.

Yango, Emelito Acoba. "Towards a Hermeneutic of Affirmation for Local Theologizing in Closed Access Communities." Doctor of Missiology thesis, Asia Graduate School of Theology,Philippines, 2009.

Yong, Amos. *Beyond the Impasse: Toward a Pneumatological Theology of Religions*. Grand Rapids, MI: Baker Academic, 2003.

———. *The Cosmic Breath: Spirit and Nature in the Christianity-Buddhism-Science Trialogue*. Boston: Brill, 2012.

———. *Discerning the Spirit(s): A Pentecostal-Charismatic Contribution to Christian Theology of Religions*. Sheffield: Sheffield Academic Press, 2000.

———. "The Holy Spirit and the World Religions: On the Christian Discernment of Spirit(s) 'after' Buddhism." *Buddhist-Christian Studies* 24:1 (2004), 191-207.

———. *The Missiological Spirit: Christian Mission Theology in the Third Millennium Global Context*. Eugene, OR: Cascade, 2014.

———. "'Not Knowing Where the Spirit Blows…': On Envisioning a Pentecostal-Charismatic Theology of Religions." *Journal of Pentecostal Theology* 14 (April 1999), 81-112.

———. *Pneumatology and the Christian-Buddhist Dialogue: Does the Spirit Blow through the Middle Way?* Boston: Brill, 2012.

———. *The Spirit Poured Out on All Flesh: Pentecostalism and the Possibility of Global Theology*. Grand Rapids, MI: Baker Academic, 2005.

Zubrzycki, Genevieve. "Religion, Religious Tradition, and Nationalism: Jewish Revival in Poland and 'Religious Heritage' in Quebec." *Journal for the Scientific Study of Religion* 51:3 (2012), 442-455.